General Editor's Introduction

This volume is published in collaboration with the Center for the Study of World Christian Revitalization Movements, a cooperative initiative of Asbury Theological Seminary faculty. Building on the work of the previous Wesleyan/Holiness Studies Center at the Seminary, the Center provides a focus for research in the Wesleyan Holiness and other related Christian renewal movements, including Pietism and Pentecostal movements, which have had a world impact. The research seeks to develop analytical models of these movements, including their biblical and theological assessment. Using an interdisciplinary approach, the Center bridges relevant discourses in several areas in order to gain insights for effective Christian mission globally. It recognizes the need for conducting research that combines insights from the history of evangelical renewal and revival movements with anthropological and religious studies literature on revitalization movements. It also networks with similar or related research and study centers around the world, in addition to sponsoring its own research projects.

Greg Crofford's study of prevenient grace in the Wesleys opens new ground in understanding this seminal doctrine of Methodism. He does so by uncovering a diversity of sources used by John Wesley in his exposition of this biblical concept. He also includes an in-depth examination of the complementary role of Charles Wesley's poetical discourse on the theme, which results in a more comprehensive presentation of its form and function in early Methodism. Finally, Crofford demonstrates major ways in which prevenient grace was deployed in the writings of selected Methodist theologians. In view of the centrality of this doctrine for an understanding of evangelism and conversion within the Wesleyan context, Crofford's definitive study demonstrates congruence with the mission of the Center and serves to advance its research objectives.

J. Steven O'Malley, Editor, Pietist and Wesleyan Studies
Director, Center for the Study of World Christian Revitalization Movements, Asbury Theological Seminary

Streams of Mercy

Prevenient Grace in the Theology of John and Charles Wesley

J. Gregory Crofford

Asbury Theological Seminary Series:
The Study of World Christian Revitalization Movements in
Pietist/Wesleyan Studies (No. 3)

EMETH PRESS
www.emethpress.com

Streams of Mercy:
Prevenient Grace in the Theology of John and Charles Wesley

Copyright © 2010 J. Gregory Crofford
Printed in the United States of America on acid-free paper

All rights reserved. No part of this book may be reproduced, or stored in a retrieval system or transmitted in any form or by any means, electronic, mechanical, photocopying, recording, scanning or otherwise, except as permitted by the 1976 United States Copyright Act, or with the prior written permission of Emeth Press. Requests for permission should be addressed to: Emeth Press, P. O. Box 23961, Lexington, KY 40523-3961. http://www.emethpress.com.

Library of Congress Cataloging-in-Publication Data

Crofford, Gregory.
Streams of mercy : prevenient grace in the theology of John and Charles Wesley / Gregory Crofford.
  p. cm. -- (Asbury Theological Seminary series: the study of world Christian revitalization movements in Pietist/Wesleyan studies ; no. 3)
Includes bibliographical references (p.   ) and index.
ISBN 978-1-60947-008-1 (alk. paper)
1. Wesley, John, 1703-1791. 2. Wesley, Charles, 1707-1788. 3. Prevenient grace--History of doctrines. I. Title.
BT761.3.C76 2010
234--dc22   2010031767

(Picture of John Wesley mounting his horse on the front cover is a copy of a painting by Richard Gilmore Douglas, Thirsk, Enlgand. Used by permission).

All scripture quotations, unless otherwise indicated, are taken from the Holy Bible, New International Version®, NIV®. Copyright ©1973, 1978, 1984 by Biblica, Inc.™ Used by permission of Zondervan. All rights reserved worldwide. www.zondervan.com

Dedication

I lovingly dedicate this book to my parents, Don and Marilyn Crofford, whose abiding love for Christ, for each other, and for their six sons is a priceless heritage;

and to

John and Bonna Lee Bean, who instilled both laughter and love for missions in the heart of their daughter, my wife, Amy Bean Crofford.

"These commandments that I give you today are to be upon your hearts. Impress them on your children. Talk about them when you sit at home and when you walk along the road, when you lie down and when you get up. Tie them as symbols on your hands and bind them on your foreheads. Write them on the doorframes of your houses and on your gates."

Deuteronomy   6:6-9

Contents

Preface..9

Acknowledgements..17

Chapter 1. Roots of the Doctrine of Prevenient Grace: Analysis of
          Selected 16th, 17th, and Early 18th Century Church of England
          and Puritan Sources..19

Chapter 2. Roots of the Doctrine of Prevenient Grace: The "Light of Christ"
          in Robert Barclay's Apology...53

Chapter 3. John Wesley on Prevenient Grace...67

Chapter 4. Charles Wesley: Preliminary Considerations.........................105

Chapter 5. Prevenient Grace in Charles Wesley:
          The Contours of a Doctrine..139

Chapter 6. Beyond the Brothers Wesley:
          Interpretation of Prevenient Grace..179

Appendix..203

Bibliography...207

Index..223

Preface

Free as air Thy mercy streams,
Thy universal grace
Shines with undistinguish'd beams
On all the fallen race:
All from Thee a power receive
To reject, or hear, Thy call;
All may chuse to die, or live;
Thy grace is free for all.

-Charles Wesley

Research Scope

The role of prevenient grace in the Wesleyan theological system is considerable. Kenneth Collins called it the key to John Wesley's ability "to hold together, without any contradiction, the four motifs of total depravity, salvation by grace, human responsibility, and the offer of salvation to all."[1] As the concept that "broke the chain of logical necessity by which the Calvinistic doctrine of predestination seems to flow from the doctrine of original sin,"[2] the doctrine of prevenient grace has become increasingly important for Wesleyan theologians. This is evidenced by the recent publication of several works on Wesley's theology, studies that included significant treatment of prevenient grace. Most notable are Randy Maddox's *Responsible Grace: John Wesley's Practical Theology* and Kenneth Collins' *The Theology of John Wesley: Holy Love and the Shape of Grace.*[3] While these scholars and others cited Charles Rogers' 1967 thesis on prevenient grace in Wesley's theology,[4] further lines of historical-theological inquiry not pursued by Rogers merit research, particularly those clarifying the nature of Wesley's appropriation of 16th, 17th and early 18th century sources in developing this idea. Furthermore, the renaissance in Charles Wesley studies facilitates the discovery of what the younger Wesley contributed to the doctrine, primarily by his voluminous hymns and poems, but also through his prose writings, including the *Sermons* and *Journal*. It is the contention of this study that Charles – though neglected in Wesleyan studies – reinforced his brother's teaching on prevenient grace, helping him lay a theological and biblical foundation for the doctrine.

Prevenient Grace Defined

It is important to establish a working definition for the term "prevenient grace." "Prevenient" stems from the Latin *prae*, meaning "before," and *venire*, signifying "to come."[5] The term "prevenient grace" originated in Augustine's *De natura et gratia* and is implied in New Testament passages such as John 1:9, 6:44, 12:32, Acts 10 and Romans 2:14-16.[6] Orton Wiley defined "grace" as "unmerited favor" and called "graces" the "various forms of the goodness and love of God."[7] Kenneth Grider asserted that prevenient grace "has to do with the many ways God favors us prior to our conversion."[8] It is the divine initiative that precedes the justification of an individual.[9] Randy Maddox defined grace as "God's loving personal presence in our lives"[10] and termed prevenient grace "the beginning of restoration."[11] All of these definitions are consistent with the understanding of prevenient grace outlined in John Wesley's 1765 sermon, *The Scripture Way of Salvation*, which related prevenient grace to the drawings of the Father, the enlightening of the Son, and the convictions of the Holy Spirit.[12]

Prevenient Grace in Wesleyan Soteriology

The prominence of prevenient grace in the thinking of Wesleyan theologians may be attributed to the desire to avoid both the Scylla and Charybdis of deterministic and moralistic theology. Richard Heitzenrater aptly described the challenge:

> In order to avoid the theological dilemma presented by a belief in both the sovereignty of God and the free will of humankind, Wesley chooses to espouse the doctrine of prevenient grace, which he usually calls "preventing grace" – the grace of God that "comes before"...any human action. Through prevenient grace, God provides universally to fallen humanity the possibility of knowing the good and thereby the potential of restoring the capability of doing the good.[13]

Choosing God is not a manifestation of unfettered human capability (Pelagius), nor is faith subsequent to God's sovereign election of the individual (Augustine, Calvin). Rather, because of the depravity resultant from original sin, it is only through the enablement of God's prevenient grace that one has the possibility – in Heitzenrater's words – to "choose properly."[14]

Review of Literature

Prevenient grace has long interested Wesleyan scholars. In his *Wesley on Religious Education*, John Prince addressed the "theory of human nature."[15] For Prince, original sin was a foundational theological reality. If depravity is the condition even of children, on what basis can one provide Christian education? The answer was prevenient grace, defined as that "ameliorating doctrine of grace whereby every man born into the world is enabled to sense his pitiable condition, to sigh for deliverance, and to make a start toward it."[16]

Writing after John Prince, George Croft Cell in *The Rediscovery of John Wesley* overstressed the Calvinistic strands in Wesley's theology. However, his work re-ignited an interest in Wesley's writings, and his observation that the "Wesleyan reconstruction of the Christian ethic of life is an original and unique synthesis of the Protestant ethic of grace with the Catholic ethic of holiness"[17] remains helpful for locating Wesley's place in the Christian tradition.

Like George Cell, Harald Lindström saw in John Wesley a traditional understanding of original sin. In *Wesley and Sanctification*, he noted that prevenient grace allowed Wesley to affirm depravity without adopting Calvinistic categories, such as unconditional election or irresistible grace.[18] Allan Coppedge concurred, seeing prevenient grace as a tool that enabled Wesley to fashion a reasonable alternative to both Pelagianism and determinism.[19]

While Colin Williams wrote after Harold Lindström, he shared a strong view of prevenient grace. Curiously, as Williams pointed out, John Wesley never made traditional arguments for God's existence. Instead, he believed that God is directly revealed in a preliminary way through prevenient grace.[20]

Albert Outler's essay, "The Place of Wesley in the Christian Tradition,"[21] explored the broader soteriological context in which Wesley's doctrine of prevenient grace finds meaning. Part of that soteriology is an appreciation for Wesley's understanding of prevenience.[22] Randy Maddox discerned in John Wesley both a "broad" and a "narrow" understanding of prevenient grace. The "broad" understanding may be termed the "prevenience of grace," i.e. "every salutary human action or virtue, from the earliest expression of faith to the highest degree of sanctification, (which is) grounded in the prior empowering of God's grace."[23] What Maddox called the "narrow" definition is "the specific Arminian doctrine about God's saving work in fallen humanity prior to justification."[24]

Like Maddox, Kenneth Collins has been at the forefront of the systematization of John Wesley's theology. In *The Scripture Way of Salvation*[25] and *Holy Love and the Shape of Grace*,[26] he outlined Wesley's *ordo salutis* and the role of prevenient grace. Theodore Runyon's *The New Creation: John Wesley's Theology Today* also addressed prevenient grace, including its relation to conscience and its value as an alternative to predestinarian theology.[27]

Apart from Scriptural allusions, where did John Wesley learn the idea of prevenient grace? Charles Rogers uncovered some of the 17th century Church of England theologians from whom Wesley inherited the concept.[28] However, Wesley's reading at Oxford included theologians not treated by Rogers who used prevenient grace or similar categories to describe divine action upon the human heart. This inquiry will evaluate additional writers, discovering to what extent they shaped Wesley's thinking on prevenient grace. Helpful as tools in that investigation are Robert Monk's *John Wesley: His Puritan Heritage—A Study of the Christian Life*,[29] and Elton Trueblood's *Robert Barclay: A portrait of the life and times of a great Quaker intellectual leader*.[30] Useful for understanding the dynamics behind the 18th century doctrinal disputes in which the brothers Wesley engaged are Allan Coppedge's *Shaping the Wesleyan Message*[31] and Herbert McGonigle's *Sufficient Saving Grace*.[32] Of special utility are details surrounding the 1739 publication of John Wesley's controversial sermon, *Free Grace*, and the Charles Wesley hymn, "Universal Redemption," which John appended to it.[33]

Often forgotten is the theological contribution of his younger brother, Charles. Barrie Tabraham lamented that "Charles Wesley has not received the attention from Methodists that he deserves."[34] Like a golden thread, prevenient grace – and particularly its universal nature – was woven throughout his nearly 9,000 hymns and poems, and especially figured in the thirteen volumes of Osborn's *The Poetical Works of John and Charles Wesley* and the original hymn collections from which the *Poetical Works* were gleaned.[35] Other primary sources include recent critical editions of his *Sermons* and *Journal*.[36] Through these materials, Charles Wesley contributed to the doctrine of prevenient grace, a contribution that until now has never been researched. Key to this venture will be the use of interpretive sources, such as John Tyson's *Charles Wesley: A Reader*,[37] Frank Baker's *Charles Wesley's Verse: An Introduction*,[38] and the Kenneth Newport/Ted Campbell compendium, *Charles Wesley: Life, Literature & Legacy*.[39]

Terminology

Following research, it became clear that the writings on prevenient grace fall into three categories, terms that will be used throughout this investigation :

1) *anthropological* – Prevenient grace is equated with or linked to conscience, or else is part of the post-fall *imago Dei*;
2) *cosmological* – Prevenient grace is a function of divine revelation in the Creation, an element of natural theology;
3) *pneumatological* – Prevenient grace is related to the universal ministry of the Holy Spirit, God at-work among all, including those who have never heard the gospel. While the activity of the Holy Spirit is accentuated, it is not severed from its Christological moorings, since the atonement is the source of prevenient grace.

Book Structure

Chapter 1 begins with an assessment of the claim that the *Homilies* of the Church of England affirmed prevenient grace. Afterwards, new insights on concepts related to prevenient grace are gleaned from the mostly Puritan writers in Felix Farley's edition of John Wesley's neglected *Christian Library*. This investigation then turns to selected sermons of William Tilly, building upon insights from Charles Rogers before addressing shades of prevenient grace in Jeremy Taylor's *Works*.

Chapter 2 examines the Quaker theologian, Robert Barclay, and how a modified understanding of his doctrine of the "light of Christ" proved useful to Wesley in honing what became a mature doctrine of prevenient grace. Together, the first two chapters uncover additional findings on prevenient grace, mined from the Wesley brothers' "general theological heritage."[40]

Chapter 3 considers what John Wesley wrote regarding prevenient grace, while Chapters 4 and 5 address Charles Wesley. The lesser celebrated and younger brother, Charles left thousands of hymns and poems, and recent critical editions of his *Sermons* and *Journal* have appeared. The key objective will be to ascertain how Charles supplemented John's prevenient grace doctrine.

How have Wesleyan scholars writing since the time of the Wesleys interpreted prevenient grace? This is the focus of Chapter 6, which is organized around answers to eight key questions raised in the literature on prevenient grace.

A summary of findings appears in the "Appendix," including suggestions for further research. This inquiry now turns to Chapter 1, in order to better understand the theological context in which the Wesleyan doctrine of prevenient grace evolved in the roughly 150 years preceding the births of John and Charles Wesley.

Notes

1. Kenneth J. Collins, *The Scripture Way of Salvation: The Heart of John Wesley's Theology* (Nashville: Abingdon Press, 1997), 45.

2. Colin W. Williams, *John Wesley's Theology Today* (New York and Nashville: Abingdon Press, 1960), 44.

3. Randy L. Maddox, *Responsible Grace: John Wesley's Practical Theology*. (Nashville: Kingswood Books/Abingdon Press, 1994); Kenneth J. Collins, *The Theology of John Wesley: Holy Love and the Shape of Grace* (Nashville: Abingdon Press, 2007).

4. Charles Allen Rogers, "The Concept of Prevenient Grace in the Theology of John Wesley" (Ph.D. thesis, Duke University, 1967).

5. Jeff Paton, "Prevenient Grace," n.p. [cited 16 June 2003]. Online: http://biblicaltheology.webhostme.com/prevenient_grace.htm.

6. On Augustine and prevenient grace, see the *De natura et gratia* in F.H. Woods and J.O. Johnston, trans., *Three Anti-Pelagian Treatises of S. Augustine* (London: David Nutt, 1887), 117-18. Thomas Aquinas took up the question of the relationship of prevenient and subsequent grace in Q. 111, Article 3, in A.M. Fairweather, trans. and ed., *Nature and Grace: Selections from the Summa Theologica of Thomas Aquinas*. In the *Library of Christian Classics* (Ichthus edition), no volume numbers (Philadelphia: The Westminster Press, 1954), 168-70.

7. H. Orton Wiley and Paul T. Culbertson, *Introduction to Christian Theology* (Kansas City, Missouri: Beacon Hill Press, 1946), 108.

8. J. Kenneth Grider, "Prevenient Grace," *Beacon Dictionary of Theology* (Kansas City, Missouri: Beacon Hill Press, 1984), 415-16.

9. Jeff Paton, "Prevenient Grace." Charles Rogers argued: "After justification, prevenient and assisting grace enable man to discern the sin remaining in him and to do good works as the means of his growth in holiness." See page (v) in Rogers' thesis abstract. Whether Rogers was correct in discerning in John Wesley a role for *prevenient* grace after justification is discussed in Chapter 6 of this study.

10. Maddox, *Responsible Grace*, 86.

11. *Responsible Grace*, 87.

12. *The Works of John Wesley*, Bi-Centennial edition (Frank Baker, ed. 35 vols. projected. Nashville: Abingdon Press, 1984 to present), 2:156-57; hereafter, *Works* [BE].

13. Richard P. Heitzenrater, "God with Us: Grace and the Spiritual Senses," in Robert K. Johnston et. al., eds., *Grace upon Grace: Essays in Honor of Thomas A. Langford* (Nashville: Abingdon Press, 1999), 93.

14. Heitzenrater, "Spiritual Senses," 93.

15. John W. Prince, *Wesley on Religious Education* (New York and Cincinnati: The Methodist Book Concern, 1926), 13-43.

16. Prince, 40.

17. George Croft Cell, *The Rediscovery of John Wesley* (New York: Henry Holt and Company, 1934), 347.

18. Harald Lindström, *Wesley and Sanctification* (London: Epworth Press, 1950; repr., Nappannee, Illinois: Francis Asbury/Evangel Publishing House, 1996), 19-37.

19. Allan Coppedge, *Shaping the Wesleyan Message: John Wesley in Theological Debate* (1987; repr., Nappanee, Illinois: Francis Asbury Press/Evangel Publishing House, n.d.), 111-13.

20. Colin Williams, *John Wesley's Theology Today* (New York and Nashville: Abingdon Press, 1964), 41.

21. Albert C. Outler, "The Place of Wesley in the Christian Tradition," in Kenneth E. Rowe, ed., *The Place of Wesley in the Christian Tradition* (1976; repr. Metuchen, New Jersey: The Scarecrow Press, 1980), 11-38.

22. Outler, reflecting on unconditional election, observed: "Prevenience always seemed for him (Wesley) a more fruitful notion than election..." Albert Outler, "John Wesley's Place," 25.

23. *Responsible* Grace, 30. This is consistent with the view of Charles Rogers, who held that – besides working prior to justification – prevenient grace is an "energy" or "power" which is "given to man to assist him in the process of sanctification." Rogers, 205.

24. *Responsible Grace*, 84.

25. See endnote 1 above.

26. See endnote 3 above.

27. Theodore Runyon, *The New Creation: John Wesley's Theology Today* (Nashville: Abingdon Press, 1998), 27-42.

28. Rogers, 25-58. Rogers evaluated selected passages from Robert Barnes, Thomas Rogers, Richard Hooker, William Beveridge, Gilbert Burnet, John Pearson, Samuel Annesley, and William Tilly.

29. Robert C. Monk, *John Wesley: His Puritan Heritage—A Study of the Christian Life* (New York and Nashville: Abingdon Press, 1966).

30. D. Elton Trueblood, *Robert Barclay: A portrait of the life and times of a great Quaker intellectual leader* (New York, Evanston, and London: Harper and Row, 1968).

31. See endnote 18 above.

32. Herbert Boyd McGonigle, *Sufficient Saving Grace: John Wesley's Evangelical Arminianism* (Carlisle, Cumbria, and Waynesboro, Georgia: Paternoster Press, 2001).

33. *Works* [BE], 4:542-63.

34. Barrie W. Tabraham, *Brother Charles* (Vol. 6 in the *Exploring Methodism* series; Peterborough: Epworth Press, 2003), 1.

35. G. Osborn, *The Poetical Works of John and Charles Wesley* (13 vols.; London: Wesleyan-Methodist Conference Office, 1868-1872). The original hymn collections from which the *Poetical Works* were culled are now available online at: http://www.divinity.duke.edu/wesleyan/texts/cw_published_verse.html.

36. Kenneth G.C. Newport, *The Sermons of Charles Wesley: A Critical Edition with Introduction and Notes* (Oxford: Oxford University Press, 2001); S.T. Kimbrough, Jr., and Kenneth G.C. Newport, eds., *The Manuscript Journal of the Reverend Charles Wesley, M.A.* (2 vols.; Nashville: Kingswood Books/Abingdon Press, 2008).

37. John R. Tyson, ed. *Charles Wesley: A Reader* (New York: Oxford University Press, 1989).

38. Frank Baker, *Charles Wesley's Verse: An Introduction* (2nd Ed.; London: The Epworth Press, 1988).

39. Kenneth G.C. Newport and Ted A. Campbell, eds., *Charles Wesley: Life, Literature, and Legacy* (Werrington, Peterborough: Epworth Press, 2007).

40. Rogers, 27.

Acknowledgements

Mrs. Amy Crofford, wife, mother, teacher, editor, author, artist, and listening ear *par excellence*;
John and Bradley Crofford, who gave up time with their dad, so that he could find out something more about "Mr. Wesley";
The Rev. Dr. Herbert B. McGonigle, Principal Emeritus of Nazarene Theological College (Didsbury, Manchester, England), my primary supervisor, who in 2001, having just returned from a whirlwind visit to Japan, complete with jet-lag, did not find it an impossible task to meet with an obscure missionary from West Africa to talk about the possibility of researching prevenient grace;
The Rev. Dr. David Rainey, who as my secondary supervisor read the thesis and made several helpful suggestions;
The Rev. Dr. Ron Benefiel, NTC classmate and President of Nazarene Theological Seminary, who helped me believe in myself and prodded me along the way;
The **Rev. Dr. John Seaman**, who encouraged me in the initial and later stages of this project;
The **Rev. Dr. Terry Ketchum**, who allowed me to carve time out of my busy schedule in Haiti, to work on the first two chapters;
The late **Rev. Dr Paul Orjala**, and the **Rev. Dr. Charles Gailey**, from whom I learned the love of missions;
The **Rev. Dr. Rob Staples**, whose course at Nazarene Theological Seminary, "Wesley's Theology," opened my eyes to a new world;
Mr. Don Maciver, librarian at Nazarene Theological College, for his patience and kindness;
The **Rev. Andrew Aveyard** and the **Rev. Sue Aveyard**, who during my research visits, taught me the delights of Yorkshire puddings in the comfort of their home;
The **staff of the Methodist Special Collections of the John Rylands library**, University of Manchester, especially **Dr. Peter Nockles** and **Dr. Gareth Lloyd**, who dug up obscure resources and still found time to visit over coffee;
Sharon Bull and the library staff of **Northwest Nazarene University,** who were helpful in locating resources by interlibrary loan, as well as printing on-line resources;
The **Rev. Dr. Hal Cauthron** and the **Rev. Dr. Howard Culbertson** of Southern Nazarene University, for their friendship and interest in this undertaking.

Chapter One

Roots of the Doctrine of Prevenient Grace: Analysis of Selected 16th, 17th, & Early 18th Century Church of England and Puritan Sources

The Contribution of Charles Rogers

In his 1967 thesis, "The Concept of Prevenient Grace in the Theology of John Wesley," Charles Allen Rogers began his examination by looking at mostly Church of England sources that would have influenced Wesley's thinking on the topic.[1] Rogers called this Wesley's "general theological heritage."[2] How does this heritage come into play in relation to prevenient grace? Rogers clarified:

> In attempting to speak of sources for his view of prevenient grace, it is not possible to mention any specific theologians from whom Wesley, at least after Aldersgate, simply and directly "borrowed" the concept. The doctrine of prevenient grace is part of the church's theological tradition present in both ancient and medieval theology, and particularly prominent in English Protestant theology in the sixteenth and seventeenth centuries.[3]

Rogers cited the *39 Articles, Liturgy* (i.e. the *Book of Common Prayer*) and the *Homilies* as *loci* of prevenient grace teaching. In addition, he uncovered important references to language akin to prevenient grace in theologians Robert Barnes, Thomas Rogers, Richard Hooker, William Beveridge, Gilbert Burnet, John Pearson, Samuel Annesley, and William Tilly. This project does not replicate in most respects Rogers' important work, though it will re-assess his position on some points. Rather, it uncovers new findings from the "English Protestant theology" referenced by Rogers.

Article X: "Of Free Will," and the *Book of Common Prayer*

A good place to begin the enquiry into the "theological tradition" of which Charles Rogers spoke is Article X of the *39 Articles* of the Church of England. Article X, titled "Of Free Will," affirmed:

> The condition of man after the Fall of Adam is such that he cannot turn and prepare himself by his own natural strength and good works to faith and calling upon God. Wherefore we have no power to do good works pleasant and acceptable to God, without the grace of God by Christ preventing us, that we may have a good will, and working with us when we have that good will.[4]

The first portion of the Article was derived from the 1552 Confession of Würtemberg.[5] The last line – "the grace of God by Christ preventing us" – drew on a comment by Augustine on the Latin of Psalm 59:1- *Deus meus misericordia eius praeveniet me.*[6] Oliver O'Donovan discerned in this phrase the divine initiative in grace, and in "working with us when we have that good will" the continuation of grace, "because there is never a time when we can become independent of God for our response to him."[7] O'Donovan seems to have had the concept of *via media* in mind, concluding: "It is satisfying to contemplate this moment in the career of the English Reformation when it drew on the tradition of Saint Thomas to ward off the influence of late-medieval voluntarism on the one hand and early Calvinist predestinarianism on the other."[8]

Selections from the *Book of Common Prayer* also employed the language of prevenient grace.[9] In the Collect for Easter-Day, the priest petitioned: "Almighty God...we humbly beseech thee, that as by thy special grace preventing us thou dost put into our minds good desires..."[10] Likewise, on the Seventeenth Sunday after Trinity, the Collect read: "Lord, we pray that thy grace may always prevent and follow us, and make us continually to be given to all good works..."[11] Finally, in the fourth Collect at the conclusion of the Order of Communion, communicants prayed: "Prevent us, O Lord, in all our doings, with thy most gracious favour, and further us with thy continual help..."[12] In all instances, the usage was what Randy Maddox has called the "broad" definition of prevenient grace, where *all* grace goes before us, regardless of its location in the *via salutis*, i.e. before or after conversion.[13] Churchgoers as observant of the *Liturgy* as were John and Charles Wesley would have by force of repetition unconsciously incorporated such language into their theological worldview.

Do the Homilies Teach Prevenient Grace?

A. Origin and Background

Published in 1547, at least five of these standard moralistic sermons were written by Thomas Cranmer (1489-1556).[14] The purpose of the *Homilies*, according to the preface of the original edition, was to instruct people in the "very word of God, that lively food of man's soul" and to keep them from the "pernicious doctrine" of the "bishop of Rome."[15] A perusal of the sermons also reveals the motive of encouraging civil obedience, as evidenced by *An Homily Against Disobedience and wilfull Rebellion*.[16]

B. The *Homilies* and Justification by Faith

The early *Homilies* attributed to Thomas Cranmer played a role in preparing John Wesley for his Aldersgate "heartwarming" on May 24, 1738. According to Wesley's *Journal*, he had contact with Peter Böhler beginning on March 4 of the same year, and met with him occasionally over the course of several weeks. On April 22, Wesley wrote: "I met Peter Böhler once more. I had now no objection to what he said of the nature of faith, viz., that it is (to use the words of our Church), 'A sure trust and confidence which a man hath in God, that through the merits of Christ *his* sins are forgiven, and *he* reconciled to the favour of God.'"[17]

These words came from Part III of the homily *Of Salvation*.[18] They became a bedrock definition of faith for John Wesley. Also in 1738, Wesley published a tract, *The Doctrine of Salvation, Faith and Good Works, Extracted from the Homilies of the Church of England*, containing abridgements of not only *Of Salvation*, but also *A Short Declaration of the True, Lively and Christian Faith*. The effort of producing the tract confirmed that Wesley still espoused the faith definition arrived at with Peter Böhler, and promulgated by the *Homilies*.[19] What was implicit became explicit in the *Farther Appeal to Men of Reason and Religion* (1745), when Wesley again used the "sure trust and confidence" terminology to define justifying faith.[20]

C. The *Homilies* and Prevenient Grace: a Re-assessment

Charles Rogers cited the *Homilies* as part of the "substantial tradition of sixteenth and seventeenth century British theology" that informed John Wesley's doctrine of prevenient grace.[21] But is this accurate? While two homilies addressed justification by faith, they were silent on prevenient grace. Even the simpler "grace" rarely appeared in the homilies Wesley referenced. When grace was included, its context was post-conversion and unrelated to prevenience.[22]

Unlike in his writings on justification, such as the *Farther Appeal,* where John Wesley directly quoted the *Homilies* to buttress his arguments, he made no reference to them to support his concept of prevenient grace. This silence is eloquent. While they had proven helpful in nudging the Oxford Wesley away from a moralistic view of justification[23] to one more Pauline in nature, it would take the heat of the predestinarian controversy with George Whitefield in the early 1740s for Wesley to elaborate the *via media* between determinism and moralism that prevenient grace would help him steer.

John Wesley's *Christian Library*: Glimpses of Prevenient Grace

Though it may be questioned to what degree the *Homilies* influenced the final form that John Wesley's doctrine of prevenient grace assumed – and though Wesley was raised a loyal son of the Church of England – there is little doubt concerning the overall influence of Wesley's Puritan heritage upon his theology.[24] Besides the Puritan heritage from John's and Charles' parents, Samuel and Susanna Wesley,[25] their maternal grandfather was Samuel Annesley, respected for his gifted preaching and non-conformist convictions.[26] Manfred Marquardt attributes John's ascetic orientation to the "Puritan tradition."[27] The role that Puritan writers played in his intellectual blossoming was also considerable, if one considers the number of Puritan writers that the young Wesley read while at Oxford.[28]

A. The *Christian Library*: Its Purpose and Editing

As the Methodist movement gained momentum in the late 1730s and through the 1740s, John Wesley not only wrote original tracts, but often extracted the writings of others that he deemed helpful for his fledgling Methodist societies. In the "Preface" to the 50 volume Felix Farley edition of the *Christian Library*,[29] Wesley explained his motive for publishing the multi-volume digest:

> I have endeavoured to extract such a collection of English divinity, as (I believe) is all true, all agreeable to the oracles of God: as is all practical, unmixed with controversy of any kind; and all intelligible to plain men...to make the man of God perfect, thoroughly furnish'd unto every good word and work.[30]

Its aim was "the most important instruction" and the promotion of "personal piety."[31] Wesley's practical purpose was re-affirmed on the occasion of the printing of the second edition, beginning in 1819:

> There is reason to believe that in the compilation of this great and important work, he had principally in view the improvement, in knowledge and piety, of those preachers who were raised up by the singular providence and grace of God, and called from their secular avocations, to assist him in the spreading vital religion through the land.[32]

John Wesley explained his method of abridgement. He felt free to "correct their mistakes" and to "add what was needful."[33] He concluded: "I therefore take no author for better, for worse (as indeed I dare not call any man Rabbi), but endeavour to follow each so far as he follows Christ, and not knowingly one step further."[34]

B. Anthropological, Cosmological, and Pneumatological Categories

What did selected writers in the *Christian Library* affirm regarding concepts related to prevenient grace? Their thoughts on conscience, revelation, the image of God in the human being, and other relevant constructs can be grouped under three headings:

1. *anthropological* – Emphasis was upon the "remnants" of the image of God in the person.[35] These "traces" post-fall were the basis of "conscience," explaining virtuous behavior among those who are not Christian.
2. *cosmological* – The divine self-disclosure to sinful persons often appeared in the Creation, or was revealed in nature.[36] The created order was viewed as the mediator of the grace of God to the individual..
3. *pneumatological* – God the Holy Spirit was the means by which the unbeliever awakened from the slumber of sin. The "drawings" of the Father, the "illumination" of the mind and related concepts were mediated by the Third Person of the Trinity.

C. An Anthropological Approach: Robert South and Edward Reynolds

The first approach to categories akin to a Wesleyan concept of prevenient grace may be termed "anthropological." Key to this understanding is the notion of "conscience." Robert South and Edward Reynolds both wrote about conscience, and appeared in John Wesley's *Christian Library*.

Robert South (1635-1716) was a Church of England clergyman and theologian. A graduate of Christ Church, Oxford, he was best known for his attack upon William Sherlock, who in South's mind had erred by defending the Trinity against Socinianism by employing rationalistic arguments.[37] Brooke Griggs commented upon South's mystical tendencies:

> Yet for South mystery and incomprehensibility were the essence of the Trinity and Christianity itself. Christianity was manifestly not reasonable...Lockean epistemology could dismantle divine right, but rationalism could never comprehend Christian mystery, however much it claimed to support orthodox doctrine.[38]

John Wesley abridged a sermon from Robert South on Luke 11:35, taken from his *Twelve Sermons Upon Several Subjects and Occasions*.[39] In the *Christian Library* abridgement, "conscience" was portrayed as "the great and sovereign gift of God to mankind for the guidance and government of their actions."[40] South described it as a "directing and distinguishing light within him"[41] or as the "candle of the Lord."[42] It is both a "light to inform" and a "law to oblige us."[43] No one was born without conscience,[44] yet conscience was impaired in many. South remarked:

> Our present business therefore shall be to show how, and by what courses, this divine light, this candle of the Lord, comes first to burn faint and dim, and so by a gradual decay fainter and fainter,' till at length and by a total extinction it quite sinks to nothing, and so dies away.[45]

While Robert South taught that conscience is present at birth, he was careful to explain ways by which conscience, "the poor remains of our fallen nature," could like a last remaining spark be turned by the devil into darkness.[46] Such a person, through the practice of sin, including perjury, drunkenness, theft, and neglecting duty to one's parents, became destitute of the light.[47]

Robert South, while considering conscience primarily a human faculty, allowed external divine influence in the moral realm. Citing Aristotle, South spoke not only of the "light of the intellect" – another anthropological term – but also of "another light, in the nature of a medium, beaming in upon it by a continual influx and emanation from the great Fountain of Light, and irradiating this intellectual faculty together with the representations of things imprinted thereupon."[48] South continued, describing this "influx" variously as "illuminations...from the Father of lights" or "blessed irradiations which the divine nature is continually darting in upon it."[49]

In this description, Robert South appeared to be positing two entities. First, there was *conscience*, a faculty of the human person, given at birth. Secondly, there were *illuminations* and *irradiations* from God, that acted upon the intellect. The difficulty arose when "sorts and degrees of guilt" formed a "huge thick blot" upon the faculty of the intellect.[50] This allowed the intellect neither to receive nor transmit the "beams" of divine origin. When sin became a "custom," it had a "strangely efficacious power to darken the conscience."[51]

Besides Robert South, Edward Reynolds (1599-1676), Lord Bishop of Norwich, also wrote about conscience. Reynolds – a graduate of Merton College, Oxford – was a prolific writer, authoring more than thirty books in his lifetime, including his *Treatise on the Passions*, still a common undergraduate text at the close of the 17th century.[52] Rector for more than thirty years in Braunston, Northhamptonshire,[53] his extensive pastoral experience lent an irenic tone to his writings. Wesley included in his *Christian Library* a sermon by Reynolds entitled *The Sinfulness of Sin*.[54] In the sermon, Reynolds evidenced a low estimation of the ability of "mere nature" – i.e. faculties like the reason, the conscience, and the will that have been corrupted by original sin – to adequately "feel the weight and curse of a sin committed above five thousand years ago before he was born" or to "feel the spirits of sin running in his blood" after the fall.[55] Speaking of the "remnants of nature in the hearts of men," Reynolds was pessimistic that these alone were sufficient to lead persons to a saving knowledge of God:

> Some things nature is sufficient to teach: God may be felt and found out, in some sense, by those that ignorantly worship him. Nature doth convince men that they are not so good as they should be: the Law is written in the hearts of those who know nothing of the letter of it: idleness, bestiality, lying, luxury, the Cretan poet could condemn in his own countrymen. But these are remnants of nature in the hearts of men, and are but like the blazes and glimmerings of a candle in the

socket; there is much darkness mingled with them. Nature cannot thoroughly convince.[56]

The revelation of God that came through the slight "glimmerings" of human nature were inadequate. To be convinced of our sinfulness, according to Reynolds, we required a separate revelation by God of the divine law.[57] Only then could what is partial and sporadic inside the human being become clear via an exterior revelation of truth.

D. A Cosmological Perspective: Stephen Charnock

In the previous section, sermons from Robert South and Edward Reynolds evoked an anthropological explanation of conscience, of why those who knew nothing of Christ could still have some notion of morality. However, some looked beyond remnants of the *imago Dei*, preferring cosmological explanations of the presence of good among those who had never heard Christian preaching. Stephen Charnock (1628-80), was one such thinker.

Stephen Charnock was a graduate of Emmanuel College, Cambridge, and later a Fellow of New College, Oxford.[58] His ministerial work included a prominent assignment at Christ Church in Dublin, Ireland (1655-60) and – following a fifteen year medical practice in London – he was co-pastor with Thomas Watson of a nonconformist chapel at Crosby Hall, Bishop Gate, London.[59] Richard Greaves described him as an "intensely private and studious man" who was widely read and conversant with Greek and Hebrew.[60] William Gordon Blaikie observed: "His theology was Calvinistic, conceiving as he did that the infinite foreknowledge of God involved divine foreordination, but assigning to man a power of distinguishing good and evil which threw on him the responsibility of his actions."[61]

John Wesley's *Christian Library* contained a two part abridgment of Stephen Charnock's *A Discourse of the Knowledge of God*.[62] Charnock's concern was to compare the inferior divine revelation in Creation to the superior revelation of God in Christ. The former was a "candle-light"; the latter was the "lustre of the day."[63] Charnock characterized our "natural knowledge" of God as "dim." Earlier in the sermon, he observed: "In the Creation God writ Himself in hieroglyphicks, in short characters; in Christ, in a plain and legible hand, which gave a substantial discovery of God."[64] Creation can only afford "languishing notions of God, and a relation to Him fit for that miserable condition, wherein the Fall of Adam has involved us."[65] Though Charnock did not have a *high* view of God's self-revelation in Creation, he nonetheless affirmed that it is possible thereby to know something of the Creator.

While the main thrust of Stephen Charnock's *Discourse* was to exalt Christ as God's ultimate revelation, one early paragraph connected "light" and "grace":

> The whole work of grace is called light, as the whole state of nature is called darkness: As the understanding is the leading faculty, so knowledge is the directing principle that leads, and the will follows. The enlightenings of the one makes men quickly capable of the quickenings of the other.[66]

Charnock's language of "enlightening" and "quickening" resembled John Wesley's terminology when discussing prevenient grace.[67]

E. Prevenient Grace through the "Lens" of Pneumatology

To this point, anthropological and cosmological emphases in the *Christian Library* as related to prevenient grace have been examined. Now begins an analysis of what is by far the most prevalent prevenient grace motif in the *Christian Library*, namely, the use of pneumatological terminology. In the process, six writers will be evaluated: John Smith, John Preston, Isaac Ambrose, John Tillotson, Richard Sibbes, and Robert Bolton.

John Smith (1618-1652)

John Smith was a philosopher and mathematics lecturer at Queen's College, Cambridge.[68] An admirer of Descartes, Smith was part of the group commonly called the "Cambridge Platonists," including Benjamin Whichcote, Ralph Cudworth, Nathaniel Culverwell, Peter Sterry, and John Worthington.[69] Sarah Hutton described Smith's theological framework: "(His) emphasis on practical Christianity, his high valuation of reason as an instrument of faith, and his optimistic view of human nature are all features of the tolerant divinity that he inherited from his teacher, Whichcote, and shared with the other Cambridge Platonists."[70] Dead of tuberculosis at a young age, Smith's *Select Discourses* was only published posthumously in 1660. An abridgment of his *A Discourse Concerning the True Method of Attaining Divine Knowledge* as well as *A Discourse Treating of Legal Righteousness, Evangelical Righteousness, or the Righteousness of Faith* appeared in John Wesley's *Christian Library*.[71]

John Smith held a negative view of the human intellect. In *Legal Righteousness,* he described our minds as "vulgar," since upon them is a "crust of impurity."[72] This "crust" was as a "thick and palpable darkness which cannot comprehend that divine light that shines in the mind of all men, but makes them deny the very truth they seem to entertain."[73] Later, he spoke of "that divine light and goodness" that had its origin in God. It was not limited in scope, but "flows forth" upon all.[74]

In *True Method*, John Smith explained that our sensitivity to this "divine light" could be increased, provided that we "shut the eyes of the sense" and open the "eye of the soul."[75] This was done in part by abstaining from "bodily things" and setting ourselves free from slavery to the flesh,[76] but more importantly, it was a work of the Holy Spirit:

> Besides in wicked men there are sometimes distastes of vice, and flashes of love to virtue, which are the faint strugglings of an higher life within them, which they crucify again by their wicked sensuality. As truth does not always act in good men, so neither doth sense always act in wicked men: they may sometimes have their sober fits; and a divine Spirit breathing upon them may then blow up some sparks of true understanding within them; though they may soon quench them again, and rake them up in the ashes of their own earthly thoughts.[77]

While this excerpt made no explicit mention of prevenient grace, it did picture the resistance that became an important element in John Wesley's doctrine of prevenient grace. Grace increased as long as the recipient of that grace did not quench it.

John Preston (1587-1628)

A student of music at King's College, Cambridge, John Preston switched to Queen's College, where he pursued the study of natural philosophy and medicine.[78] Named a Fellow in 1609, he was converted in 1611/12 under the preaching of John Cotton, who became a lifelong friend. As an ordained priest, his ministry varied, including service as master of Emmanuel College, Cambridge, preacher at the Honourable Society of Lincoln's Inn, and a lectureship at Holy Trinity Church, Cambridge.[79] Jonathan Moore called Preston a "conforming reformer," one who appears to have straddled the divide between Puritans and Episcopalians in the Church of England, particularly in his support of both extemporaneous and formal prayers, but also by establishing devotional publications as a new spiritual genre.[80] John Wesley's *Christian Library* contains an abridgement of John Preston's *The Breast-Plate of Faith and Love*.[81] In select quotes, one can discern a three-fold work of the Holy Spirit: 1) drawing the sinner; 2) preparing the sinner for conversion, through "humiliation," and 3) making faith effectual.

Drawing the sinner. Under the general heading of faith, John Preston spoke of the "drawing" effectuated by the Spirit of God:

> Seeing then the will hath a part in faith, as well as the understanding and this must be drawn, the question is, who must draw it? This is the work of God; He only hath the sovereignty over the will and affections of man...so saith our LORD, John 6:44 – No man can come to me except the Father draw him. But how shall that be done? It is not such a drawing as when man is drawn by force; but it is a drawing by changing the will and affections...Draw me and I will run after thee, saith the desiring soul...[82]

Preparing the sinner for conversion through humiliation. John Preston continued to describe the work of the Holy Spirit prior to conversion: "There must go always a work of humiliation before the testimony of the Spirit."[83] The Spirit was symbolized for Preston by a "wind that rends the rocks." Only when the mountains come down and the way is made plain could God come to us in a "soft voice."[84]

Making Faith Effectual. A final way in which the Spirit of God acted preveniently was through faith: "We are not able to believe of ourselves, nay, we are so far from it, that we strive against it; so that, if God Himself put not his hand to the work, no man can believe."[85]

Isaac Ambrose (1604-64)

A graduate of Brasenose College, Oxford, Isaac Ambrose served pastorates in Castleton, Derbyshire, and Clapham, Yorkshire.[86] Roger Pooley credited him for playing a prominent role in the establishment of Presbyterianism in Lancashire in the 1740s.[87] Ejected from the Anglican ministry in 1662 due to non-conformity, Ambrose has been called "the most meditative Puritan of Lancashire."[88]

Isaac Ambrose's writings were largely "free of controversy and doctrinal refutation," instead drawing upon the "affectionate strain of Puritanism, weaving together such writers as Rutherford, Bolton, and Baxter with Ambrose's own style of warmth and urgency."[89] John Wesley abridged Ambrose's *The Doctrine of Regeneration* and from it came many insights into the work of the Holy Spirit in the period immediately prior to conversion.[90] Ambrose laid the groundwork for his discussion of the new birth by first describing the person apart from Christ. What was his or her condition? Ambrose clarified:

> In a word, the understanding is darkened, the will enthralled, the affections disordered, the memory defiled, the conscience benumbed, all the inner man is full of sin, and here is no part that is good, no not one. How needful is a new birth to a man in this case? Can he enter into heaven, that favours all of earth? Will those precious gates of gold and pearls open to a sinner? No, he must be new moulded and sanctified.[91]

The unregenerated person had a measure of wisdom, knowing the "light of reason" and may have been "furnished with store of rare and excellent learning." For all this, he or she was without "true spiritual wisdom."[92] The conscience acted as a "herald," bringing warning, but also as an "accuser." Ambrose described conscience as a "serjeant to arrest him"[93] and as an "executioner" to warn a person of hell.[94] Conscience could be active in such a person, but often he or she paid it no attention, and would quickly "lull it to sleep again" by sinning, resulting in despair.[95] For the new birth to take place, the will of the individual had to first be quickened and revived by God's grace.[96]

Isaac Ambrose employed the images of "light" and "drawing" to describe the gracious action of the Holy Spirit. God "lets the light into the soul of a poor sinner," and "draws with the cord of his mercy."[97] Ambrose delineated two kinds of divine drawing:

- *moral drawing* – This was the enlightenment of the mind, the moving of the will "to embrace things offered";
- *physical drawing* – Powerless left to oneself, it was the Lord who "enables the soul to lay hold of the things offered."[98] God was able to "pluck" the sinner away from "those sins that harbour in it unto himself."[99]

The regeneration of the sinner was effected by the agency of preaching and the work of the Holy Spirit. Wherever the "doctrine of the Gospel" was preached, the Holy Spirit "comes to regenerate."[100] The new birth transpired by "the Spirit of God dropping grace into their hearts betimes."[101]

John Tillotson (1630-94)

A graduate of Clare College, Cambridge, and later Archbishop of Canterbury, John Tillotson was a talented preacher. H.R. McAdoo called him the most influential of the Latitudinarians.[102] Alexander Gordon noted regarding his influence: "Hitherto the pulpit had been the great stronghold of puritanism, under Tillotson it became a powerful agency for weaning men from puritan ideas."[103] Noting that while Tillotson early rejected his Calvinistic upbringing, he still harbored a deep sympathy with nonconformity to the end of his life,[104] Isobel Rivers remarked:

> To adherents and Catholics he stressed the rational grounds of faith and the close connection between natural and revealed religion; to nonconformists that justification included obedience and faith included works; and to Socinians that Christianity required the acceptance of mysteries incomprehensible to reason.[105]

John Wesley included in his *Christian Library* excerpts from John Tillotson's *Sermons*.[106] In Tillotson, one encountered a mix of grace and Spirit language more clearly than in any other *Christian Library* writer. "Repentance unto life" could be obtained by "complying with that grace which God affords them."[107] The Archbishop continued:" And though he that accepts it does not save himself, yet he that refuseth it destroys himself."[108] While for Tillotson much of the language of the Holy Spirit's assistance applied to believers, so they could perform "what the Gospel requires of us,"[109] unbelievers were not excluded:

> And though the Spirit be said to be given to them that already believe, that is, so as to dwell and reside, to take up his constant habitation and abode only in these; yet this doth not exclude a preventing influence and operation of God's Holy Spirit upon the minds of those to whom the Gospel is offered, disposing them to embrace and entertain it, and working faith in them. And in this sense it is, that "faith" in Scripture is said to be the "gift of God," because it is first wrought in them by the influence and operation of the blessed Spirit, which is promised to dwell and reside in them after they believe.[110]

Tillotson clarified that the Holy Spirit gave the unbeliever "strength and assistance," working all that is necessary for salvation, as long as the Spirit was not resisted.[111]

John Tillotson was significant for the development of John Wesley's thought. Wesley read Tillotson's *Sermons* in 1732 while at Oxford.[112] The 1740s were a period of confrontation over the doctrine of "free grace" with George Whitefield, the "imputed righteousness" debate with James Hervey, and a renewal of the predestinarian controversy with Augustus Toplady.[113] Wesley's inclusion of Tillotson's view on the gracious work of the Holy Spirit in the *Christian Library* in the early 1750s may have reflected his desire to further fortify the Methodist societies against Calvinistic teaching.

Richard Sibbes, or Sibs/Sibbs (1577-1635)

The author of more than thirty volumes, Richard Sibbes – hobbled by a speech impediment – nevertheless rose to renown beginning in 1610 as one of the Sunday afternoon lecturers at Holy Trinity Church, Cambridge.[114] Appointed in 1626 to the mastership of St. Catherine's College, Cambridge, he was considered a moderate Puritan, opposing kneeling during communion, the wearing of surplices, and the signing of the cross during baptism.[115] The importance of the operation of the Holy Spirit in Sibbes' theology was underscored by R.T. Kendall, who affirmed that Sibbes "gave but perfunctory attention to the doctrine of temporary faith – and never uses the expression itself – and stresses instead the positive work of the Holy Spirit in the soul who is weary with sin – 'the bruised reed.' "[116]

Richard Sibbes was best known for his 1638 *The Fountaine Opened, or the Mysterie of Godlinesse*.[117] Appearing in John Wesley's *Christian Library*, Sibbes used the metaphor of "light" to describe God's work in the mind of the Christian. The objective was to "come to know this mystery as we ought, and to carry ourselves answerable."[118] Sibbes advised:

> We must desire God to open our eyes, that as the light hath shined, so we may discern it. Though the mystery be now revealed by preaching, books, and other helps, yet to see this mystery, and make right use of it, there is required a spiritual light, to join with this outward light. And hence comes a necessity of depending upon God's Spirit.[119]

While this selection applied to the understanding of Scripture by converted persons, a later passage in *Mysterie of Godlinesse* speculated that the Spirit may be involved even before conversion: "For it (faith) draws all other graces after it; it enlivens and quickens the soul; it is the spring of spiritual life in us; it is the first grace of all. There are some degrees of the Spirit, perhaps, before it, but all graces have their quickening from faith..."[120] Richard Sibbes juxtaposed the language of Spirit and grace, though prevenient grace was never explicit in his treatise.

Robert Bolton (1572-1631)

The sixth son of his father, Adam Bolton, Robert Bolton graduated from Lincoln College, Oxford, and later was named Fellow of Brasenose College, Oxford, teaching logic and both moral and natural philosophy.[121] Thomas Peacock was influential in Bolton's conversion to a strict form of Protestantism which he was to follow for the remainder of his life."[122] Bolton was best known for his public lectureship at Kettering – where he was outspoken against corruption – but also for his service as pastor beginning in 1610 at Broughton, Northamptonshire.[123] John Wesley abridged Bolton's 1631 *A Discourse About the State of True Happiness*,[124] showing his esteem for the Puritan divine by including a nineteen page summary of his life in the *Christian Library*.[125]

Robert Bolton's primary concern in *True Happiness* was to discuss saving grace. Nevertheless, in so doing, he provided glimpses of the work of grace mediated by the Holy Spirit prior to the moment of conversion. His teaching on the pneumatology of grace in *True Happiness* may be summarized as follows:

The Holy Spirit Enlightened the Understanding. A "formal hypocrite," though not yet converted, could still profit from the "spirit of illumination":

> Concerning other parts of divine knowledge, and other points of religion, he may be furnished with store of rare and excellent learning, in fathers, schoolmen, commentaries, controversies; he may be endued with subtilty (sic) in disputing and defending the truth of God; yea, and in resolving cases of conscience too:

nay, besides this, the formal hypocrite may be made partaker of some degrees of the spirit of illumination, for the good of his children. For I doubt not, but many have much light of judgment, that have little integrity of conscience; and are inspired by the spirit of illumination for the good of others, that have no part in the spirit of sanctification.[126]

The "sanctifying Spirit" or the "Spirit of God" was characterized by Robert Bolton as a "general influence concur (sic) to the illumination of the understanding with knowledge."[127] Though these "kinds and measures of inward graces" were only a "shadow of true regeneration,"[128] yet this "illumination" could result in "a civil reformation of the will even in the unregenerate."[129]

God's grace unresisted saved, but grace resisted condemned. In a passage retained nearly word for word by John Wesley's Christian Library, Robert Bolton explained the gracious operation of the Holy Spirit:

> It is not difference of degrees and measure that takes away the nature of faith. A small drop of water is as truly water as the whole ocean. A little spark is as truly fire, as the mightiest flame. The hand of a little child may receive a pearl, as well as the hand of the greatest giant, though not hold to it strongly. A weak faith may be a true faith. This only must I advise, that if this grain of mustard seed, watered with the dew of grace, grow not towards a great tree; if this spark, enkindled by the Spirit of God, spread not into a big flame; if this small measure of faith be not edged with a longing fervency after fulness of persuasion, and seconded with an assiduous and serious endeavour after more perfection, it is no sound and saving faith but only a counterfeit show, and a deceiving shadow.[130]

For Bolton, a "gross hypocrite" was one who "sinneth against the light of conscience."[131] In the same paragraph, he spoke of the Spirit of God, who was both "softening" and "sanctifying."[132] While "some good motion of God's Spirit" could be "stirred up in him by the preaching of the Word,"[133] nonetheless, "resistance to godly motions" and "sin" could lead to "hardness."[134] The "formal hypocrite," though the recipient of "inward graces," had to experience the "truth of regeneration" and a "sound conversion," without which he or she would be "cut off forever from all hope of immortality, and shall never be able to stand firm and sure in the day of the Lord Jesus."[135]

F. Anthropological/Pneumatological Blending: Samuel Annesley's Two "Lights"

Samuel Annesley (1620-1696) – a graduate of Queen's College, Oxford – also earned a doctorate in civil law (1648).[136] Best known today as the maternal grandfather of John Wesley, Annesley fathered twenty-four or twenty-five children,[137] all the while earning a solid reputation as an able preacher and pastor, first in 1657 as a lecturer at St. Paul's in London, then beginning in 1658 as pastor at St. Giles, Cripplegate.[138] In 1662, along with two thousand other non-conformists, he was ejected from his pulpit, following the Restoration of King Charles II.[139] Characterized by Newton Key as "an unbending presbyterian," a defiant Annesley held conventicles and was active in the erection of public meeting houses long before the indulgence of 1672.[140] A collection of his sermons – *The Morning Exercises at Cripplegate* – proved popular, going into four editions by 1677.

John Wesley's *Christian Library* included a selection from the *Morning Exercises*, an abridgement of *How we may be universally and exactly conscientious*, a sermon from Acts 24:16.[141] Samuel Annesley's homily was also quoted at-length in Wesley's 1788 sermon, *On Conscience*.[142] Annesley defined "conscience" as self-judgment of one's "estate and actions, as they are subject to the judgment of God."[143] Quoting Brochmand's definition, he maintained that it was "a kind of silent reasoning of the mind, whose definitive sentence is received by some affection of the heart, whereby those things which are judged to be good and right, are approved of with delight, but those things which are evil and naught, are disapproved with grief and sorrow."[144] Conscience was universal; it was a "tribunal erected in the breasts of men" that serves to "accuse delinquents" but also to "excuse those who do what is right."[145] Conscience "surveys" our duties toward both God and others.[146] In all of these descriptions, conscience was an anthropological category.

Having defined "conscience," Samuel Annesley attempted to explain its function in relation with two "lights," the "light of nature" and "divine revelation":

> In general, the proper office of conscience is discursively to apply that light which is in the mind unto particular actions, or cases. The light which is in the mind is the light of nature, or the light of divine revelation. By the light of nature, I understand those common notions, which are written in the heart of men, which (as a brand plucked out of the common burning) are the relics of the image of God after the Fall...By divine revelation I mean both the standing rule of Scripture and God's extraordinary discoveries of himself, whether by dreams or visions, or prophecies, or other spiritual communications...[147]

It is important to compare this original statement with John Wesley's abridgement of Annesley in the *Christian Library*:

> In general, the proper office of conscience is to apply that light which is in the mind, to particular actions or cases. The light which is in the mind, is either the light of nature, or rather preventing grace; or the light of divine revelation. By the light of nature, I understand those common notions, which are written in the hearts of men, which (as a brand plucked out of the common burning) are the relics of the image of God after the Fall.[148]

The phrase "or rather preventing grace" was an interpretive gloss added by John Wesley to Samuel Annesley's original sermon. By adding this phrase, Wesley appears to have affirmed that prevenient grace was an anthropological phenomenon, not to be confused with divine revelation. Charles Rogers concluded: "It is the duty or business of conscience to apply the principles of the law known to man inwardly by prevenient grace and outwardly by revelation to his own thoughts and actions, thereby bringing judgment upon himself concerning his moral condition."[149]

Both John Wesley and Charles Rogers made prevenient grace a strictly internal matter. However, Samuel Annesley's metaphor was "light," and he spoke of *two* lights, not one. There were both the internal "light of nature" and the external "light of divine revelation." There were the moral "relics" of the fall remaining in the human heart, yet there were also diverse channels of God's self revelation, including visions and prophecy. Rather than inferring that only the internal relics of the fall are "preventing grace," per Wesley and Rogers, it would be a more accurate reading of *Universally and Exactly Conscientious* to conclude that prevenient grace had both internal and external *loci*, i.e. two lights, the internal relics of the fall and the external "spiritual communications" alluded to by Annesley. In other terms, prevenient grace functioned both anthropologically *and* pneumatologically.

G. An Eclectic Approach: Richard Lucas and the *Enquiry After Happiness*

Richard Lucas (1648-1715) was a graduate of Jesus College, Oxford, and a highly reputed preacher and writer.[150] Edward Vallance maintained that Lucas had a "high reputation for piety," noting his service first as pastor (1678-83) at St. Stephen, Coleman St., London, and later as lecturer of St. Olave, Southwork.[151] Though his eyesight had never been strong, in 1683, it failed him totally. Inspired by the dictum of Thomas Lamb – "The life of a man is to be estimated by its usefulness to the world" – Lucas shunned self-pity, and focused his attention in a positive direction by composing his 1685 *Enquiry After Happiness*.[152]

In the *Enquiry* – abridged by John Wesley in the *Christian Library*[153] – Lucas defined his objective as determining "the notion of happiness," and steering his life accordingly.[154] For Lucas, the goodness and holiness of God were foundational to any consideration of human happiness:

> It is evident therefore of what importance it is to propagate and settle in the minds of men a right understanding of the divine nature; and of all the attributes of God, there are none that have a more immediate and powerful influence, either upon the conduct of men's life, or the life of his mind, than those two, his holiness and goodness; these make us willing and desirous to believe that there is a God; these make us love him and depend upon him, as one from whom we may rationally expect all that is good.[155]

Having established the goodness of God, in a later chapter, Richard Lucas took up the question of fate. He defined the word as "one's present and future state being fix'd and determined by a fatal and inexorable necessity."[156] If God was the "Author" and the "instrument" of faith, then what could be said of those who demonstrate no faith at all? Whatever the solution, Lucas refused predestinarian formulas:

> This decree supposes him (God) so utter an enemy to, and hater of, mankind, that he made the far greater part to no other end, but only to make him miserable. Let any unprejudiced person judge now, whether this be not as contradictory to the Scripture as it is to sense; nor is it possible that any one, unless prejudiced, should look into holy writ, and not discern evidently that man's ruin is the effect of sin…God is so far from being fond of our sufferings and calamities, that he is

ever and anon bewailing the disappointment of his love, the defeat of his grace and mercy by our obstinacy and impenitence...[157]

Lucas later warned that if we "debar" individuals from God's grace, then the notion of fate is inevitable: "For what more fatal necessity can a wretched creature lie under, than *natural impotence*, utterly destitute and for ever forsaken of divine assistance?"[158] If God's grace is not "universal" and "sufficient" to help us attain virtue and happiness, then we simultaneously deny God's power, goodness, and sincerity.[159]

A few pages earlier, Richard Lucas had affirmed that it is in our power to be "virtuous and happy." However, he qualified the statement: "Nor can I think this assertion any ways injurious to the honour and goodness of God, if it be remembered, that whatever power I attribute to man, I acknowledge derived from God."[160] But how is that power derived? Here Lucas synthesized strands of the anthropological, cosmological, and pneumatological approaches to grace. He asked: "Why are men not good? Why are they not happy? Shall we say, that God doth not vouchsafe his grace? Shall we impute men's misery to God?"[161] Answering his own question, he listed five ways in which God's grace manifests itself: 1) through the "sufferings of his Son"; 2) by the "vigorous attempts and endeavours of his Spirit"; 3) by heaven and earth, which are "stamped with the impress of his *power* and *goodness*"; 4) by "various methods of his providence"[162] that both "contrive" and "pursue" our happiness, and 5) through the presence of conscience.[163]

Richard Lucas was curious about the ancient philosophers, such as Pythagoras, Socrates, and Plato. How were they able to live virtuously and happily? The answer was *divine assistance*:

> They were extremely sensible of that opposition which virtue met with from the world and the body; they were extremely sensible that the inclination of the one, and the affluence and troubles of the other did naturally tend to engage them in vice; and therefore though they do sometimes magnify human nature, yet they were not so forgetful of their own infirmities, or the condition of this life, as not to judge the assistance of God indispensably necessary to render them virtuous and happy...[164]

Though most of their contemporaries worshipped devils, the philosophers worshipped good spirits. How was this possible? Lucas credited the "light of nature," the "image of God," and "divine providence."[165] These may be seen as cosmological, anthropological, and pneumatological interpretations of God's gracious interaction with humanity.

Summary:
The Christian Library and Prevenient Grace

Having examined eleven writers who appeared in John Wesley's *Christian Library*, two conclusions suggest themselves:

1. While the term "preventing" was rare, related terms were frequent. Other than the two instances examined, the first where John Wesley inserted the phrase "preventing grace" into Samuel Annesley's sermon, and the second in John Tillotson, this expression was nearly absent from the *Christian Library*. Nevertheless, words that denote some aspect of prevenient grace were repeatedly employed. These included "light," "conscience," "law," "spark," "illumination," "quickening," and "drawing." This cluster of concepts re-appeared in the writings of John Wesley, where he gathered them up like individual cords to weave a "rope," the "rope" of a more highly developed doctrine of prevenient grace.

2. **Most writers in the *Christian Library* preferred pneumatological language when talking about pre-conversion divine/human interaction.** While some described God's self-revelation using anthropological or cosmological categories, more were comfortable with pneumatological terminology.[166] For writers in the *Christian Library*, the function of prevenient grace was largely subsumed under the rubric of the work of the Holy Spirit.

William Tilly Revisited[167]

William Tilly was a Church of England clergyman, and Fellow of Corpus Christi College, Oxford.[168] While little is known of this Queen Anne supporter and high churchman disliked by Non-jurors,[169] Richard Heitzenrater noted that Wesley owned Tilly's 1712 *Sixteen Sermons* and later extracted and published it.[170] Herbert McGonigle speculated that Wesley's 1732 reading of Tilly may have been preparation for preaching at the university church of St. Mary's.[171] Whatever his motive, Tilly's impact upon John Wesley's concept of prevenient grace was unmistakeable.[172]

A. Analysis of Selected Sermons from William Tilly

1. *The Folly and Danger of Being Conceited of our Spiritual Knowledge*

This sermon on 1 Cor. 8:2 was preached before Oxford university in January 1710.[173] According to Tilly, what was the source of spiritual knowledge? It was a gift of God's grace:

> (Spiritual knowledge) is the mere gift of God's free grace and bounty, in the revelation of himself by his Word without, and the assistance and inspirations of his Holy Spirit within our minds, and therefore to presume and vaunt ourselves upon it, is a great sin; because it implies we vainly ascribe it to ourselves.[174]

This "grace" was a "revelation" that came both from Scripture and the inspiration of the Holy Spirit. Without God's self-revelation to us, "we can hardly have known anything either of the divine nature, or our own duty."[175]

Wiiliam Tilly described anthropologically the pitiful human condition apart from the grace of God. In the "old heathen world," he wrote, "all the light that could be struck out, in so many ages, by the utmost pains of men...amounted to little more than a faint suspicion of some religious truths."[176] According to the "Gentile philosophy," the soul was immortal, and there was some notion of the "gods." Nonetheless, the "wits of men" were extremely limited. They were "entangled in doubts and difficulties." Without "the assistance of God's enlightening grace, there was darkness."[177]

2. Of Grieving the Holy Spirit

Based on Eph. 4:32, this 1708 sermon was particularly helpful in explaining how God's grace can be resisted.[178] It was noteworthy for its juxtaposition of the language of grace with the activity of the Holy Spirit. The Holy Spirit was

> the great spring and fountain from whence are derived all that grace and virtue, by which the stains of our corrupt nature are cleansed, and by which we are endued with those divine qualities, and that heavenly disposition of mind, whereby we come to resemble God himself in his perfections, and are enabled to conform our actions to his will.[179]

Sin occurred "despite all his powerful assistances, in defiance of all his rebukes."[180] Through the commission of sins, we could "forfeit and diminish, and even lose this blessed influx of *divine grace* upon our minds."[181] The symptoms of this diminished presence of grace were "dryness" and "barrenness of spirit," both the result of wilful sinning.[182]

William Tilly depicted the Holy Spirit as a "vigourous light from heaven." This light could not be stifled by what he terms "the weakness of our present nature." Only high-handed sin, and a neglect of "spiritual improvements" could grieve the Holy Spirit.[183] On the other hand, we were responsible to pursue a "sobriety of mind." How was this possible? Tilly explained that this was "in our own power by virtue of his *general preventing grace* to form and prepare within ourselves; and he expects we should do so, it being the ground and foundation upon which he is to proceed with on his after-workings."[184] Was it only the Holy Spirit that Tilly linked with prevenient grace? No; to a pneumatological frame-of-reference he added an anthropological one, i.e. conscience. The "sin of presumption" meant not only disobeying Scripture, but "resolutely going against the...lively, full, and intimate convictions of his own mind and conscience."[185]

It is not always obvious in this sermon whether William Tilly was describing the state of the unregenerate or the regenerate since he spoke alternately of our "improvement in holiness," as well as of our "regeneration."[186] This point will become more clear following an examination of two final selections from *Sixteen Sermons*.

3. The Grace of God and the Liberty of Man's Will [187]

Based on Phil. 4:13, this 1702 sermon from William Tilly provided the clearest statement of his doctrine of prevenient grace.[188] Tilly's methodology was a precursor to John Wesley's *via media*. He described then rejected two extreme positions, positing that the truth lies somewhere in-between. What were the extreme positions?

1) *Christian fatalism* – This was the viewpoint that "the mind of man (is) to be purely passive and ineffective in the work of his conversion and duty."[189]

2) *Pelagianism* – Here too much "loose" was given to the "freedom" of a "depraved will." This was based upon an overestimation of the will's power, and was in opposition to any concept of God's grace.[190]

Having identified the extreme positions, the rest of the sermon was given to developing a doctrine of grace that protected the meaning of Paul's call to "work out your salvation with fear and trembling." William Tilly observed that this phrase only made sense if we have "some kind of liberty in our wills, and a possibility of our own endeavours in the matters of our obedience."[191] It remained to be seen how this "liberty" was effected in the human soul.

For William Tilly, the fall was a difficult subject. At first, he appeared to waver whether the "liberty of man's will to good" had been entirely forfeited because of Adam's sin. Why this reticence? First, Tilly suggested that we could not be sure "from what perfection we are fallen."[192] Secondly, it was not always clear "into what degree of degeneracy and corruption we are sunk."[193] Despite this hesitancy, his conclusion seemed Augustinian:

> In general, I think we may determine safely, that the powers of our soul are so exceedingly bruised and enfeebled by the prevarication of our first parents, that our natural inclinations run only to evil, and that, before our new birth and regeneration in Christ our Saviour, to do good, and thereby to procure the favour of God, we have no power.[194]

Tilly was hardly optimistic about human possibility apart from grace. Persons who were "unregenerate" or "natural" had "no free will or liberty to produce good works."[195] And so-called "liberty" remaining after the fall tended only toward evil.[196]

What was the remedy for this miserable, grace-less condition? The only answer for William Tilly laid in what he called "baptismal grace." Tilly clarified: " 'Tis the Spirit of God in baptism that revives and rekindles those sparks and remainders of life, which have escaped the deluge of original corruption, and recovers them once more into a perfect way."[197] This baptism was infant baptism, for it occurred "before we can remember."[198]

Where did this leave the discussion of human liberty? Only the Christian possessed liberty. Liberty was not "the result of our being men" but a "consequent of our spiritual birth."[199] In baptism only was the liberty of the will "restored and confirmed to us, by second covenant, which was so entirely lost and forfeited by our prevaricating with the conditions of the first."[200] While the new covenant conveyed prevenient grace, its foundation was the "merits and death of our blessed Saviour."[201] The doctrine of prevenient grace was for William Tilly the *via media*, the resolution of the age-old problem of how divine and human wills interact in the salvation encounter. He explained:

> But for now for a man to assert, that from a principle of preventing grace laid and hidden in our nature, at our regeneration in baptism, we are enabled to move our selves without any other help some of the first degrees towards our amendment, is a doctrine that does not in the least derogate from the grace of God, because it does not advance the strength of nature above its due proportion, in that it supposes nature to work only in the power and efficacy of grace itself.[202]

B. Summary of Findings from William Tilly's Sermons

Having examined the selections from *Sixteen Sermons* that are germane to our topic, it is possible to summarize their teaching on prevenient grace as follows

"Liberty" was a reality only for the Christian. Tilly was pessimistic about the condition of the unregenerate. The only liberty was "Christian liberty," i.e. the ability to fulfil our duty to God and others through the prevenient grace activated in baptism and the assisting grace communicated by the Holy Spirit to the regenerate.

Prevenient grace, though anthropological, was also pneumatological. While Tilly alluded to "conscience," "sparks and remainders of life" in the unregenerate, as well as a grace that is "hidden in our nature," he emphasized the work of the Holy Spirit. Spirit language was laced throughout the sermons examined. Indeed, prevenient grace would remain latent without the Spirit's activity in baptism.

The prevenient operation of the Holy Spirit could be resisted. This was particularly clear in the sermon *Of Grieving the Holy Spirit*. Deliberate sinning diminished the effectiveness of prevenient grace.

Jeremy Taylor on Prevenient Grace

Having seen the contours of prevenient grace in William Tilly, this inquiry turns to one of the most celebrated minds of 17th century Anglicanism, Jeremy Taylor (1613-1667).[203] A graduate of both Gonville and Caius College, Cambridge, and University College, Oxford, Taylor became a protégé of Bishop Laud.[204] When Taylor preached before him for the first time, Laud remarked that he was "very young," upon which Taylor "humbly begged his grace to pardon that fault, and promised, if he lived, to mend it."[205] Taylor in 1736 was named a Fellow at All Souls, Oxford, and later taught in Wales, before ascending in 1660 to the bishopric of Down and Connor, Ireland, under appointment from King Charles II.[206]

Possessed of a prolific pen, Jeremy Taylor is classed among the "Caroline writers," those who promoted "the centrality of a simple and unadorned concept of holiness for everyman in the Anglican scheme of spiritual direction."[207] W.C. de Pauley affirmed that Taylor "is not a speculative thinker, but essentially a practical man."[208] This did not deter Taylor – described as a "combative preacher" – from participating in debates, including extended correspondence regarding the doctrine of original sin.[209] This included Taylor's rejection of the concept of a corrupted human nature inherited from Adam; Taylor accepted only physical death as the enduring consequence of Adam's sin.[210] Having examined Taylor's doctrine of original sin, Cary Balzer concluded: "Jeremy Taylor described the fall as serious, but not as intolerable as some would describe it, and not so tragic that grace cannot overcome it."[211]

While Jeremy Taylor had a lasting impact upon the theology of John Wesley,[212] little has been written about what Taylor believed regarding prevenient grace.[213] In one passage, Taylor asked: "For let it be seriously weighed, to what purpose is the variety of God's grace? What use is there of *preventing*, restraining, concomitant, subsequent, and persevering grace, unless it be in order to religious conversation?"[214] Taylor rarely used the phrase "preventing" in relation to grace, though concepts akin to it served an important purpose, occasionally appearing in his writings.

A. The "Law of Nature" as Conscience

In the preface to *The Life of our Blessed Lord and Saviour Jesus Christ*, Jeremy Taylor observed: "Now God, who takes more care for the good of man, than man does for his own, did not only imprint these laws in the hearts and understandings of man, but did take care to make this light shine clear enough to walk by, by adopting some instances of the natural laws into religion."[215] Here, God's "laws" were part-and-parcel of the human being at creation.

In the same preface, Jeremy Taylor wrote of the "two great natural laws," i.e. loving God and neighbor. Did knowledge of these laws depend upon "special revelation"? Could they be known by those who had "lost all memory of tradition"? Taylor answered affirmatively. Even the person devoid of special revelation had both "natural reason" and "conscience." The first was "sufficient ability to do all that should be necessary to live well and happily."[216] The second was not a fear of hell, but "a dissatisfaction, a disease, a removing out of the place, a unquietness of spirit, even when there is no monitor or observer."[217]

In Book 2 of the obscure *Ductor Dubitantium*,[218] Jeremy Taylor interestingly defined "the law of nature in general" not in cosmological terms, but anthropologically, as being "the universal law of the world, or the law of mankind, concerning common necessities to which we are *inclined by nature*, invited by consent, prompted by reason, but is bound upon us only by the commands of God."[219] Likewise, in *The Rule and Exercises of Holy Living*, Taylor described God as "specially present in the consciences of all persons, good and bad, by way of testimony and judgment: that is, he is there a remembrancer to call our actions to mind, a witness to bring them to judgment, and a judge to acquit or condemn."[220]

The scope of conscience was impressive. The "law of nature" was universal, present among "very many men and nations" who had "no entercourse (sic) with God as a lawgiver."[221] Good and evil were discernible only because God was the "lawgiver" and "Lord of his conscience."[222] In Taylor, though conscience was part of the human fabric, it was "primarily intellectual rather than emotional."[223]

B. The Necessity of Revelation as Supplementary to Conscience

Timothy Sedgwick, while acknowledging the role that conscience played in Jeremy Taylor's moral theology, maintained that for Taylor, "natural law" (or conscience) was inadequate.[224] If it were sufficient, all nations would admit of the same laws, but they did not.[225] Revelation was the ground of the Christian moral life.[226] To the "law of nature" had to be added the "law of Christianity," i.e. "the express voice of God, tradition, providence, education, and all sorts of influence from God, and intercourse with man."[227]

For Jeremy Taylor, this "influence" was both Scripture and the Holy Spirit. In conscience, God's laws had been written upon people's hearts, but the laws had to be re-inscribed "with a quill taken from the wings of the holy Dove,"[228] i.e. the Spirit of God, who was "the great engraver and scribe of the new covenant."[229] The restoration of conscience by the work of the Holy Spirit was affirmed elsewhere by Taylor:

> The law of nature is a transcript of the wisdom and will of God written in the tables of our mind...written with the finger of God, first in the tables of our hearts. But those tables we, like Moses, brake with letting them fall out of our hands, upon occasion of the evil manners of the world: but God wrought them again for us, as He did for Moses by His spirit, in all the ages of the world, more or less, by arts of instruction and secret insinuation, by all the ways proportioned to a reasonable nature...[230]

That for Taylor the Holy Spirit and Scripture were intimately connected is clear. "Holy Writ," wrote Raymond Peterson, "republishes and clarifies the natural law."[231] Revelation was the ground of the Christian moral life.[232]

C. Characteristics of Prevenient Grace

Beyond references to nature, conscience, Scripture, and the Holy Spirit, Jeremy Taylor also wrote about grace. As noted above, the word "prevenient" rarely fell from Taylor's pen. Nonetheless, several passages revealed images that later seemed to influence the thinking of the Wesley brothers regarding the doctrine.

Grace could be accepted or resisted. In a sermon on 2 Peter 3:18, *Of Growth in Grace*, Jeremy Taylor dealt not only with the progress of the new believer, but first portrayed the awakening of the sinner:

> But when the grace of God begins to work upon a man's spirit, it makes the conscience nice and tender: and although the sin, as yet, does not displease the man...yet he will not endure to be used so ill by his sin...But while the Spirit of God is doing this work in man, man must also be...a "fellow worker with God;" he must entertain the Spirit, attend his inspirations, receive his whispers, obey all his motions, invite him farther...When we leave every sin, when we resolve never to return to the chains, when we have no love for the world but such as may be a servant of God; then I account that we are entered into a state of grace, from whence I am not to begin to reckon the commencement of this precept, "Grow in grace, and in the knowledge of our Lord Jesus Christ."[233]

Likewise, in *The Deceitfulness of the Human Heart*, a sermon on Jeremiah 17:9, Taylor portrayed how individuals could resist "the violence of God's grace." When God graciously advises that sin is "transient and vain, unsatisfying and empty," the "heart of man shuffles all these discourses into disorder." Taylor warned:

> And if such incogitancy comes to be habitual, as it is in very many men – first by resisting the motions of the Holy Spirit, then by quenching him – we shall find

the consequence to be, first an indifferency, then a dullness (sic), then a lethargy, then a direct hating the ways of God and it commonly ends in a wretchedness of spirit, to be manifested on our death bed.[234]

Grace not resisted would increase. Jeremy Taylor, in his *The Mercy of Divine Judgments*, a sermon based on Romans 2:4, used the metaphors of seeds, light, and heat to explain the progress of grace in the human heart:

> For as the sun sends forth a benign and gentle influence on the seeds of plants, that it may invite forth the active and plastic power from its recess and secrecy...so doth the Almighty Father of all creatures...send forth his blessings upon us, that we, using them aright, should make ourselves capable of greater...And if we, by despising such gracious rays of light and heat, stop their progress, and interrupt their design, the loss is not God's, but ours; we shall be the miserable and accursed people.[235]

We only had "choice" because it was Spirit enabled. Earlier, we saw that Jeremy Taylor rejected Calvinistic predestination. In the *Ductor Dubitantium*, he explained the basis of this rejection. Rule # 1 affirmed that "an action is neither good nor evil, unless it be voluntary and chosen."[236] God had placed a choice between good and evil before us, but how could we choose what is good? This could only transpire because the human will had been enabled "by all the aids of the spirit of grace."[237] Taylor then equated the "spirit of grace" with the "Spirit of God."[238] Elsewhere, Taylor affirmed that "without God's grace we can do nothing, so by His grace strengthening us we can do everything."[239] In the same way, even an unregenerate individual could do "moral good things" if one was willing to be "taught by the Spirit of grace."[240]

Earlier, we saw how William Tilly attempted to reconcile human "liberty" with the grace of God. In a section entitled "liberty of choice in spiritual actions and moral effects," Taylor took up the same topic. In what sense did the human individual have "liberty"? He replied:

> It is very easy to reconcile God's grace with our liberty, because by this grace it is that we have this liberty. For no man can choose what he does not know, and no man can love that which hath in it no amiability. Now because we have all notices spiritual and the arguments of invitation to obedience in duties evangelical from the revelation and the grace of God, therefore to this we owe the liberty of our will, that is, a power to choose spiritual things.[241]

Cary Balzer cited an important passage from Jeremy Taylor's sermon, *The Miracles of Divine Mercy*, where the utter necessity of prevenient grace for our salvation came into full view. In the sermon, "preventing grace" was mentioned by name as "working the first part or our pardon before we are capable of pardon." Taylor described prevenient grace as a "mercy of forgiveness" that was at work among those who were "given over to a reprobate sense."[242]

The question of the conscience and its capabilities is again in view. Despite his seeming optimism regarding the conscience in other passages, in a comment on Romans 7:23, Jeremy Taylor had little good to say about the "law of the mind" apart from grace:

The law of the mind has been so rased and obliterated, and we, by some means or other, so disabled from observing it exactly, that until it was turned into the law of grace, (which is the law of pardoning infirmities, and assisting us in our choices and elections), we were in a state of deficiency from the perfective state of man, to which God intended us.[243]

Taylor spoke in the same context of the "law of nature and right reason," synonymous with conscience.[244] It is critical to note in this passage that the "law of grace" is what made moral choice a possibility. Prevenient grace restored to the individual the capacity for moral decision making.

Conclusion

Charles Rogers was correct to assert that John Wesley did not invent the prevenient grace concept. It has been shown that numerous writers adopted a position that Wesley came to label "prevenient grace." In the *39 Articles* and the *Book of Common Prayer*, the notion that God graciously goes before us found clear expression. The anthropological, cosmological, and pneumatological expressions of concepts related to prevenient grace in-turn can be found in diverse theologians that appeared in John Wesley's *Christian Library* or in other authors that Wesley read or abridged under separate auspices. But Wesley's reading led him beyond his dual nonconformist and Church of England heritage to the pages of Robert Barclay's celebrated *Apology*. It is to this Quaker work that this inquiry now turns its attention in further pursuit of the roots of Wesley's doctrine of prevenient grace.

Notes

1. See Charles Allen Rogers, "The Concept of Prevenient Grace in the Theology of John Wesley" (Ph.D. thesis., Duke University, 1967), 25-58.
2. Rogers, 27.
3. Rogers, 27. Rogers' allusion to ancient and medieval sources for prevenient grace is only a passing mention. Likewise, this inquiry does not investigate prevenient grace doctrine during those time periods. Nevertheless, it would be a logical area for further research as prevenient grace is traced back through the centuries. See the "Appendix" of this book.
4. In Gilbert Burnet, *An Exposition of the 39 Articles of the Church of England* (Oxford, England: Clarendon Press, 1814), 160; emphasis added. E.J. Bicknell commented: "The title appears at first unsuitable. The Article does not deal with free-will but asserts the need of grace against Pelagian Anabaptists. But in reality the connexion is very close." See E.J. Bicknell, *A Theological Introduction to the Thirty-Nine Articles* (2nd edition; New York: Longmans, Green, and Co., 1925), 219.
5. Oliver O'Donovan, *On the Thirty-Nine Articles: A Conversation with Tudor Christianity* (Exeter: Paternoster Press, 1986), 73.
6. Bicknell, 243.
7. O'Donovan, 75.
8. O'Donovan, 75.
9. For a general treatment of the *Book of Common Prayer* as related to John Wesley's theology, consult Jerald Brian Selleck, "The Book of Common Prayer" (Ph.D. Thesis,

Drew University, 1983), 203-94. Selleck treats soteriology generally, making no mention of prevenient grace.

10. *The Book of Common Prayer* (Glasgow: Collins' Clear-Type Press, n.d.), 134; hereafter, *BCP*.

11. *BCP*, 174.

12. *BCP*, 232.

13. See discussion in the "Preface" of this investigation.

14. "The Homilies," n.p [cited August 1, 2005]. Online: http:// www. anglicanlibrary .org/homilies. Diarmaid MacCulloch asserted that Cranmer, anxious to combat "popish error," wrote four homilies, including the opening homily on Scripture and subsequent sermons on faith and good works. See Diarmaid MacCulloch, *Thomas Cranmer: A Life* (New Haven and London: Yale University Press, 1996), 372.

15. *Certain Sermons or Homilies or Homilies appointed to be read in churches in the time of Queen Elizabeth of famous memory* (Oxford: University Press, 1844), xi; hereafter, *Homilies*.

16. *Homilies*, 489-533.

17. Frank Baker, ed., *The Works of John Wesley* (Bi-Centennial Edition; 35 vols. projected; Nashville: Abingdon Press, 1984 to present), 18:233-34; hereafter, *Works* [BE].

18. The emphasis was Wesley's. The full citation affirmed: "For how can a man have this true faith, this sure trust and confidence in God, that by the merits of Christ his sins be forgiven, and he reconciled to the favour of God, and to be partaker of the kingdom by Christ, when he liveth ungodly, and denieth Christ in his deeds?" *Homilies*, 26-7.

19. In Albert C. Outler, ed., *John Wesley* (New York: Oxford University Press, 1964), 123-33.

20. *Works* [BE], 11:107.

21. Rogers, 28. See also endnote 2 above.

22. For example, *Of Faith* exhorted: "For the very sure and lively Christian faith is, not only to believe all things of God, which are contained in holy scripture, but also is an earnest trust that he is careful over us…(and that) our offenses (are) continually washed and purged, whensoever we, repenting truly, do return to him with our whole heart, steadfastly determining with ourselves, through his grace, to obey and serve him…" *Homilies*, 31-32.

23. For an understanding of the dominant understanding of salvation taught in the later half of the 17th century and afterwards, and which greatly affected John Wesley's thinking prior to Aldersgate, see C. Fitzsimons Allison, *The Rise of Moralism: The Proclamation of the Gospel from Hooker to Baxter* (Vancouver: Regent College Publishing, 1966).

24. Puritanism's influence on Wesley was detailed in Robert C. Monk, *John Wesley, His Puritan Heritage: A Study of the Christian Life* (Nashville and New York: Abingdon Press, 1966), especially chapter 1, "John Wesley and Puritan Literature," pp. 29-63. Also relevant is Frank Baker, "Wesley's Puritan Ancestry," *London Quarterly and Holborn Review* 187 (1962), 180-86.

25. Samuel was an Anglican priest, and Susanna had joined the Church of England independently before her marriage to Samuel. Notwithstanding, Kenneth Collins remarks: "The theological setting in which John Wesley thrived as a child was marked, of course, by Anglicanism; but it was also shaped, to some extent, by a heritage of dissent mediated to him through the lineage of both his mother and his father." In *John Wesley: A Theological Journey* (Nashville: Abingdon Press, 2003), 13.

26. Collins, *Theological Journey*, 14.

27. Manfred Marquardt, *John Wesley's Social Ethics: Praxis and Principle* (trans. John E. Steely and W. Stephen Gunter; Eugene, Oregon: Wipf and Stock Publishers, 2000), 41.

28. For a comprehensive list of what John Wesley read between 1725 and 1735, see Richard Paul Heitzenrater, "John Wesley and the Oxford Methodists, 1725-35" (Ph.D. thesis., Duke University, 1972), 493-526. Also useful is V.H.H. Green, *The Young Mr. Wesley* (London: Edward Arnold Publishers, 1961), 305-19. Many of the Puritan writers whom Wesley later abridged for his *Christian Library* appeared on Heitzenrater's and Green's lists, evidence that the young theologian was pondering their ideas, though not always adopting them.

29. Robert Monk referenced the second edition of the *Library*, which was published in 30 volumes by T. Cordeaux for T. Blanshard in London, 1819-27. The first edition of 50 volumes, published in Bristol by Felix Farley and Son (1751-55) and housed in the Special Collections of the Rylands library of the University of Manchester, England, was consulted for this research. All references hereafter will be to the Farley edition, noted as *CL* [FE].

30. John Wesley, *A Christian Library* [FE], 1:iv-v. To facilitate reading, where updating does not change the meaning, modernization in capitalization and punctuation of quotations cited in this chapter has been made. This procedure has also been adopted for other 17th and 18th century sources, though non-inclusive language has been left unchanged.

31. See Didymus, in " Mr. Wesley's Christian Library," *The Wesleyan Methodist* XXVII (Vol. 50, from the beginning, or Vol. 6 in the 3rd series, No. 27, 1827), 315.

32. Didymus, 310. Despite his high purpose, Wesley appears to have lost money on the venture. See Monk, 36, fn. 14.

33. In defense of Wesley's method, Robert Monk commented: "Such liberties with the materials of other authors, while questionable by modern standards, were quite common before the days of copyright laws." In *John Wesley: His Puritan Heritage*, 34.

34. *CL* [FE], 1:v.

35. John Miley differentiated between "scientific anthropology," which enumerates specific characteristics of the human being, and "theological anthropology," which is concerned with one's "religious constitution and history as related to Christian doctrine." In John Miley, *Systematic Theology* (2 vols.; New York: Hunt & Eaton, 1892; repr., Peabody, Massachusetts: Hendrickson Publishers, 1989), 1:353.

36. Theological cosmology refers to God's self-revelation in nature: "The perfection and greatness, the power and wisdom of the Creator, his goodness, but also his wrath can be deduced *from nature*." In Walter Klaiber and Manfred Marquardt, *Living Grace: An Outline of United Methodist Theology* (trans. and adapted by J. Steven O'Malley and Ulrike R.M.Guthrie; Nashville: Abingdon Press, 2001), 36.

37. Brooke Griggs, "South, Robert," *Oxford Dictionary of National Biography, from the Earliest Times to the year 2000* (H.C.G. Matthew and Brian Harrison, eds. 60 vols.; Oxford: Oxford University Press, 2004), 51:679; hereafter, *ODNB*.

38. Griggs, 679. South was celebrated for his use of humor in the pulpit, a characteristic for which he was criticized by John Tillotson. See Alexander Gordon, "South, Robert, D.D.," *Dictionary of National Biography* (Leslie Stephen and Sidney Lee, eds.; 22 vols.; London: Smith, Elder, & Co., 1908), 18:683-5; hereafter, *DNB*.

39. Robert South, *Twelve Sermons Upon Several Subjects and Occasions* (London: Thomas Warren, 1698), 53-107. The sermon was preached at Christ Church (Oxford) on October 29, 1693, and appears in the *Christian Library* [FE], 43:150-77.

40. *CL* [FE], 43:151.

41. *CL* [FE], 43:153

42. *CL* [FE], 43:155.

43. South, *Twelve Sermons*, 58.
44. South wrote: "No man living, in respect of conscience is born blind, but makes himself so. None can strike out the eye of conscience but himself..." *CL* [FE], 43:155.
45. South, 155; *CL* [FE], 43:155.
46. *CL* [FE], 43:154-55.
47. *CL* [FE], 43:153, 160.
48. South, 68-9; *CL* [FE], 43:156. It is not easy to classify this as either cosmological or pneumatological, but it seems similar to prevenient grace in its effects.
49. South, 70-1; *CL* [FE], 43:157.
50. South, 70; *CL* [FE], 43:157.
51. South, 78-81; *CL* [FE], 43:160. South at times appeared to make no distinction between "intellect" and "conscience." If the two were inter-dependent, this would be problematic when addressing the moral development of those born with cognitive disabilities.
52. Ian Atherton, "Reynolds, Edward," *ODNB*, 46:530.
53. Atherton, 529.
54. For the original sermon, see Edward Reynolds, *The Whole Works of Edward Reynolds* (6 vols.; London: Printed for Holdsworth, 1826). Wesley's abridged version appeared in *CL* [FE], 41:215-89.
55. *CL* [FE], 41:218. While Reynolds used the term "nature," it is clear in-context that he was referring to *human* nature, and not to the Creation in general. His approach was anthropological, not cosmological. The Lord Bishop's terminology in relation to original sin was Augustinian, much like John Wesley's.
56. *CL* [FE], 41:218.
57. *CL* [FE], 41:218.
58. Richard L. Greaves, "Charnock, Stephen," *ODNB*, 11:203.
59. Greaves, 204.
60. Greaves, 204.
61. William Gordon Blaikie, "Charnock, Stephen," in *DNB*, 4:134-5.
62. For the original work from Charnock, consult Griffith Williams, *Discourses upon the existence and attributes of God, abridged from the writings of the late learned and venerable Stephen Charnock, B.D.* (London: W. Smith, 1797). Wesley's abridgement appeared as "A Discourse of the Knowledge of God" (*CL* [FE] 39:101-50) and "A Discourse of the Knowledge of God in Christ" (*CL* [FE] 39:151-204).
63. *CL* [FE]: 39:168.
64. *CL* [FE], 39:164.
65. *CL* [FE], 39:164-65.
66. *CL* [FE], 39:121, emphasis added.
67. For further details, see Chapter 3 of this study.
68. Sarah Hutton, "Smith, John," *ODNB*, 51:200.
69. Hutton, 200.
70. Hutton, 200.
71. See *CL* [FE], 19:279-97, and 20:61-138, respectively. For a collection of Smith's writings, see Henry Griffin Williams, *Select Discourses by John Smith, M.A., Formerly Fellow of Queen's College, Cambridge* (Cambridge, England: University Press, 1859).
72. *CL* [FE], 20:64.
73. *CL* [FE], 20:64.
74. *CL* [FE], 20:98.
75. *CL* [FE], 19:192. Henry Griffin Williams saw this as an allusion to Plotinus. The "eye of the soul" is our intellectual capacity. See Williams, *Select Discourses by John*

Smith, 16.
76. *CL* [FE], 19:192.
77. *CL* [FE], 19:191, emphasis added.
78. Jonathan D. Moore, "Preston, John," *ODNB*, 45:261.
79. Moore, 261-62.
80. Moore, 264.
81. John Preston, *The Breast-Plate of Faith and Love* (London: R.Y. for Nicholas Bourne, 1634). See also *CL* [FE], 9:221-319.
82. *CL* [FE], 9:273-74.
83. *CL* [FE], 9:308.
84. *CL* [FE], 9:308.
85. *CL* [FE], 9:297.
86. Roger Pooley, "Ambrose, Isaac," *ODNB*, 1:921.
87. Pooley, 921.
88. John Eglinton Bailey, "Ambrose, Isaac," *DNB*, 1:350-51.
89. Pooley, 921.
90. It appears in *CL* [FE], 13:55-175. For the original work, consult Isaac Ambrose, *The Complete Works of Isaac Ambrose* (London: Printed for R. Chiswel, B. Tooke, and T. Sawbridge, 1689).
91. *CL* [FE], 13:58.
92. *CL* [FE], 13:63.
93. *CL* [FE], 13:127.
94. *CL* [FE], 13:128.
95. *CL* [FE], 13:66.
96. *CL* [FE], 13:63.
97. *CL* [FE], 13:122. Both images occurred in the theology of John and Charles Wesley.
98. Isaac Ambrose, *Complete Works*, 34. In the context of the discourse – and in contrast with Wesleyan theology – Ambrose would apply this enablement only to those elected by God to salvation.
99. *CL* [FE], 13:121.
100. *CL* [FE], 13:83.
101. *CL* [FE], 13:73. This is a reference to saving grace, not prevenient grace.
102. H.R. McAdoo, *The Spirit of Anglicanism: A Survey of Anglican Theological Method in the Seventeenth Century* (New York: Charles Scribner's Sons, 1965), 171-79.
103. Alexander Gordon, "Tillotson, John," *DNB*, 19:874.
104. Isobel Rivers, "Tillotson, John," *ODNB*, 54:791.
105. Rivers, 795.
106. *CL* [FE], 45:293-347; from John Tillotson, *Sermons* (London: Printed for R. Chiswell, at the Rose and Crown in St. Paul's Church-yard, 1701).
107. *CL*, 45:318-19.
108. *CL* [FE], 45:319.
109. *CL* [FE], 45:299. See also 45:306, where the "powerful assistance of divine grace" was the means of mortifying "evil and corrupt inclinations," of breaking off "vicious habits" and of walking in the "way of God's commandments."
110. *CL* [FE], 45:309, italics added.
111. *CL* [FE], 45:304-5.
112. Green, 314; Heitzenrater, "Oxford Methodists," 522.
113. Allan Coppedge, *Shaping the Wesleyan Message: John Wesley in Theological Debate* (1987; Repr., Nappanee, Illinois: Francis Asbury Press/Evangel Publishing House, n.d.), 99-145; also Herbert Boyd McGonigle, *Sufficient Saving Grace: John*

47 Analysis of Selected Church of England and Puritan Sources

Wesley's Evangelical Arminianism (Carlisle, Cumbria, and Waynesboro, Georgia: Paternoster Press, 2001), 282-87.

114. Mark E. Dever, "Sibbes, Richard," *ODNB*, 50:487.
115. Dever, 488.
116. R.T. Kendall, *Calvin and English Calvinism to 1649* (rev. ed.; New York: Oxford Univ. Press, 1981), 104.
117. Alexander Gordon, "Sibbes, Sibbs, or Sibs, Richard, D.D.," *DNB*, 18:182-83.
118. *CL* [FE], 10:121.
119. *CL* [FE], 10:121.
120. *CL* [FE], 10:153.
121. Alexander Balloch Grosart, "Bolton, Robert," *DNB*, 2:792-94; also, Stephen Wright, "Bolton, Robert," *ODNB*, 6:491.
122. Wright, 491-92.
123. Wright, 492.
124. Robert Bolton, *A Discourse About the State of True Happiness* (London: John Dawson, 1631). See *CL* [FE], 7:181-286. The discourse was originally five sermons.
125. See "The Life and Death of Mr Bolton," *CL* [FE], 7:161-80.
126. *CL* [FE], 7:237.
127. Bolton, *True Happiness*, 22.
128. *CL* [FE], 7:209-10.
129. Bolton, 22.
130. *CL* [FE], 7:198; Bolton, 16, italics added. The only phrase that Wesley struck from Bolton appeared after "and so a saving faith." The original read: "A weak faith may be a true faith, and so a saving faith, as well as the full persuasion and height of assurance."
131. Bolton, 30.
132. Bolton, 31.
133. *CL* [FE], 7:222.
134. Bolton, 31.
135. Bolton, 34.
136. Newton E. Key, "Annesley, Samuel," *ODNB*, 2:238.
137. Robert Monk noted that Susanna Wesley, John's mother, was Dr. Annesley's twenty-fifth child. In *John Wesley: His Puritan Heritage*, 21.
138. Key, 238.
139. Alexander Balloch Grosart, "Annesley, Samuel," *DNB* 1:480. See also Frank Baker, "Wesley's Puritan Ancestry," 183.
140. Key, 238.
141. *CL* [FE], 38:297-338; from Samuel Annesley, ed. *The Morning Exercises at Cripplegate, or, Several Cases of Conscience Practically Resolved, by Sundry Ministers* (London: T. Milbourn and Joshua Johnson, 1671), 1-32.
142. *Works* [BE], 3:479-90. Albert Outler noted (p. 479): "It was as if grandfather and grandson were able to speak with one voice on one of the basic presuppositions of Christian ethics."
143. Annesley, *Universally conscientious*, 3.
144. Annesley, 3.
145. Annesley, 3.
146. Annesley, 4. Annesley seemed conflicted whether conscience could be rendered inoperative by a person's actions. In a section deleted by Wesley (*CL* [FE], 38:309), he observed that in a person with a "seared conscience," one may "deaden his conscience unto an insensible senselessness" (p.10). Earlier, he had affirmed that it is impossible to "blow out God's candle of conscience" (p. 5).

147. Annesley, 4-5, emphasis added.
148. *CL* [FE], 38:302, emphasis added.
149. Rogers, 55.
150. John Henry Overton, "Lucas, Richard, D.D.," *DNB*, 12:239-40.
151. Edward Vallance, "Lucas, Richard," *ODNB*, 34:688-89.
152. Vallance, 688. See Richard Lucas, *An Enquiry After Happiness in Several Parts* (6th ed. London: Printed for R. Gosling, 1734). At Oxford, John Wesley read the *Enquiry* in March of 1730. See Heitzenrater, "Oxford Methodists," 511, and Green, , 311.
153. *CL* [FE], 40:3-346 and 41:3-114.
154. Lucas, *Enquiry*, 2.
155. Lucas, 56.
156. Lucas, 119.
157. Lucas, 142.
158. Lucas, 156.
159. Lucas, 156-57.
160. Lucas, 153.
161. Lucas, 157.
162. For Lucas, "providence" was a synonym of divine assistance. See *Enquiry*, 80-81.
163. Lucas, 158.
164. Lucas, 78.
165. Lucas, 80-81, fn. 152.
166. Of the theologians addressed in Chapter 1, Richard Lucas was an anomaly, since he made balanced use of anthropological, cosmological, and pneumatological terminology.
167. For a summary of William Tilly's view of prevenient grace, see Rogers, 55-57. The analysis presented here supplements Rogers' treatment.
168. McGonigle, 101. See also Charles A. Rogers, "John Wesley and William Tilly," *Proceedings of the Wesley Historical Society* 35 (June 1966): 137-41.
169. McGonigle, 101.
170. Heitzenrater, "Oxford Methodists," 523. The full name of the edition used in this research is *Sixteen Sermons Upon Several Occasions, All (except One) Preached Before the University of Oxford at St. Mary's Church (*2nd ed.; London: Printed for John Osborn, 1737).
171. McGonigle, 101.
172. Charles Rogers cautioned: "We must be careful not to over-emphasize the significance of these extracted sermons. They do not have quite the same authoritative value as expressions of Wesley's own thought in this period as do the known original sermons, such as *Circumcision of the Heart*. Nevertheless, they should be taken seriously, for in abridging them carefully and preaching them on several occasions Wesley made them his own." See Rogers, "Wesley and Tilly," 140. In a September 30, 1735 letter to Richard Morgan, Wesley wrote: "Dr. Tilly's sermons on free will are the best I ever saw." See *Works* [BE], 25:438.
173. It appeared in *Sixteen Sermons*, 370-95.
174. Tilly, *Sixteen Sermons*, 374.
175. Tilly, 379.
176. Tilly, 379.
177. Tilly, 380.
178. The full text of the sermon appeared in *Sixteen Sermons*, 312-38.
179. Tilly, 313.
180. Tilly, 319.
181. Tilly, 324.

182. Tilly, 324.
183. Tilly, 324.
184. Tilly, 326; emphasis added.
185. Tilly, 330.
186. Tilly, 327.
187. The full title of the sermon was: "The grace of God shown to be not only consistent with the liberty of man's will, but the strongest obligation to our own endeavours in our duty." The sermon appears in *Sixteen Sermons*, 226-54. See pp. 255-82 for a second sermon with the same title. For the purposes of this discussion, both sermons are considered as one.
188. John's Wesley's own 1785 sermon on Phil. 4:13, *On Working Out Our Own Salvation*, would provide his clearest statement on the nature of prevenient grace. See *Works* [BE], 3:199-209.
189. Tilly, 227.
190. Tilly, 227.
191. Tilly, 230.
192. Tilly, 232.
193. Tilly, 232.
194. Tilly, 232.
195. Tilly, 234.
196. Tilly, 234-5.
197. Tilly, 235.
198. Tilly, 237. "It is not surprising," McGonigle observed, "that a high churchman like Tilly believed that this awakening came through baptismal regeneration." In H.B. McGonigle, *Sufficient Saving Grace*, 321.
199. Tilly, 237.
200. Tilly, 238.
201. Tilly, 239.
202. Tilly, 242. Later in the sermon (pp. 248-54), Tilly described "assisting grace" in pneumatological terms, as something distinct from preventing grace, that allowed the Christian to fulfil his or her duty. On the other hand, God's grace and Holy Spirit could be "removed" if they were "neglected" or "despised" (p. 276). Tilly's heightened hypostatic use of language to describe prevenient grace sets him apart from other writers examined in this chapter.
203. For useful biographical details on Taylor, see Alexander Gordon, "Taylor, Jeremy, D.D.,"*DNB*, 19:422-29; also C.J. Stranks, *The Life and Writings of Jeremy Taylor* (London: S.P.C.K., 1952), 27-68.
204. John Spurr, "Taylor, Jeremy," *ODNB*, 53:922.
205. Spurr, 921.
206. Spurr, 921.
207. H.R. McAdoo, *The Structure of Caroline Moral Theology* (London, New York, and Toronto: Longmans, Green, and Co., 1949), 135
208. W.C. de Pauley, *The Candle of the Lord: Study in the Cambridge Platonists* (London: SPCK, 1937), 42.
209. John Spurr, "Taylor, Jeremy," *ODNB*, 53:922.
210. Herbert Boyd McGonigle, "Christianity or Deism? John Wesley's Response to John Taylor's Denial of the Doctrine of Original Sin." Unpublished paper, June, 2005.
211. Cary Balzer, "John Wesley's Developing Soteriology and the Influence of the Caroline Divines" (Ph.D. thesis, University of Manchester, England, 2005), 111.
212. Wesley first read Taylor's *Rules and Exercises of Holy Living and Dying* at age twenty-three, in 1725. Its impact upon him was mentioned in Wesley's *A Plain Account*

of Christian Perfection, in *The Works of John Wesley* (3rd ed.; 14 vols.; 1872; reprint, Kansas City, Missouri: Beacon Hill Press, 1978), 11: 366. Kenneth Collins noted Wesley's criticism of the lack of assurance that Taylor's *Rules* promoted. See *Theological Journey* , 34-5. For an analysis of the *Rules*, consult C.J. Stranks, *Anglican Devotion: Studies in the Spiritual Life of the Church of England between the Reformation and the Oxford Movement* (London: SCM Press Ltd., 1961), 64-95.

213. Balzer, 101-24. Balzer analyzed Taylor's soteriology, including some mention of prevenient grace.

214. In Reginald Heber, ed., *The Whole Works of the Right Rev. Jeremy Taylor* (15 vols.; London: Printed for C. and J. Rivington, and others, 1828), 2:434; italics added; hereafter, *Works* [HE]. The later edition of Taylor's *Works* was by Charles Page Eden, ed., *The Whole Works of the Right Rev. Jeremy Taylor, D.D., Lord Bishop of Down, Connor, and Dromore* (10 vols.; London: Longman, Brown, Green, et. al., 1847-52), hereafter *Works* [EE]. More accessible is Thomas K. Carroll, ed., *Jeremy Taylor: Selected Works* (in *The Classics of Western Spirituality: A Library of the Great Spiritual Masters*; ed. Bernard McGinn; New York and Mahwah, New Jersey: The Paulist Press, 1990).

215. *Works* [HE], 2:xxxiv.
216. *Works* [HE], 2:xxviii.
217. *Works* [HE], 2:xxix.

218. The work was alternatively titled: "The Rule of Conscience in all her General Measures." For an analysis of 17th century Anglican casuistry, including Taylor's 1660 *Ductor Dubitantium*, see Camille Slights, "Ingenious Piety: Anglican Casuistry of the Seventeenth Century," *Harvard Theological Review* 63 (1970): 409-32. Slights (p. 410) calls the *Ductor* "all but unknown." John Wesley owned the *Ductor*, and read it in 1732. See Heitzenrater, "Oxford Methodists," 521.

219. *Works* [EE], 9:279. Emphasis added. Taylor was already hinting at the incompleteness of conscience apart from divine revelation.

220. *Works* [HE], 4:33.
221. *Works* [EE], 9:298.
222. *Works* [EE], 9:298.

223. Raymond A. Peterson, "Jeremy Taylor in Conscience and Law," *Anglican Theological Review* 48 (July '66): 246.

224. Timothy F. Sedgwick, "Revisioning Anglican Moral Theology," *Anglican Theological Review* 63 (1981): 11.

225. *Works* [EE], 9:288.
226. Sedgwick, 11.
227. *Works* [EE], 9:298-99.
228. *Works* [HE], 2:xxxviii.
229. *Works* [HE], 2:xxxviii; italics added.
230. *Works* [EE], 9:295-6; italics added.
231. Peterson, 252.
232. Sedgwick, 11.
233. *Works* [HE], 6:4-6; italics added.
234. *Works* [HE], 5:513-14.
235. *Works* [HE], 5:572.
236. *Works* [EE], 10:548.
237. *Works* [EE], 10:548-49.
238. *Works* [EE], 10:549.
239. *Works* [EE], 1:121.
240. *Works* [EE], 9:150.
241. *Works* [EE], 10:552.

242. *Works* [EE], 5:342; cited by Balzer, 107.
243. *Works* [HE], 2:xlviii.
244. *Works* [HE], 2:xlviii.

Chapter Two

Roots of the Doctrine of Prevenient Grace: The "Light of Christ" in Robert Barclay's *Apology*

Introduction

Robert Barclay (1648-90) is considered the foremost theologian of the Quaker movement.[1] Although he later became a disciple of the better known Quaker, George Fox (1624-91),[2] Barclay as a child lived for four years in Paris, where he came under the influence of his uncle, a Roman Catholic. Only through the intervention of his father, repatriating him to his native England, did the young Barclay avoid becoming an adherent of Rome.[3] After his conversion to Quakerism in 1667, Barclay became an eloquent defender of Quaker faith. Imprisoned on more than one occasion, he eventually was appointed co-governor with William Penn of East Jersey.[4] Though he died at a relatively young age, Barclay – through his children and even more so through his ideas – left an enduring imprint not only on Quakerism, but as we shall see, also on the thinking of John Wesley.

Background of the *Apology* [5]

Robert Barclay's *Apology* was first published in Latin in 1676 in Amsterdam, an English edition appearing in England two years later.[6] Its influence on both sides of the Atlantic was widespread. By 1800, the *Apology* had been reprinted nine times in England, three in Ireland, three in Philadelphia, and three in New England.[7] It became the standard book given to inquirers about the beliefs of the Quakers, also know as the Society of Friends.[8]

Structure of the Work

The strength of the *Apology* was its logical organization. Voltaire, the French écrivain, remarked: "At last Robert Barclay, a native of Scotland, presented to the King in 1675 His apology for the Quakers, a work as well drawn up as its subject could possibly admit."[9] Jackson Cope called the scholastic *theses theologicae* of the *Apology* "thoroughly organised."[10] William Frost characterized it as a "coherent biblically based, and solidly argued statement of Quaker doctrine."[11]

The *Apology* opens with a brief statement of fifteen "propositions."[12] The first six propositions are germane to our topic, and include discussion of knowledge, revelation, the Scriptures, the Fall, Universal Redemption, and Spiritual Light, respectively.[13] After presenting the propositions, Robert Barclay systematically considered each proposition at-length, carefully developing the historical and Scriptural basis of each.

The following pages will examine a handful of themes related to prevenient grace that emerge in the *Apology*. The discussion will conclude with an analysis of John Wesley's 1741 tract *Serious Considerations on Absolute Predestination as Extracted from a Late Author*, an abridgement of the early section of the *Apology*. By discovering what Wesley kept and what he excised, some appreciation of what ideas Wesley accepted and rejected will be gained. [14]

Knowledge, Immediate Revelation, the Holy Spirit, and Scripture

The First and Second Propositions introduced the epistemological foundation for the remainder of Barclay's theological "building."[15] Not until the Second Proposition, however, did he begin to divulge the marrow of his thinking. How could one have "the true knowledge of God"? This was only by the "revelation" of God's Spirit manifested to humans. Divine revelation came through four channels, namely, "outward voices," "outward appearances," "dreams," and "objective manifestations in the heart."[16] Barclay had little to say about the first three,[17] yet provided great detail concerning the fourth. These "objective manifestations" were defined as "inward illumination." They were not optional, but "absolutely necessary for the building up of true faith."[18] Through them, "God could present knowledge not in the Bible to an individual."[19]

Having posited the necessity of such revelation, Robert Barclay realized the importance of establishing the trustworthiness of the same. While inward illumination would not contradict Scripture,[20] neither should it be considered an inferior source of religious authority. Barclay clarified:

> Moreover, these divine inward revelations, which we make absolutely necessary for the building up of true faith, neither do nor can ever contradict the outward testimony of the Scriptures, or right and sound reason. Yet from hence it will not follow, that these divine revelations are to be subjected to the outward testimony of the Scriptures, or of the natural reason of man, as to a more noble or certain rule or touchstone; for this divine revelation, and inward illumination, is that

which is evident and clear of itself, forcing, by its own evidence and clearness, the well-disposed understanding to assent...[21]

The Third Proposition, "Concerning the Scriptures," shed light on the relative worth of Scripture and immediate divine revelation. The Scriptures issued from the "fountain," but were not the fountain itself. What, then, was the fountain? None other than the Holy Spirit. Scripture is "a secondary rule, subordinate to the Spirit."[22] The Spirit was "that guide by which the saints are led into *all truth*." We only believed the Scriptures because they "proceeded from the Spirit."[23]

How was knowledge obtained? While Quakers generally held a low view of reason,[24] Robert Barclay admitted the value of "head knowledge," but at the same time called it "soaring" and "airy."[25] While the devil could "deceive the outward senses," saints of old like Abraham could only know he was encountering angels through "the secret persuasion of God's spirit in his heart."[26] In spiritual matters, the physical senses were wholly inadequate:

> We do distinguish betwixt the certain knowledge of God, and the uncertain; betwixt the spiritual knowledge, and the literal; the saving knowledge, and the soaring, airy head knowledge. The last, we confess, may be divers ways obtained, but the first, by no other way than the inward immediate manifestation and revelation of God's Spirit, shining in and upon the heart, enlightening and opening the understanding.[27]

In a later passage, Robert Barclay approvingly quoted Philip Melanchthon. Christianity's power to redeem from sin was based not upon knowledge in general, but uniquely "that which proceeds from the warm influence of God's Spirit upon the heart, and from the comfortable shining of his light upon their understanding."[28]

The Holy Spirit assumed huge proportions in Robert Barclay's system. The very definition of "Christian" was narrowed to Romans 8:9, as one who, in Barclay's words, "hath the Spirit, and is led by it."[29] Christianity without the Holy Spirit was moribund:

> For take but away the Spirit, and Christianity remains no more Christianity, than the dead carcass of a man, when the soul and spirit is departed, remains a man; which the living can no more abide, but do bury out of their sight, as a noisome and useless thing, however acceptable it hath been when actuated and moved by the soul.[30]

The relationship between the Holy Spirit and immediate revelation was exposed in one of many syllogisms laced throughout the *Apology*. Barclay affirmed: "That which is spiritual can only be known and discerned by the Spirit of God. But the revelation of Jesus Christ, and the true saving knowledge of him, is spiritual: Therefore the revelation of Jesus Christ, and the true saving knowledge of him, can only be known and discerned by the Spirit of God."[31] Such knowledge was "inward, immediate, and objective."[32] Beyond saving knowledge, the Holy Spirit also gave guidance to individuals in specific circumstances in ways that the general principles of Scripture, while important, could not hope to match.³³

Above all, the foundation of Robert Barclay's version of Quakerism was experiential. Because of the disproportionate emphasis upon our inward experience of the Holy Spirit, William Frost questioned whether the historic nature of the Christ event had been neglected in Quaker thinking, resulting in a type of docetism.³⁴ In any case, Barclay's first Three Propositions paved the way for a fresh consideration of the human condition in the Fall (Proposition Four) as well as the extent of the Redemption and the nature of the Spiritual Light (Propositions Five and Six) that "lightens everyone coming into the world" (John 1:9).

On Depravity and Two Types of "Seed"

Proposition Four, entitled "Concerning the Condition of Man in the Fall," was a mediating statement regarding human depravity. It was noteworthy not only for avoiding both the excesses of Pelagianism and a doctrine of infants being damned for original sin,³⁵ but also because it introduced metaphors akin to prevenient grace, namely, "seed" and "light."³⁶

Robert Barclay took pains to present Quaker teaching as consistent with the historic sweep of doctrine regarding the human condition. While he avoided the term "original sin," calling the phrase unscriptural and an invitation to abuse by those who would teach the "barbarism" of sins being imputed to infants,³⁷ Barclay nonetheless affirmed traditional interpretations. Commenting on the phrase "there is none righteous" from Romans 3:10, he observed:

> What more positive can be spoken? He seemeth to be particularly careful to avoid that any good should be ascribed to the natural man; he shews how he is polluted in all his ways; he shews how he is void of righteousness, of understanding, of the knowledge of God; how he is out of the way, and in short unprofitable; than which nothing can be more fully laid to confirm our judgment: for if this be the condition of the natural man, or of man as he stands in the Fall, he is unfit to make a right step to heaven.³⁸

There could be no doubt about the lamentable condition of the human being. We were "fallen, degenerated, and dead."³⁹ Nonetheless, there was a "seed of God" that exists in the human heart, though it could not be sensed by the unbeliever, and its power was mitigated by the seed of the serpent. The solution was to be "disjoined from this evil seed, and united to the Divine Light."⁴⁰

Robert Barclay explained the origin of the "seed of God." Decidedly, his argument was not anthropological, i.e. identifying the "seed" as a remnant of the *imago Dei* post-fall. Rather, he criticized the idea that there are "reliques (sic) of the heavenly image left in Adam" as being Socinian and Pelagian, making Christ's coming unnecessary.⁴¹ He cited Romans 2:14 as signifying the "spiritual law that is written in the heart."⁴² Barclay commented:

> If they object that which the same apostle saith in the foregoing chapter, ver. 14, to wit, that the Gentiles do by nature the things contained in the law, and so consequently do by nature that which is good and acceptable in the sight of God,

I answer: This nature must not, neither can be understood as man's own nature, which is corrupt and fallen; but of the spiritual nature, which proceedeth from the seed of God in man, as it receiveth a new visitation of God's love, and it quickened by it...[43]

It was only through the Spirit of God that the things of God could be known.[44] Accordingly, Barclay specifically rejected a Pelagian view that ascribed the capacity for things spiritual to the inherent nature of the individual.

The Nature and Activity of the Light of Christ[45]

This study now turns to a brief analysis of Propositions Five and Six.[46] Proposition Five was entitled: "Concerning the Universal Redemption by Christ, and also the Saving and Spiritual Light, wherewith every Man is enlightened." The proposition itself claimed:

> God, out of his infinite love, who delighteth not in the death of a sinner, but that all should live and be saved, hath so loved the world, that he hath given his only Son a LIGHT, that whosoever believeth in him should be saved, John iii.16. who enlighteneth EVERY man that cometh into the world, John i.9. and maketh manifest all things that are reproveable, Ephes.v. 13 and teacheth all temperance, righteousness, and godliness; and this Light enlighteneth the hearts of all for a time, in order to salvation; and this is it which reproves the sin of all individuals, and would work out the salvation of all, if not resisted. Nor is it less universal than the seed of sin, being the purchase of his death, who tasted death for every man: for as in Adam all die, even so in Christ all shall be made alive, 1 Cor. xv. 22.[47]

On the basis of this proposition, as interpreted in reference to Proposition Six[48], what can be said about the light of Christ?

The light of Christ was universal in reach. Robert Barclay framed his arguments in contrast to Calvinistic teaching. The marginal note at the beginning of his extended treatment read: "Absolute probation, that horrible and blasphemous doctrine, described."[49] On the other hand, the light of Christ reached all because the death of Christ was *for* all. Barclay asserted: "This doctrine of *universal redemption*, or *Christ's dying for all men*, is of itself so evident from the Scripture testimony, that there is scarcely found any other article of Christian faith so frequently, so plainly, and so positively asserted."[50] Demonstrating his propensity for syllogisms, Barclay affirmed:" Those for whom our Saviour gave himself a ransom, to such salvation is possible. But our Saviour gave himself a ransom for all; therefore, salvation is possible."[51] At the end of Proposition Six, Barclay explicitly tied together the universality of both the redemption and the light of Christ. Though appreciative of their correction of Calvinism, he criticized Holland's remonstrants for not having "placed the extent of this salvation in that divine and evangelical principle of light and life wherewith Christ hath enlightened every man that cometh into the world..."[52]

The language was taken from John 1:9, what Barclay called "the Quaker Text."[53] The three adjectives that Barclay ascribed to "light" were "supernatural," "saving," and "sufficient."[54] In addition, it shone upon all, without exception:

> It is plain there comes no man into the world, whom Christ hath not enlightened in some measure, and in whose dark heart this light doth not shine; though the darkness comprehend it not, yet it shineth there; and the nature thereof is to dispel the darkness, where men shut not their eyes upon it.[55]

Elsewhere, Barclay affirmed that "God hath communicated and given unto every man a measure of the light of his own Son, a measure of grace, or a measure of his Spirit."[56] As the sin of Adam had universally negative effects upon humankind, so Christ's "coming in the flesh," his "whole obedience" and his "sufferings" allow "many…to feel the influence of this holy and divine seed and light, and to be turned from evil to good by it…"[57]

Though universal, the light of Christ could be resisted.[58] The last phrase of the citation above – "where men shut not their eyes upon it" – indicated another truth regarding this light, namely, that it was resistible. To the words "seed" and "light," Robert Barclay added "grace." Every human being "hath a measure of it, which strives with him in order to save him…"[59] Adopting the synonymous language of the "seed," defined as an "invisible principle, in which God, as Father, Son, and Spirit, dwells,"[60] Barclay portrayed the seed as that "which of its own nature draws, invites, and inclines to God."[61] Unfortunately, not all submitted to the salutary influence of the seed: "And as every unrighteous action is witnessed against and reproved by this light and seed, so by such actions it is hurt, wounded, and slain, and flees from them; even as the flesh of man flees from that which is of a contrary nature to it."[62] Supplementing biblical arguments with those of early Christians, Barclay quoted Chrysostom on John 1:9, arguing the possibility of resisting God's grace:

> If he enlightens every man coming into the world, how comes it that so many men remain without light? For all do not so much as acknowledge Christ. How then doth he enlighten every man? He illuminates indeed so far as in him is; but if any of their own accord, closing the eyes of their mind, will not direct their eyes unto the beams of this light, the cause that they remain in darkness is not from the nature of the light, but through their own malignity, who willingly have rendered themselves unworthy of so great a gift. Why believed they not? Because they would not. Christ did his part.[63]

The doctrine of the light of Christ attributed all good to God. As was clarified previously regarding the human condition after the fall, Robert Barclay rejected the optimistic Socinian and Pelagian interpretation of the natural capacity of the human being for the things of God.[64] How then could one explain what appeared to be good tempers or actions performed by one who makes no profession of Christian faith? The Apologist replied: "It (the light of Christ) exalts above all the grace of God, to which it attributeth all good, even the least and smallest actions that are so; ascribing thereunto not only the first beginnings and motions of good, but also the whole conversion and salvation of the soul."[65] Virtue in the unbeliever, according to Barclay, was not a sign that human nature was good. Rather, it was indicative of the enlightening grace of God, as mediated by the Holy Spirit.[66]

The light of Christ protected the justice of God. Unlike the Calvinistic doctrine of predestination – which Robert Barclay protested made God "the author of sin"[67] – through the Christ light, "the mercy of God is excellently and well exhibited, in that none are necessarily shut out from salvation; and his justice is demonstrated, in that he condemns none but such to whom he really made offer of salvation, according them the means sufficient thereof."[68] Salvation wholly depended upon the grace of God, while condemnation was entirely the responsibility of the individual.[69]

The light of Christ offered salvation to those lacking gospel preaching. Robert Barclay thought deeply about the fate of those who were born prior to Christ, or lived in parts of the earth untouched by the preaching of the gospel. The "old philosophers" might have been saved, said Barclay, "if they receive and resist not that grace, a manifestation whereof is given to every man to profit withal."[70] Elton Trueblood observed:

> Unless we accept some such position as that stated by Barclay, we cannot escape the conclusion that Socrates is in hell! But, if Barclay's thesis is accepted, the gospel is indeed good news, since it means that Socrates, when he listened obediently to the inner voice, clearly had what Barclay calls his "day of visitation"… if the new insight is a valid one, the absolute barrier to belief in God's outgoing love is removed.[71]

Not only did the Christ light explain problems of time; it also addressed difficulties of geography and opportunity. Those "living in parts of the world where the outward preaching of the Gospel is unknown" still had the possibility of salvation.[72] In an extended passage, Barclay addressed the importance of the light of Christ doctrine for those whom he called "infidels":[73]

> It wonderfully commends us as well the certainty of the Christian religion among infidels, as it manifests its own verity to all, in that it is confirmed and established by the experience of all men; seeing there was never yet a man in any place of the earth, however barbarous and wild, but hath acknowledged, that at some time or another, less or more, he hath found somewhat in his heart reproving him for some things evil which he hath done, threatening a certain horror if he continued in them, as also promising and communicating a certain peace and sweetness, as he has given way to it, and not resisted it.[74]

With such a strong understanding of the light, one may question what value Robert Barclay placed upon preaching. If the light of Christ was sufficient for the salvation of those who did not resist it, was preaching superfluous? Was knowledge of the Christ event, i.e. his birth, life, miracles, sufferings, resurrection, and ascension optional? Not at all; the value of preaching, even to those who have come to Christ through his universal light, was threefold:

1) They were strengthened in their faith;
2) Knowing the story of Christ was a great comfort;

3) Only through knowledge of Christ could one become Christlike, and follow in his footsteps.[75]

Barclay concluded in a flurry of wit: "The *history* then is profitable and comfortable with the *mystery*, and never without it; but the *mystery* is and may be profitable without the explicit and outward knowledge of the *history*."[76]

The light of Christ was not to be confused with reason or conscience. Reason was one of the "faculties" of the human being.[77] It was a "natural and rational principle" useful in learning many things, such as the "arts and sciences," but in things spiritual, may have proven a hindrance rather than a help:

> Indeed the great cause of the apostasy hath been, that man hath sought to fathom the things of God in and by this natural and rational principle, and to build up a religion in it, neglecting and overlooking this principle and seed of God in the heart; so that herein, in the most universal and catholic sense, hath Anti-Christ in every man set up himself, and sitteth in the temple of God as God, and above every thing that is called God.[78]

Robert Barclay illustrated the relationship between the divine light and reason by comparing the sun with the moon. The sun was the greater light, and illuminated the moon. Likewise, "the light of (God's) Son, a spiritual and divine light" enlightened human reason. While reason might prove "useful" in spiritual things, it was "still subservient and subject to the other."[79]

Beyond reason was the question of conscience. How was conscience related to the light of Christ? The two should not be equated. "Conscience" was defined as "that knowledge which ariseth in man's heart, from what agreeth, contradicteth, or is contrary to any thing believed by him, whereby he becomes conscience to himself, that he transgresseth by doing that which he is persuaded he ought not to do."[80] Barclay spoke of a Turk who is taught that drinking wine is wrong, but that keeping concubines is lawful. Should such a man drink wine, his conscience would "reprove" him, but would leave him undisturbed when he commits "fornication."[81] The content of conscience, therefore, was determined by socialization; as such, it could be "defiled and corrupted."[82] It was culturally conditioned and subjective, varying according to the environmental factors by which it was formed. These factors differed depending upon the *milieu* in which one was educated. Though conscience, "when rightly informed and enlightened," might serve as a lanthorn to magnify the light of a candle, it was not the candle itself.[83]

What then was the "candle" that enlightens the conscience? The candle was the light of Christ.[84] Whereas conscience was subjective and culturally conditioned, the Christ light was *objective* and *consistent* across cultures. Returning to the illustration of the Turk, Robert Barclay noted that where conscience might leave him undisturbed, the light of Christ would not:

> Whereas if the light of Christ in him were minded, it would reprove him, not only for committing fornication, but also, as he became obedient thereunto, inform him that Mahomet was an imposter; as well as Socrates was informed by it, in his day, of the falsity of the heathens (sic) gods.[85]

Barclay observed that a lanthorn was only useful when "a clear candle burns and shines in it."[86] The light of Christ served a three-fold purpose: 1) it removed the blindness of the judgment; 2) it opened the understanding and 3) it rectified the judgment and the conscience.[87] As such, the light of Christ was "a most certain guide unto life eternal."[88]

The Apology and John Wesley's Serious Considerations

John Wesley abridged relevant portions of Barclay's work, publishing it in 1741 under the title *Serious Considerations on Absolute Predestination.*[89] At the height of the unfortunate controversy over predestination with George Whitefield, Wesley distributed the abridgement not only to his own adherents at the Foundry in London, but also to Whitefield's followers at the Tabernacle.[90]

Just twenty-four pages long, *Serious Considerations* was drawn mostly from Robert Barclay's treatment of his Fifth and Sixth Propositions, grouped under the title "Of Universal and Saving Light." John Wesley edited out most of Barclay's confusing description of the "seed" but kept a reference to the parable of the sower.[91] Clearly, he preferred the metaphor of "light," including large swaths of Barclay's discussion of the light of Christ, especially from Johannine writings.[92]

Equally important in both Robert Barclay's *Apology* and John Wesley's abridgement were the concepts of the *universality* and *resistibility* of grace. For Barclay, the "day of visitation" represented the active striving of the Spirit of God with an individual, calling all unbelievers to repentance.[93] However, refusal of the salvation offer was an option. After examining numerous passages of Scripture, Barclay concluded:

> If there was a day when the obstinate Jews might have known the things that belonged to their peace, which, because they rejected it, were hid from their eyes; if there was a time wherein Christ would have gathered them, who, because they refused, could not be gathered; then such as might have been saved do actually perish, that slighted the day of God's visitation towards them, wherein they might have been converted and saved.[94]

Robert Barclay argued from the parable of the talents in Matthew 25 that the talents symbolized God's grace in Christ extended to all.[95] Though in the parable not all the servants received the same number of talents from the master, "yet there is given to all that which is sufficient, and no more is required than according to that which is given."[96] John Wesley included this passage in *Serious Considerations,* thus acknowledging the validity of Barclay's hermeneutical link between the availability of grace and the metaphor of talents.[97]

John Wesley's *Serious Considerations* ended with a paragraph that did not appear in Robert Barclay's *Apology*. In it, he gathered up the threads, affirming again that:

1) The gospel is good tidings of great joy for all people;
2) Ministers were to preach to all;
3) Christ died for all;
4) God gives to all a day or time of visitation;
5) A measure of saving grace is available to all;
6) Those who might have come to Christ but did not had their blood on their own heads.[98]

Through his careful elucidation of the *logos* doctrine, Robert Barclay provided an alternative system to the strong Calvinism of his day.[99] When the predestinarian controversy arose in his own time, John Wesley did not hesitate to adapt the arguments that the Quaker theologian had made years before. Though at the time of the first predestinarian controversy (1739-41) Wesley's conception of prevenient grace was not fully developed, Barclay's doctrine of the universal light of Christ had already left its mark. The "Quaker text" (John 1:9) became Wesley's favorite passage when confronting the inroads of predestinarian ideas among his Methodist societies.

Conclusion

In Robert Barclay's *Apology*, John Wesley encountered ideas that resonated with his own developing understanding of the economy of God's grace. The light of Christ, universal in scope, was a compelling metaphor that he employed in the sometimes heated discussions with those who limited the reach of grace to those predestined to eternal life. Yet *Serious Considerations*, while important, was just once piece of a much broader theological puzzle. What were the final contours of Wesley's doctrine of prevenient grace as they developed over the course of fifty years of itinerant ministry? It is to this broader question that Chapter 3 of this investigation is dedicated.

Notes

1. Earle Edwin Cairns, *Christianity Through the Centuries: A History of the Christian Church* (3rd ed.; Grand Rapids: Zondervan Publishing Co., 1996), 381. Leslie Stephen noted that Barclay possessed "a degree of learning very unusual among the early quakers." See "Barclay, Robert," *Dictionary of National Biography* (Leslie Stephen and Sidney Lee, eds.; 22 vols.; London: Smith, Elder, & Co., 1908), 1:1088. William Frost observed: "The contrast between Quaker and Puritan theological attainment is striking. After the initial outpouring of works by the 'First Publishers of Truth' and the more orderly expositions of the faith by William Penn, Robert Barclay, and George Keith – all of whom had created their most significant writings between 1664 and 1695 – the Friends produced no original able thinkers for the next one hundred years." In J. William Frost, "The Dry Bones of Quaker Theology," *Church History* 39:4 (December 1970): 503.

2. T.A. Burkill, *The Evolution of Christian Thought* (Ithaca and London: Cornell University Press, 1971), 277.

3. D. Elton Trueblood, *Robert Barclay: A portrait of the life and times of a great Quaker intellectual leader* (New York, Evanston, and London: Harper and Row, 1968), 26-7. Trueblood's favorable biography remains the best work on Barclay's life.

4. Trueblood, 95-110. For a discussion of the Quaker refusal to take oaths and the gradual gains made by Quakers in the political realm, see Ethyn Williams Kirby, "The Quakers' Efforts to Secure Civil and Religious Liberty, 1660-96," *The Journal of Modern History* 7:4 (December 1935), 401-21.

5. The full name of Barclay's treatise was *Apology for the True Christian Religion, as the Same is Set Forth and Preached by The People Called in Scorn "Quakers."* Burkill, 277.

6. Burkill, 277.
7. Frost, 503, fn. 2.
8. Frost, 2.
9. Trueblood, 1.
10. Jackson I. Cope, "Seventeenth Century Quaker Style," *PMLA* 71:4 (September 1956), 752.
11. Frost, 504.
12. The 1780 version of the *Apology* referenced in this inquiry is by Kessinger Publishing's Rare Mystical Reprints (www.kessinger.net) and was entitled *An Apology for the True Christian Divinity Being an Explanation and Vindication of the Principles and Doctrines of the People Called Quakers;* hereafter, all references are to the Kessinger edition.
13. Capitalization here reflects the usage in the *Apology* and not modern conventions.
14. The same procedure was followed by Herbert Boyd McGonigle, *Sufficient Saving Grace: John Wesley's Evangelical Arminianism* (Carlisle, Cumbria, and Waynesboro, Georgia: Paternoster Press, 2001), 131-36.
15. Elton Trueblood observed: "Barclay saw that he should start, not with knowledge about God and man, but with the way in which such knowledge can be reached." Trueblood, 134.
16. Barclay, *Apology*, 3.
17. Barclay later called the ministry of angels "circumstantial" and "accidental," whereas inner revelations were "universal" and "substantial." See *Apology*, 35.
18. *Apology*, 3.
19. Frost, 518-19. For a more extended discussion on how Quakers used the Bible, see pp. 519-23.
20. The *Apology* was replete with Scripture references, a testimony to the Apologist's familiarity with the Bible and ease in mustering texts to buttress his arguments.
21. *Apology*, 4. Regarding reason, William Frost observed: "Friends, although never affirming that revelation went contrary to reason, were more in the Tertullian stream of Christian thought which refused to admit even the relevance of reason in spiritual matters." Frost, 507.
22. *Apology*, 5. Elton Trueblood noted: "Barclay valued the Bible because it enables us to extend the fellowship of verification to past ages and to see how our direct experiences of God's power compare with the reported experiences of God's power at other times." Trueblood, 136.
23. *Apology*, 5.
24. See endnote 22 above. Comparing reason unfavorably with the "inward and immediate guide," i.e. the Spirit, Barclay asked: "Why need we set up our own carnal and corrupt reason for a guide to us in spiritual matters, as some will needs do?" *Apology*, 46.
25. *Apology*, 20. Barclay later compares the light of God's Son to the sun, i.e. "the greater light, to rule the day," whereas human reason is like the moon, "the lesser light to rule the night." *Apology*, 145.
26. *Apology*, 36.
27. *Apology*, 20.

28. *Apology*, 23.
29. *Apology*, 25.
30. *Apology*, 42.
31. *Apology*, 30.
32. *Apology*, 51.
33. *Apology*, 48, 74. Barclay later argued that there is no reason to believe that the Canon of Scripture is closed, though any such new revelation would be consistent with what has already been revealed, i.e. "the good old gospel and doctrines." *Apology*, 91.
34. Frost, 509.
35. The final section of Proposition Four read: "Nevertheless, this seed is not imputed to infants, until by transgression they actually join themselves therewith; for they are by nature *the children of wrath,* who walk according to the *power of the prince of the air, the spirit that now worketh in the children of disobedience,* having their conversation in the lusts of the flesh, fulfilling the desires of the flesh, and of the mind." *Apology*, 95.
36. These metaphors appeared again in Propositions Five and Six.
37. *Apology* , 108.
38. *Apology*, 99.
39. *Apology*, 94.
40. *Apology*, 94-95. William Frost observed: "At times Quakers became almost Manichaean in discussing an innate seed of righteousness contending with a seed of evil." Frost, 511. Likewise, Leif Eeg-Olofsson remarks that Barclay is "often guilty of a strongly spiritualized exegesis,' not letting the word "seed" in the Parable of the Sower (Matthew 13) refer to the historic word of Jesus. See Leif Eeg-Olofsson, *The Conception of the Inner Light in Robert Barclay's Theology: A Study in Quietism* (Lund: CWK Gleerup, 1954), 30.
41. *Apology*, 101. Barclay reiterated this point in his treatment of Propositions Five and Six (144). Leif-Eeg Olofsson viewed Barclay as inconsistent, since he sometimes seemed to treat what Olofsson termed the "Inner Light" as a "vestige" remaining after the fall. See Leif-Eeg Olofsson, 72-73.
42. *Apology,* 101.
43. *Apology*, 100.
44. *Apology*, 102.
45. The term, "light of Christ," is characteristic of the writings of George Fox, William Penn, and Robert Barclay, and thus more accurate than "Inner Light." The former was chosen by Elton Trueblood for the title of chapter nine of his biography of Robert Barclay. On the concept itself, Trueblood wrote: "This basic theology may rightly be called the theology of the Holy Spirit" (p. 163). Trueblood further remarked that, while appealing to the *Logos* doctrine was nothing new, Barclay "was the first Christian thinker to make it both explicit and central" (p. 155).
46. These two propositions are of special interest, as this section of the *Apology* was what John Wesley abridged for distribution in tract form during the 1741 predestinarian controversy. Barclay allotted eighty-seven pages to his explication of these two propositions, more than given to any other proposition.
47. *Apology,* 6-7, 108.
48. *Apology,* 7-8, 109-10. The length of Proposition Six precludes reproducing the full text.
49. *Apology*, 110.
50. *Apology*, 118.
51. *Apology* , 121.
52. *Apology*, 110.
53. *Apology*, 160. Regarding the prologue to John's Gospel, including John 1:9, Jackson Cope remarked: "No amount of repetition seemed able to dry the spiritual

marrow out of those verses for the early Quakers, who adapt them to every circumstance." Jackson I. Cope, 729. This passage was also John Wesley's preferred proof-text when referencing the doctrine of prevenient grace.

54. *Apology*, 162.
55. *Apology*, 161.
56. *Apology*, 132. This quote coupled the metaphor of "light" with the language of grace and pneumatology. Trueblood observed: "The Holy Spirit is not spirit in general, but that which is consistent with Christ's earthly life, teaching, death, and resurrection. The historic revelation of Christ gives precision; the revelation of the Holy Spirit in each contemporary life gives universality; and it is the combination which makes vital Christianity possible." Trueblood, 163.
57. *Apology*, 141-42.
58. This is an important point that distinguished Puritan from Quaker theology: "The Calvinist could not stop God; the Quaker could." (Frost, 513).
59. *Apology*, 137.
60. Barclay's description of "seed" blurred the line between the unbeliever, upon whom the light of Christ shone, and the believer, in whom God the Holy Spirit dwelt. When Barclay described "this seed, light, or grace" as "a real spiritual substance," he introduced ideas that exceeded biblical warrant.
61. *Apology*, 138.
62. *Apology*, 138. On the contrary, for the one in whom "the seed is received in the heart," in whom there is no resistance, "Christ comes to be formed and raised, of which the Scripture makes so much mention, calling it the *new man, Christ within, the hope of glory*."
63. *Apology*, 126.
64. No one can act, move, or work on his or her own "until he first be quickened, raised up, and actuated by God's Spirit." *Apology*, 134.
65. *Apology*, 133-4.
66. In a convoluted passage (pp. 142-43), Barclay attempted to explain in what sense Christ is in all persons, even the unbeliever. While he insisted that Christ is in all as a "seed" or "light," these can be "pressed down" or "crucified." Still, only the "saints" know "union" with Christ or can speak of his "inhabitation."
67. *Apology*, 112.
68. *Apology*, 133.
69. *Apology*, 134.
70. *Apology*, 109.
71. Trueblood, 156.
72. *Apology*, 109.
73. Barclay reflected the occasionally insensitive use of language typical of his era.
74. *Apology*, 134.
75. See discussion in *Apology*, 141-42. Though he did not use the word, Barclay was discussing the work of sanctification, which he made dependent upon preaching.
76. *Apology*, 142.
77. *Apology*, 144.
78. *Apology*, 144-45. William Frost commented: "Both Friends and Puritans required the necessity of something besides reason in religion, but with this difference: the Puritans defended all possible tools of man in learning about and communicating the contents of revelation; the Friends admitted only supernatural means in evaluating supernatural matters." Frost, 507.
79. *Apology*, 145.
80. *Apology*, 146.

81. *Apology*, 146.
82. *Apology*, 145. Barclay cited Titus 1:15 to buttress his claim.
83. *Apology*, 147.
84. *Apology*, 147.
85. *Apology*, 146.
86. *Apology*, 147.
87. *Apology*, 146-47.
88. *Apology*, 147.
89. Allan Coppedge, *Shaping the Wesleyan Message: John Wesley in Theological Debate* (1987; repr., Nappanee, Indiana: Francis Asbury Press/Evangel Publishing House, n.d.), 83. The full title of Wesley's abridgement was: *Serious Considerations on Absolute Predestination extracted from a late author* (Bristol: S. and F. Farley, 1741).
90. Coppedge, 83.
91. John Wesley, *Serious Considerations*, 22-23.
92. *Serious Considerations*, 20-22.
93. *Apology*, 153-160.
94. *Apology*, 160. In *Serious Considerations*, Wesley devoted pages 15-24 to excerpts from Barclay explaining both God's indiscriminate offer of salvation (the "day of visitation") and the insistence that Christ died for all.
95. *Apology*, 167.
96. *Apology*, 167.
97. *Serious Considerations*, 23. The talent metaphor was most fully developed by John Fletcher in his *Third Check to Antinomianism*. See Joseph Benson, ed., *The Works of the Rev. John Fletcher, Late Vicar of Madeley* (9 vols.; London: Wesleyan Conference Office, 1877), 2:405-406; also 4:295-299.
98. *Serious Considerations*, 24.
99. See full discussion in Trueblood, 154-56.

Chapter Three

John Wesley on Prevenient Grace

Introduction

How do God and the individual relate to each other in the salvation encounter? This has long been a crucial soteriological question. On the one hand was the formulation of Tridentine Roman Catholicism, with its emphasis upon human merit. On the other hand was the response of John Calvin, who re-appropriated Augustine's accent upon God's sovereignty, especially predestination to eternal life of the elect. John Wesley was never at ease with either possibility. While he sympathized with the concern to guard an important place for the pursuit of holiness, always a strength of the Roman tradition, his own experience before 1738 was an eloquent reminder of the pitfalls of moralism,[1] especially the uncertainty of one's salvation that seemed to be a common experience of those who pursued this difficult path. Calvin's solution to this problem appeared to create a new set of difficulties, positing a God who unilaterally decided the fate of individuals. From Wesley's perspective, this robbed the individual of moral responsibility, and since all were not predestined to heaven, made God into a creature worse than the devil.

Was there no third possibility, a doctrine that would guard both the reality of our human helplessness, but also the necessity of holiness and response to the divine initiative? Indeed, such a *via media* lay readily at-hand in Wesley's theological heritage.[2] It is here that Wesley discovered the key, the doctrine of prevenient grace, a doctrine that became increasingly important as his thinking developed, particularly in debate with theological opponents.[3]

In Chapters 1 and 2 of this investigation, consideration was given to selected Puritan, Church of England, and Quaker theologians who in varying degrees appear to have influenced John Wesley's thinking on prevenient grace. In Chapter 3, the goal is to present Wesley's own thinking on prevenient grace by examining primary sources. Prior to this study, an outline of Wesley's beliefs about the image of God and original sin creates a theological context for situating prevenient grace in his larger thought.

A Procedural Note: the Early and Later Wesley

Interpreters of the writings of John Wesley (1703-91) are faced with a methodological challenge. Because Wesley wrote over a period of sixty years, which period in his life is considered doctrinally authoritative? While the contours of Wesley's theology remained remarkably consistent after his Aldersgate Street "heartwarming" in 1738, there was ongoing refinement in his thinking as the century progressed. It is for this reason that Randy Maddox, following Albert Outler who first proposed this insight,[4] has suggested dividing the extant writings from Wesley's life into three distinct periods:

> 1) the "early Wesley" (1733-38);
> 2) the "middle Wesley" (1738-65),
> 3) the "late Wesley" (1765-91).[5]

This methodology was also explained by Richard Heitzenrater:

> With regard to specialist studies on Wesley, then, an adequate study in the light of the principles just listed, would consider the early and late (as well as the middle) Wesley, would consider the change as well as the continuity in his development, would take seriously the criticism of anti-Wesleyan views as part of the whole picture, would recognize the incongruities and analyze the resulting tensions, and would look for the precursors and precedents of his thoughts and actions.[6]

As the image of God, original sin/depravity, and prevenient grace are evaluated, in each case the study will be conducted chronologically, from the earliest sources to the latest. However, because there is little difference between Wesley's middle and late views as touching upon these areas, a simpler classification of "early" and "later" will be maintained.[7]

Imago Dei: The Image of God in John Wesley's Thought

Prevenient grace finds its *raison d'être* as part of the divine solution to the human dilemma. It is necessary, accordingly, to carefully determine what John Wesley believed about the tragedy that necessitated lavish grace. Only when the "sickness" is diagnosed can the "cure" be applied. The logical place to begin, therefore, is by examining what Wesley believed regarding the image of God in humanity both before and after the fall.

John Wesley frequently alluded to the image of God in his sermons. In *The Image of God* (1730), based on Genesis 1:27, Wesley explained what it means to be created in God's image, how that image was lost, and how it can be recovered. Humanity prior to the fall possessed "an unerring understanding, an uncorrupt will, and perfect freedom."[8] The understanding was without error, just and clear. Perception was always accurate, everything appearing "according to its real nature."[9] Humans were possessed of epistemological perfection. Furthermore, the will was perfect. Affections were "rational, even, and regular."[10] Chief among these emotions was love. Wesley described this love in glowing terms:

> Love filled the whole expansion of his soul; it possessed him without a rival. Every movement of his heart was love: it knew no other fervour. Love was his vital heat; it was the genial warmth that animated his whole frame. And the flame of it was continually streaming forth, directly to him from whom it came, and by reflection to all sensitive natures, inasmuch as they too were his offspring; but especially to those superior beings who bore not only the superscription, but likewise the image of their Creator.[11]

Besides an epistemological and affective perfection was another, that of perfect freedom. This liberty was "implanted in his nature, and interwoven with all its parts."[12] There was no prior constraint placed upon the decision-making process.

John Wesley detailed how Adam's disobedience wreaked havoc in these three areas. Because of the physical consequences of the fall, including sickness and eventual death,[13] the understanding could no longer count upon "suitable organs," by which Wesley seemed to mean the physical senses were no longer fully dependable. Both doubt and error for the first time clouded human perception. Negative affections previously unknown became troublesome, including grief, anger, hatred, fear, and shame. The will was set upon by "the whole train of earthly, sensual, and devilish passions."[14] The inevitable consequence of enslavement to a "depraved understanding" and a "corrupted will" was the loss of freedom and happiness.[15]

A significant advance was made in John Wesley's thinking about the image of God in the sermon, *The New Birth* (1760).[16] Here, Wesley picked up the three elements already alluded to (i.e. understanding, will, and freedom) and classified them as the "natural image."[17] However, to the natural image he added the "political image" and the "moral image." Wesley explained how God created humans:

> Not barely in his natural image, a picture of his own immortality, a spiritual being endued with understanding, freedom of will, and various affections; not merely in the political image, the governor of this lower world, having "dominion over the fishes of the sea, and over the fowl of the air, and over the cattle, and over all the earth," but chiefly in his moral image, which, according to the Apostle, is "righteousness and true holiness."[18]

Having presented the perfection of humanity before Adam's sin, John Wesley again elucidated the consequences of human rebellion. The love of God was "extinguished in his soul."[19] Adam's and Eve's hiding from God symbolized their loss of knowledge of the Creator. Where "freedom of the will" had existed as part of the natural image of God, the individual was now subject to the tyranny of "self-will."[20] Wesley concluded: "So had he lost both the knowledge and love of God, without which the image of God would not subsist."[21] The "foundation" of the new birth is the "entire corruption of our nature" brought on by the fall.[22] Regeneration was the means by which the restoration of the natural and moral image begins.[23]

A third sermon where John Wesley addressed the *imago Dei* is *The General Deliverance* (1781).[24] Loosely based on Romans 8:19-22, he began by describing "the original state of the brute creation."[25] Consistent with the other sermons examined to this point, Wesley defined the "natural image" as consisting of understanding, will, and liberty.[26] The perfections apparent in each of these domains were characteristic of humans, but also of other creatures. The animals possessed "some shadowy resemblance of even *moral goodness*" manifested by gratitude toward humans for the benefits they provided and a "reverence" toward them.[27] While he neglected to reiterate the term "political image," the concept of the human governance of nature was present. Importantly, the "dominion" exercised by humans toward the Creation was beneficent and not abusive. Humanity was to be "God's vicegerent upon earth, the prince and governor of this lower world; and all the blessings of God flowed through him to the inferior creatures. Man was the channel of conveyance between the Creator and the whole brute creation."[28] The sinfulness of humanity, however, caused the animal kingdom to descend into savageness. Only at the end of time would God restore to the non-human creation its lost understanding, will, and liberty.

Another sermon that shed light on John Wesley's doctrine of the image of God was *The End of Christ's Coming* (1781).[29] Beginning with his text, 1 John 3:8,[30] Wesley's design was soteriological. Near the conclusion, he remarked:

> Here then we see in the clearest, strongest light, what is real religion: a restoration of man, by him that bruises the serpent's head, to all that the serpent deprived him of; a restoration not only to the favour, but likewise to the image of God; implying not barely a deliverance from sin but the being filled with the fulness of God. It is plain, if we attend to the preceding considerations, that nothing short of this is Christian religion.[31]

Earlier portions of the sermon had elucidated the meaning of the *imago Dei*. The "natural image" was expanded to include humans created as "spirit," like unto God, who is also spirit.[32] The strong terms used in earlier sermons to describe the perfect nature of the understanding prior to the fall were softened. Even then, humans were "capable of mistaking, of being deceived, although not necessitated to it."[33]

The remainder of the sermon addressed the "moral image" of God, i.e. how "the life of God was extinguished in his soul" including the loss of "righteousness and true holiness."[34] John Wesley presented justification and sanctification as "a restoration not only to the favour, but likewise to the image of God."[35] This restoration appeared at first to be limited to the moral image, but there were hints – consistent with the sermon *The New Birth* – that God also restored elements of the natural image. It is the "Son of God" who "begins his work in man by enabling us to believe in him. He both opens and enlightens the eyes of our *understanding*."[36] Also, it is only the divine destruction of "self-will" that enabled the humbled sinner to say "Not as I will, but as thou wilt."[37]

In summary, the original capacity to rightly *know* and *love* God – both components of the natural image – were re-ordered.

Consistent with his prior views, John Wesley maintained his understanding of "will" as "various affections," including love. To this he added the familiar "liberty":

> It seems therefore that every spirit in the universe, as such, is endued with understanding, and in consequence with a will and a measure of liberty; and that these three are inseparably united in every intelligent creature. And observe: 'liberty necessitated,' or overruled, is really no liberty at all. It is a contradiction in terms. It is the same as 'unfree freedom,' that is, downright nonsense.[38]

What is the nature of this "liberty"? Noting that Robert Chiles had lamented the apparent shift away from "free grace" (Wesley) to "free will" (American Methodism), John Knight countered: "The *first* subtle step in this shift from free grace to free will can be found, not in Richard Watson…but in John Wesley himself."[39] In addition to the sermon, *The End of Christ's Coming*, this appeared in the 1790 sermon, *Heavenly Treasure in Earthen Vessels*.[40] There, Wesley spoke of what "Christian believers" have in common with "other men," namely, "the remains of the image of God." These included "a degree of liberty, of self-moving, yea, and self-governing power," without which Wesley asked whether we would be "mere machines, stocks and stones?"[41] Nevertheless, such liberty was limited to the mundane decisions of human existence and should not be construed in a Pelagian sense, i.e. that there was an innate human capacity for choosing God that remained even after the fall.[42] This became clear in Wesley's 1788 sermon, *What is Man?* Having defined "liberty" as a "power of self-determination," he spoke of human ability to "move this or that part of his body, to move it or not, and to move this way or the contrary, just as he pleases."[43] However, Wesley introduced an important caveat:

> And although I have not an absolute power over my mind, because of the corruption of my nature, yet through the grace of God assisting me I have a power to choose and do good as well as evil. I am free to choose whom I will serve, and if I choose the better part, to continue therein even unto death.[44]

Randy Maddox cast this concern under the larger heading of what he calls John Wesley's "holistic psychology."[45] Interpreting Wesley, he argued that humans have liberty because we have been "*graced* with liberty."[46] As will be argued below in connection with Wesley's understanding of original sin, the results of the fall are such that only the prior grace of God can enable the individual to respond to divine overtures.

Original Sin and Depravity

Though John Wesley appears to have given little consideration to the condition of the political image after the fall, there is no doubting his pessimistic view of the moral image. The sin of Adam and Eve, traditionally termed "original sin," resulted in alienation from God and the attendant loss of righteousness, a corruption (usually termed "depravity") that was radical in scope, affecting subsequent generations.

A. Importance and Role of the Doctrine

It is difficult to exaggerate the central role original sin played in John Wesley's theological system. Harald Lindström considered original sin a "marked soteriological element in his theology,"[47] and Herbert Boyd McGonigle viewed it – along with prevenient grace – as foundational in Wesley's thinking on the related doctrines of universal grace and salvation by faith.[48] In an April 6, 1761 letter to George Downing, Wesley spoke of "the three grand scriptural doctrines – Original Sin, Justification by Faith, and Holiness consequent thereon."[49] Seeking greater cooperation among the clergy, Wesley in a March 29, 1764 letter identified the same three teachings as "essentials" in the pursuit of unity.[50] Such was his concern for the impact that the Socinian John Taylor's denial of original sin was making that in 1757 Wesley took time out from his busy schedule to produce his longest writing, *The Doctrine of Original Sin according to Scripture, Reason and Experience.*[51] In this treatise, Wesley showed that – like John Calvin – he was Augustinian in his view of original sin.

Having established the importance of the doctrine of original sin for John Wesley, the question remains: How is original sin relevant to our study of prevenient grace? Simply put, prevenient grace has no *raison d'être* for one who denies human depravity. Harald Lindström clearly understood the symbiotic relationship between original sin and prevenient grace:

> Since the whole of mankind is involved in guilt and punishment and since human nature has been utterly perverted, man has no chance at all of saving himself by his own efforts. Instead he is referred exclusively to God's grace in Christ. In this way the doctrine of original sin safeguards the idea of grace. The doctrine is necessarily linked up with the essential purpose of the Gospel, which he (Wesley) declared was to humble mankind and to ascribe the whole of his salvation to God's free grace instead of to man's free will.[52]

Cary Balzer expressed the same viewpoint, noting that "Wesley's doctrine of prevenient grace followed directly from a firm commitment to the reality of original sin, a condition which Wesley likened to a sickness from which only faith can provide a remedy."[53] Prevenient grace was a solution to a problem, namely, the incapacity of the human being to respond to divine drawings, due to the effects of the fall. Only when the nature of depravity as taught by Wesley comes clearly into focus can the value and role of prevenient grace be put in proper perspective.

B. Selected Passages from John Wesley on Original Sin

From the earliest days of his ministry, John Wesley consistently accorded a key place to the doctrine of original sin.[54] The 1746 sermon *Justification by Faith* unfolded in four major sections, the first of which described Adam's state both before and after his rebellion against God.[55] He was created in the image of

God, "an incorruptible picture of the God of glory. He was accordingly pure, as God is pure, from every spot of sin."[56] However, by eating of the fruit of the forbidden tree, Adam came under the judgment of God. What was the consequence of Adam's sin? Alluding to Romans 5:12, Wesley explained it primarily in terms of *physical* and *spiritual death*:

> Thus "by one man sin entered into the world, and death by sin. And so death passed upon all men," as contained in him who was the common father and representative of us all. Thus "through the offence of one" all are dead, dead to God, dead in sin, dwelling in a corruptible, mortal body, shortly to be dissolved, and under the sentence of death eternal. For as "by one man's disobedience all were made sinners," so by that offence of one "judgment came upon all men to condemnation."[57]

Wesley later in the sermon called original sin "the general ground of the whole doctrine of justification."[58] In *Justification by Faith*, Wesley presented the problem of original sin and its resultant depravity extended to the descendents of Adam, as well as the solution of potential forgiveness provided through the sacrifice of the Second Adam, Jesus Christ.

The negative tableau of the human condition painted by John Wesley exuded still darker tones in two 1746 sermons, *The Righteousness of Faith*[59] and *The Way to the Kingdom*.[60] In the former sermon, he compared "the righteousness which is of the law" with "the righteousness which is of faith." The first righteousness is tied to the old covenant, a call to perfect obedience given by God to humanity in paradise. The second righteousness, on the other hand, referred to the "condition of justification," the holiness possible through the covenant of grace provided by the suffering of Christ.[61] The necessity of God's provision in Christ was the result of human inability to perfectly obey. But what was the source of this inability? It may be traced back to Adam's sin. Wesley described our hopeless condition apart from grace:

> But to waive this, the wisdom of the first step hereto, the disclaiming of our own righteousness, plainly appears from hence, that it is acting according to truth, to the real nature of things. For what is it more than to acknowledge with our heart as well as our lips the true state wherein we are? To acknowledge that we bring with us into the world a corrupt, sinful nature; more corrupt indeed than we can easily conceive or find words to express? That hereby we are prone to all that is evil, and averse from all that is good; that we are full of pride, self-will, unruly passions, foolish desires; vile and inordinate affections; lovers of the world, lovers of pleasure more than lovers of God?[62]

In the sermon, *The Way to the Kingdom*, John Wesley described the depravity that characterizes every sinner previous to faith. Echoing the language of his sermons on the image of God, Wesley spoke of the "understanding" and the "will." Of the former, he maintained that the "eyes of thine understanding are darkened." He spoke of ignorance and error as "clouds" that "rest upon thee, and cover thee with the shadow of death."[63] The will was "perverse and distorted, averse from all good, from all which God loves, and prone to all evil, to every abomination which God hateth."[64] Wesley went further, describing the "inbred corruption of the heart, of thy very inmost nature."[65] This was the evil "tree" upon which only the evil "fruit" of gluttony, drunkenness, fornication, and other sins could grow.[66] Without using the language of *imago Dei*, Wesley graphically depicted the severe damage that the fall had done to the natural image, and the corruption of the moral image (holiness) in humanity. In such a sorry state, the only "way to the kingdom" was through divine intervention, through the grace of God revealed in Christ.

In 1759, John Wesley published *Original Sin*[67], a sermon reviewing the salient points from his 1757 treatise, *The Doctrine of Original Sin according to Scripture, Reason, and Experience.*[68] Based on Genesis 6:5, Wesley exposed humanity's depravity from antiquity to his own day. This depravity was due in part to the utter inadequacy of what is sometimes called "natural theology," a limited knowledge of God from nature that tells us of God's existence, but remains superficial.[69]

In the closing section of the sermon, he drew several inferences. The first and second spoke of the "total corruption" of humanity due to the fall. While the "ancient heathens" admitted of some vices, they supposed that "in some the natural good much overbalances the evil."[70] The "fundamental difference" between this belief and that of Christianity was that the latter could admit of no good thing in the unconverted human heart, that instead it was characterized only by evil.[71] Wesley asked a pointed question:

> But here is the shibboleth: Is man by nature filled with all manner of evil? Is he void of all good? Is he wholly fallen? Is his soul totally corrupted? Or, to come back to the text, is "every imagination of the thoughts of his heart evil continually?" Allow this, and you are so far a Christian. Deny it, and you are but a heathen still.[72]

The third inference was that a human sickness demanded a divine cure. For the malady of sin in all of its manifestations, John Wesley prescribed the "great Physician of souls." The task was none other than to restore us to holiness: "Ye know that the great end of religion is to renew our hearts in the image of God, to repair that total loss of righteousness and true holiness which we sustained by the sin of our first parent."[73] To seek a cure, one had to first admit being sick. Wesley assured the reader: "By nature ye are wholly corrupted; by grace ye shall be wholly renewed."[74]

One year later, John Wesley returned to the theme of original sin in his sermon, *The New Birth* (1760), based on John 3:7.[75] Much like in *Justification by Faith*, Wesley carefully detailed the nature of the problem before unveiling the divine solution, in this case, regeneration. Commenting on the classic Romans 5 passage, Wesley explained:

> And "in Adam all died," all humankind, all the children of men who were in Adam's loins. The natural consequence of this is that everyone descended from him comes into the world spiritually dead, dead to God, wholly "dead in sin"; entirely void of the life of God, void of the image of God, and of all that "righteousness and holiness" wherein Adam was created.[76]

What image did the newborn bear? He or she bore the "image of the devil, in pride and self-will; the image of the beast in sensual appetites and desires." Wesley called original sin "the foundation of the new birth." Because our nature was utterly corrupted, all that are "born of a woman must be born of the Spirit of God."[77]

Besides his published sermons, John Wesley spoke elsewhere about original sin and its effects. The June 25, 1744 Minutes recorded the following interchange at the Conference:

> Q.15. In what sense is Adam's sin imputed to all mankind?
>
> A. In Adam all die; that is, (1.) Our bodies then become mortal. (2) Our souls die, that is, were disunited from God. And hence, (3). We are all born with a sinful, devilish nature. By reason whereof, (4). We are children of wrath, liable to death eternal (Romans v.18; Ephes. ii.3).[78]

A July 3, 1759 letter from John Wesley to John Taylor revealed Wesley's belief that nothing less than the integrity of the Christian system was at-stake in the debate over original sin. Taylor had avoided formally responding to Wesley's treatise, ostensibly to avoid controversy between them. Despite this, Wesley chided Taylor:

> How gladly, were it indeed no other than a personal controversy! But certainly it is not: it is a controversy *de re*, if ever there was one in this world; indeed, concerning a thing of the highest importance—nay, all the things that concern our eternal peace. It is Christianity or heathenism! for, take away the Scriptural doctrine of Redemption or Justification, and that of the New Birth, the beginning of sanctification, or (which amounts to the same) explain them as you do, suitably to your doctrine of Original Sin, and what is Christianity better then heathenism? wherein, save in rectifying some of our notions, has the religion of St. Paul any pre-eminence over that of Socrates or Epictetus?[79]

Kenneth Collins concluded that John Wesley's teaching on original sin was similar to that of both Luther and Calvin.[80] For all three, it was only in contrast with the dark shades of human depravity that the bright light of God's grace could become apparent.

Having seen the traditional understanding that John Wesley had of original sin, it is important to remember the equally vital place he left for the work of God's grace, particularly *prevenient* grace. Umphrey Lee laid down a crucial marker:

> To understand how Wesley could hold to the doctrine of original sin and at the same time reject Calvinism, one must grasp this essential fact, that, for Wesley, the "natural man" is only a logical fiction. In this world man exists as a natural man plus the prevenient grace of God. And this grace is not the forgiving favor of God granted in what the Reformed theologians called justification; this grace is empowering grace.[81]

John Peters concurred, calling Wesley's concept of total depravity a "qualified concept." Because of prevenient grace, this depravity was "total in extent...but not in degree." It was this "high doctrine of grace which makes possible in a single system a synthesis of total depravity and Christian perfection. It is by the grace of God that man can find the power to move from extended depravity to limited perfection."[82]

Summary

What may be concluded? Despite the theological ferment of his day, John Wesley remained remarkably traditional in the way he addressed the doctrines of the *imago Dei* and original sin. Adam's sin severely damaged both the political and natural images in humankind, and radically corrupted the moral image. Ron Benefiel observed: "The evidence of humanity across time and across cultures combined with his reading of Scripture provided all the fuel that he (Wesley) needed not only to hold consistently to his understanding of total depravity, but also to defend the faith against any who hold opposing views."[83] For Wesley, the consequences of original sin echoed down to our day, and included atheism, idolatry, pride, and self-will.[84] The physical and spiritual death consequent upon the fall resulted in a total incapacity on the part of a human being – left to his or her own devices – to pursue the life of God. Fortunately, in Wesley's thought, no person throughout space or time had ever been left in such dire circumstances. The mitigating factor was prevenient grace, and it is to Wesley's understanding of this universal light that this chapter now turns.

John Wesley and the Concept of Prevenient Grace

Prevenient grace has today become a vital category for Wesleyan theologians.[85] This was clearly not always the case for John Wesley himself. Indeed, the earliest decades of his ministry accorded little place to prevenient grace as a theological construct. However, as time unfolded – and especially as Wesley entered into protracted debate with those of a Calvinistic persuasion – he came to depend upon it in greater measure as a viable alternative to both predestinarian and moralistic points of view. In conformity with our methodology, let us attempt to reconstruct the increasing role that prevenient grace played in Wesley's thinking, beginning during his days at Oxford and ending in his most mature statements on the matter, published in the 1780s.

A. The Early Wesley: 1733-1738

In his introduction to the four volumes of sermons included in the critical edition of John Wesley's *Works*, Albert Outler was careful not to overvalue Wesley's early sermons. Nonetheless, he discerned in them an enduring value, noting that:

> ...they contain many a seed of Wesley's later, mature ideas. His conception of the essence of "holiness" as love of God and neighbor is there, along with his view of sanctification as more of a process than a state. There is also his platonizing theory of religious knowledge as more intuitive than discursive, along

with his distinctive sense of the personal, prevenient action of the Holy Spirit in all authentic spirituality.[86]

The clearest instance of prevenient grace in John Wesley's early writings was the sermon, *The Circumcision of the Heart* (1733).[87] What was this heart "circumcision" to which Wesley referred? Referencing Romans 2:29, Wesley equated it with holiness. It was perfection in love and renewal of the mind, a cleansing from sin and an acquiring of "those virtues which were also in Christ Jesus."[88] But how was the individual to achieve such a blessed state? Wesley clarified:

> At the same time we are convinced that we are not sufficient of ourselves to help ourselves; that without the Spirit of God we can do nothing but add sin to sin; that it is he alone "who worketh in us" by his almighty power, either "to will or do" that which is good – it being impossible for us even to think a good thought without the supernatural assistance of his Spirit as to create ourselves, or to renew our whole souls in righteousness and true holiness.[89]

While the term "prevenient grace" was absent here, the concept was implicit in the language chosen. Firstly, humans on their own were incapable of spiritual progress. John Wesley affirmed that we are "not sufficient of ourselves to help ourselves." Only with divine help can our hearts be circumcised. Secondly, the depravity that results from original sin included a thought life that would be wholly negative were it not for "the supernatural assistance of his Spirit." Finally, the pneumatological nature of prevenient grace came into focus, for it is the Holy Spirit who was the agent of spiritual renewal.

Later in the sermon, what was implicit became explicit: "He (the Spirit of Christ) alone can quicken those who are dead unto God, can breathe into them the breath of Christian life, and so *prevent*, accompany, and follow them with his grace as to bring their good desires to good effect."[90] This was the first explicit mention of prevenient grace in John Wesley's writings. Also significant were the words "dead" and "quicken." As seen earlier in connection with Wesley's doctrine of original sin, all were born spiritually dead, alienated from the life of God. The Holy Spirit's work was to "quicken," to bring life where none existed. This word took its place among a family of related terms that Wesley increasingly used to describe the action of prevenient grace.

The early writings of John Wesley did not prominently feature the doctrine of prevenient grace. Nonetheless, he acknowledged the necessity of divine quickening in order for humanity to have spiritual life. The implications of this fact will be further developed during the subsequent period of Wesley's ministry.

B. The Middle and Later Wesley: 1738-1791

The second major period of John Wesley's theological development followed his May 24, 1738 Aldersgate experience. Much of Wesley's theological energy in the months following his "heartwarming" was given to elucidating the doctrine of justification by faith. It was only in the heat of an ensuing debate with George Whitefield over the doctrine of predestination that Wesley was forced to elucidate what he believed about God's grace, including its availability to sinners and human ability to resist it.[91]

Was God's grace available to all without exception, or was it reserved only for the "elect," those whom God had predestined to salvation? This was the central concern of John Wesley's sermon, *Free Grace* (1739).[92] Taking Romans 8:32 as his text, Wesley structured his sermon around two points: 1) the grace (or love) of God is free in all, and 2) it is free for all.[93] Almost all of the sermon was a wide-ranging attack upon the "decree of predestination" and its twin doctrine of reprobation. Christ died for all, so grace is "free for all," but what did Wesley mean when he said that God's grace is "free in all"? He explained that it "does not depend on any power or merit in man; no, not in any degree, neither in whole, nor in part."[94] Wesley was sensitive to the charge of Pelagianism, and in this declaration, he steered clear of it. However, to avoid the error of Pelagius, was the theologian forced to call "evil" what appeared to be "good"? In Wesley's view, this was exchanging one error for another. What was good could genuinely be classified as such, for it was a reflection not of human merit, but of divine activity:

> They (good tempers, good desires, etc.) are the fruits of free grace, and not the root. They are not the cause, but the effects of it. Whatsoever good is in man, or is done by man, God is the author and doer of it. Thus is his grace free in all, that is, no way depending on any power or merit in man, but on God alone, who freely gave us his own Son, and "with him freely giveth us all things."[95]

Charles Allen Rogers found in this passage some of the Christological underpinnings of prevenient grace. For the sake of Christ and his being delivered up for us all (Romans 8:32), God had freely given us all things, and as Rogers noted, this included the gift of a universal prevenient grace.[96] Clearly, Wesley viewed prevenient grace as a provision of the atonement.[97]

Two years after the publication of *Free Grace*, John Wesley penned a preface to *An Extract on the Life and Death of Mr. Thomas Haliburton*.[98] His subject was how God sets up the Kingdom in the heart of the believer:

> A sinner, being drawn by the love of the Father, enlightened by the Son, ("the true light which enlighteneth every man that cometh into the world,") and convinced of sin by the Holy Ghost; through the preventing grace which is given him freely, cometh weary and heavy laden, and casteth all his sins upon Him that is "mighty to save."[99]

This paragraph exuded a Trinitarian flavor. The Father drew, the Son enlightened, and the Holy Spirit convicted of sin. But how did this conviction transpire? It was accomplished by means of prevenient grace. Also interesting is this early indication of John Wesley's preference for John 1:9 as a proof text whenever he elaborated his prevenient grace doctrine. Though he did not use the term itself, Wesley's concept was akin to the "light of Christ" of the Quaker theologian, Robert Barclay.[100] Finally, it is crucial to note the nature of divine/human interaction. In grammatical terms, the human being was primarily a direct object acted upon by the three-fold subject of Father, Son, and Holy

Spirit. It was not until the end of the sentence that the sinner became a subject in his or her own right, capable of coming to God or casting sins upon "Him that is mighty to save." Clearly, even this capability was nothing inborn; instead, it was the result of prior divine initiative.

Divine initiative was again evidenced in the 1742 treatise, *The Principles of a Methodist*.[101] Approvingly quoting his opponent, Josiah Tucker, John Wesley wrote: "For the preventing grace of God, which is common to all, is sufficient to *bring* us to Christ, though it is not sufficient to carry us any *further* till we are justified."[102] In one sentence, Wesley established two important facts about "preventing grace." First, it was "common to all," i.e. universal in scope. Secondly, it operated prior to conversion. Its role was to "*bring* us to Christ" at which time justifying grace became operative.

Prevenient grace attracted not only Josiah Tucker's attention but apparently was also a topic of interest for the early Methodist preachers, especially as related to original sin. The Conference Minutes for June 25, 1744 contained an exposition of Romans 5:19 where John Wesley taught that we are "cleared from the guilt of Adam's actual sin" by virtue of the "merits of Christ." Furthermore, Christ's obedience and death provided five benefits: 1) immortal bodies, following the resurrection; 2) our souls received a "capacity of spiritual life"; 3) a genuine "spark" or "seed" of this spiritual life was accorded; 4) reconciliation to God as "children of grace," and 5) we were made to be partakers of the divine nature.[103] Here was another clear indication that Wesley understood the atonement to be the ground of prevenient grace's availability to all humankind. His use of "seed" appears to have been borrowed from Robert Barclay's *Apology*, though it is a metaphor for prevenient grace that Wesley used less frequently than "light."[104]

Though John Wesley was close to John Calvin in his understanding of original sin, a gulf separated them in their teaching on predestination. Indeed, the late 1730s and early 1740s witnessed an ongoing debate between the Calvinistic and Wesleyan wings of the Methodist Revival.[105] This seems to be the context for a question and answer from the August 1, 1745 Conference Minutes:

Q. 23. Wherein may we come to the very edge of Calvinism?

A. (1.) In ascribing all good to the free grace of God. (2) In denying all natural free-will, and all power antecedent to grace. And, (3.) In excluding all merit from man; even for what he has or does by the grace of God.[106]

The Minutes, though helpful, were limited in how deeply they could delve into questions of doctrine.[107] Though all "power" was attributed to grace, the disciples of Calvin and Wesley divided over the question of who were recipients of that grace. For the Calvinist, grace was primarily saving grace, and as such, was reserved for the elect.[108] On the other hand, Wesley believed and taught that a measure of prevenient grace was extended to all individuals throughout time and space. Because of this, in the same Minutes, he refused to label the works of Cornelius (Acts 10) as "splendid sins," since they were not done "without the grace of Christ."[109]

In the sermon, *The Spirit of Bondage and Adoption* (1746),[110] John Wesley developed the teaching of Romans 8:15. The contrast was between the natural, legal, and evangelical states. By this, Wesley meant respectively persons who were spiritually asleep, awakened to their need of God but yet unconverted, or those who have been justified. It is significant that Wesley used no metaphors indicative of prevenient grace to describe the "natural man."[111] Instead, this person was totally ignorant of God and their own person. They were servants of sin and constantly excused it as part-and-parcel of human frailty.[112] Importantly, Wesley located prevenient grace at the second step, i.e. in the "legal man," a person who had been awakened by the working of the Holy Spirit:

> By some awful providence, or by his Word applied with a demonstration of his Spirit, God touches the heart of him that lay asleep in darkness and in the shadow of death. He is terribly shaken out of his sleep, and awakes into a consciousness of his danger. Perhaps in a moment, perhaps by degrees, the eyes of his understanding are opened, and now first (the veil being in part removed) discern the real state he is in. Horrid light breaks in upon his soul...He at last sees the loving, the merciful God is also "a consuming fire"...[113]

Based upon this sermon alone, there was no indication – apart from the phrase "by some awful providence" – why some responded to the grace of God and others did not, why some remained "natural men" while others went on to the next step of awakening, and became "legal men." Why were some touched by the divine, becoming examples of "a demonstration of his Spirit," while others remained fast asleep? Was grace extended only to some, but not to others? Wesley in this sermon provided no answer. It would remain for later writings to clarify this crucial question.[114]

Also in 1746, the sermon *The Witness of Our Own Spirit* was published.[115] Taking 2 Cor. 1:12 as his text, John Wesley clarified various meanings of "grace." Sometimes, "grace" was God's "free love" or "unmerited mercy." However, in the text cited, Wesley discerned the concept of *divine enablement*:

> But in this place it rather means that power of God the Holy Ghost which "worketh in us both to will and to do of his good pleasure." As soon as ever the grace of God (in the former sense, his pardoning love) is manifested to our soul, the grace of God (in the latter sense, the power of his Spirit) takes place therein. And now we can perform, through God, what to man was impossible.[116]

It is clear that the operation of this grace was post-conversion, and therefore could not be described as "preventing grace" in the narrow sense of the term. Nonetheless, this was an important passage in that it juxtaposed the language of grace and the Spirit. To these two concepts, Wesley just one paragraph later spoke of the "light of God that shines in my heart" as the source of our "power to walk in his ways."[117] "Grace," "Spirit," and "light" were becoming increasingly prominent in Wesley's vocabulary, in this instance, to delineate the believer's spiritual progress. With time, the same categories would be pushed further back in the *via salutis* to describe divine interaction with the person not yet justified.

But how did God the Holy Spirit reach out to the person who was not yet Christian? The sermon, *The Means of Grace* (1746),[118] provided some interesting clues. John Wesley defined "means of grace" as "outward signs, words, or actions ordained of God, and appointed for this end – to be the *ordinary* channels whereby he might convey to men preventing, justifying, or sanctifying grace."[119] The primary "means" were prayer, the study of Scripture, and observing the Lord's Supper.[120] However, elsewhere in the sermon, Wesley allowed for other means that awakened the spiritually sleeping:

> A stupid, senseless wretch is going on in his own way, not having God in all his thoughts, when God comes upon him unawares, perhaps by an awakening sermon or conversation, perhaps by some awful providence; or it may be an immediate stroke of his convincing Spirit, without any outward means at all.[121]

In the section that followed, Wesley traced how the individual – awakened by the prevenient grace received via the means of grace mentioned and yielding to God's conviction – may incrementally move closer to faith. Simultaneously, he or she continued to observe all the means of grace, namely, "hearing, reading, meditating, praying, and partaking of the Lord's Supper," until God, "in the manner that pleases him, speaks to his heart, 'Thy faith hath saved thee; go in peace.'"[122]

John Wesley lived at a time and in a country where the means of grace were readily available to those who wanted them. No one lived far from a church building, and sermons were often printed and offered for sale. Furthermore, social convention encouraged church attendance, and though many were absent on any given Sunday, important events such as baptisms, weddings, or funerals brought the masses in contact with the ecclesiastical apparatus. It is not surprising therefore to see Wesley connect the working of prevenient grace with these conventions. But what of places that lacked such an infrastructure, locations where the Bible – either because of illiteracy or unavailability – remained a closed book, or where churches were prohibited from operating? Where such *ordinary* channels were absent, Wesley allowed for what may be termed *extraordinary* measures, what he called the "immediate stroke of his convincing Spirit without any outward means at all."[123] God the Holy Spirit, though most often working through the standard means of grace, was not limited to them. In the same way, the wide-ranging workings of prevenient grace could not be geographically circumscribed.

Two years later, John Wesley published the sermon, *Upon our Lord's Sermon on the Mount, Discourse the Third* (1748).[124] Commenting upon the persecution of Christians mentioned in the Beatitudes (Matthew 5:11-12), Wesley spoke of the "scandal of the cross." However, the hatred toward believers of "those who are yet in their sins" might be mitigated to the degree that "the Spirit of God may be striving with them," or by the workings of "preventing grace" or "the peculiar providence of God."[125] Noting the correlation between providence and grace, Albert Outler observed that "preventing" in this case – while not excluding "anticipating" – more closely approximates the common meaning of "hindering."[126]

At the same time that he was pondering the persecution of believers, John Wesley was reflecting upon the atonement and its relationship to the reach of grace. In a February 10, 1748 letter to Thomas Whitehead, Wesley approvingly paraphrased Proposition VI from Robert Barclay's *Apology*:

> The benefit of the death of Christ is not only extended to such as have the distinct knowledge of his death and sufferings, but even unto those who are inevitably excluded from this knowledge. Even these may be partakers of the benefit of His death, though ignorant of the history, if they suffer His grace to take place in their hearts, so as of wicked men to become holy.[127]

Wesley's agreement is sealed at the conclusion of the letter: "In these points there is no difference between Quakerism and Christianity."[128]

In this letter, John Wesley laid down three important markers concerning prevenient grace. First, it was provided for by the atonement of Christ. Secondly, by alluding to "those who are inevitably excluded from this knowledge," i.e. of the death and sufferings of Christ, Wesley referenced those who had never enjoyed a hearing of the gospel. Thirdly, this grace could only be effective when seconded by the non-resistance of the recipient, since he or she had to "suffer His grace to take place in their hearts."

In coming years, as Wesley wrestled with the fact that not all who heard the gospel responded in saving faith, he would revisit the theme of God's grace as both universal *and* resistible. This explanation became a viable alternative to John Calvin's "horrible decree" of reprobation, that some were not elected by God to salvation and therefore assigned to perdition.

The theme of predestination arose again in John Wesley's treatise, *Predestination Calmly Considered* (1752).[129] Wesley was unwilling to ascribe to fallen humanity freedom of the will. Instead of crediting nature, Wesley credited grace:

> But I do not carry free-will so far: (I mean, not in moral things:) Natural free-will, in the present state of mankind, I do not understand: I only assert, that there is a measure of free-will supernaturally restored to every man, together with that supernatural light which "enlightens every man that cometh into the world."[130]

Wesley believed that "God nevertheless may have all the glory" even if the individual worked together with God for his or her own salvation.[131] How is this so? Wesley replied: "Why, the very power to 'work together with Him' was from God. Therefore to Him is all the glory."[132] Likewise, responding to the Calvinistic critique, Wesley asked: "How is it more to the glory of God to save man irresistibly, than to save him as a free agent, by such grace as he may either concur with or resist?"[133] Wesley noted that this "measure of free will" was "not by nature."[134] Herbert McGonigle concluded that Wesley was attempting to construct a "theological synergism" that respected Scripture, saving a place for both divine initiative and human response.[135]

Two years earlier, John Wesley published the sermon, *A Caution against Bigotry* (1750).[136] In the context of defending his extraordinary ministry that respected no parish bounds, he spoke of those in need of liberation from Satan's chains. Through the work of the Holy Spirit, "the understanding of the sinner is now enlightened, and his heart sweetly drawn to God."[137] The activity of grace appeared in another 1750 sermon, *Satan's Devices*.[138] Wesley designed to "point out the several ways whereby Satan endeavours to destroy the first work of God in the soul..."[139] While the sermon was largely descriptive of the believer longing for sanctification, not the unbeliever drawn by prevenient grace, it was nonetheless significant as it appears to be Wesley's first use of the parable of the talents (Matthew 25:14-30) as a metaphor of grace:

> Buy up every opportunity of growing in grace, or of doing good. Let not the thought of receiving more grace tomorrow make you negligent of today. You have one talent now. If you expect five more, so much the rather improve what you have. And the more you expect to receive hereafter, the more labour for God now. Sufficient for the day is the grace thereof. God is now pouring his benefits upon you. Now approve yourself a faithful steward of the present grace of God.[140]

Albert Outler discerned in this image an anticipation of Wesley's later teaching on prevenient grace as expounded in the 1785 sermon, *On Working Out Our Own Salvation*.[141]

Both the universality of prevenient grace and the possibility of resisting it appeared again in Wesley's treatise, *The Doctrine of Original Sin* (1757).[142] The context is Romans 1:19-21, a discussion of the Gentiles in God's economy of salvation. Interpreting Paul, Wesley affirmed that "the Gentiles had light sufficient to have seen God's eternal power and Godhead."[143] What was the source of this "light"? Its origin was not anthropological, i.e. unassisted human reason, but rather was *divine*: "If they had assistance from God, and did not use it, they were equally without excuse."[144] Wesley insisted that "...our nature is deeply corrupted, inclined to evil, and disinclined to all that is spiritually good; so that, without *supernatural grace*, we can neither will nor do what is pleasing to God."[145] But did all possess this grace, and if so, was it enough? Wesley replied: "If you ask, 'Why, how are they capable of performing duty?' I answer, By grace; though not by nature. And a measure of this is given to all men."[146]

The year 1757 saw the first reprinting of John Wesley's popular *Explanatory Notes Upon the New Testament* (1755).[147] In Romans 1:19, Paul wrote regarding the Gentiles: "For what is to be known of God is manifest in them; for God hath showed *it* to them." But what is the mechanism of this revelation? Consistent with his remarks in *The Doctrine of Original Sin*, Wesley explained that it is "By the light which enlightens every man that cometh into the world." John 1:9, the so-called "Quaker text," became Wesley's verse of choice for interpreting Scripture with Scripture when discussing prevenient grace.

John Wesley's comments on John 1:9 in the *New Testament Notes*, while characteristically brief, are nonetheless revealing. To the phrase "who lighteth every man," Wesley responded: "By what is vulgarly termed natural conscience pointing out at least the general lines of good and evil. And this light, if man did not hinder, would shine more and more to the perfect day." Not only was it affirmed that prevenient grace can be thwarted by human resistance, but here Wesley added the important qualification that grace unresisted lead to more grace.

But how did God draw the sinner? In a note on John 6:44, John Wesley answered: "No man can believe in Christ, unless God give him power. He draws us first by good desires, not by compulsion, not by laying the will under any necessity; but by the strong and sweet, yet still resistible, motions of his heavenly grace." Here Wesley protected both a traditional understanding of depravity *and* human responsibility, finding a *via media* between Pelagianism and determinism. Commenting on the phrase, "I will draw all men" (John 12:32), Wesley likewise steered clear of universalism, noting the verse referred to "Gentiles, as well as Jews. And those who follow my drawings Satan shall not be able to keep." He thereby implied that not all follow God's drawings, affirming again that God's grace, though powerful, does not dictate outcomes at the expense of human responsibility. Importantly, Wesley here again tied the provision of prevenient grace to the atoning work of Christ.

A final noteworthy section in the *New Testament Notes* was John Wesley's comments on Romans 2:14-15. Paul spoke of Gentiles who "do by nature the things contained in the law." Wesley explained: "That is, without an outward rule; though this also, strictly speaking, is by preventing grace." The Ten Commandments, given to the Jews, were "only the substance of the law of nature." What did Paul mean when he said that the Gentiles, "not having the law, are a law unto themselves?" Wesley responded: "That is, what the law is to the Jews, they are, by the grace of God, to themselves; namely, a rule of life." Even if Wesley was willing to concede that the "conscience" spoken of in verse 15 might be a human "faculty," he cautioned: "There is none of all its faculties which the soul has less in its power than this." The Gentiles had the "law written on their hearts," but Wesley insisted that this was "by the same hand which wrote the commandments on the tables of stone." This echoed his earlier sentiment from the sermon, *The Original Nature, Property, and Use of the Law* (1750): "And yet God did not despise the work of his own hands; but being reconciled to man through the Son of his love, he in some measure re-inscribed the law on the heart of his dark, sinful creature."[148] Two observations are in order. Firstly, this "re-inscription" of the law was predicated upon the atonement, as implied by the reconciliation only made possible "through the Son of his love." Secondly, he clearly insisted on crediting God for the moral inclinations found in the unbeliever.

In 1759, John Wesley published the sermon, *Original Sin*.[149] Espousing the dark portrait of humanity painted by Augustine, Wesley concluded: "By nature ye are wholly corrupted; by grace ye shall be wholly renewed."[150] Addressing the first point, he earlier spoke of "men of learning and education." Even these he described as "beasts," since "sensual appetites, even those of the lowest kind, have, more or less, the dominion over him."[151] But can no difference be discerned *between* persons? Here Wesley was willing to concede that there is sometimes a "considerable difference." From what did these differences arise? He gave three explanations: 1) constitution; 2) education, and 3) preventing grace.[152] The third point was parenthetical; Wesley does not elaborate.[153] However, in the context of our discussion to this point, it would be reasonable to interpret Wesley here as meaning that moral qualities in the unbeliever were evident in proportion to one's non-resistance to the drawing grace of God.[154]

On April 9, 1765, John Wesley addressed a letter to John Newton. In it, Wesley encapsulated the essence of his soteriology: "Incite them everywhere to insist upon one point – Faith that worketh by love, or (in other words) Christ *enlightening*, justifying, sanctifying, reigning in the believing soul."[155] Here in full evidence was the *via salutis* of prevenient, justifying, sanctifying, and victorious grace. These were the theological emphases that would dominate the final period of Wesley's itinerant ministry.

A large part of that ministry was preaching, and in 1765, John Wesley published *The Scripture Way of Salvation*,[156] a sermon that Albert Outler called "the most successful summary of the Wesleyan vision of the *ordo salutis* in the entire sermon corpus."[157] Prevenient grace, while not to be confused with justification, nevertheless is properly classified as a soteriological doctrine. Wesley clarified:

> If we take this (salvation) in its utmost extent it will include all that is wrought in the soul by what is frequently termed "natural conscience," but more properly, "preventing grace"; all the "drawings of the Father," the desires after God, which, if we yield to them, increase more and more; all that "light" wherewith the Son of God "enlighteneth everyone that cometh into the world," showing every man "to do justly, to love mercy, and to walk humbly with his God"; all the convictions which his Spirit from time to time works in every child of man. Although it is true the generality of men stifle them as soon as possible, and after a while forget, or at least deny, that ever they had them at all.[158]

Here Wesley taught that "preventing grace" is universal, since it "works in every child of man." What is striking, however, was the practical limitation of this grace. While *some* might live in its light, and thereby lead an ethical life, *most* would "stifle" its workings, ending up in a state of spiritual amnesia. By carefully delineating the boundaries of God's prevenient activity, Wesley was by default leaving a key role for the proclamation of the gospel.

On September 15, 1770, John Wesley addressed a letter to Miss March. Pastoral in tone, he advised that the "certain way to obtain more grace" is to "use the grace given." How was this done? Simply by the "full exercise of every talent wherewith we are entrusted."[159] Likewise, a December 14, 1771 letter to "Rev. S.L." equated "talents" with "a measure of (God's) grace" that had to be put to good use and not buried in the earth.[160] In both letters, the juxtaposition of "talent" and "grace" was a reprise of the language of his 1750 sermon, *Satan's Devices*. As in that case, prevenient grace was not explicitly mentioned. However, by continuing to relate the two terms, Wesley set up a more explicit usage that his associate, John Fletcher, would employ in his *Checks to Antinomianism*.[161]

The reason John Fletcher had to take pen in-hand to defend his mentor and friend was the so-called "Minutes controversy" that began in August 1770.[162] Attempting to guard against antinomianism, John Wesley had inadvertently left the impression in the Conference Minutes that humans in some way merit salvation. This interpretation, however, flew in the face of more than thirty years of Wesley's preaching on justification by faith.[163] George Whitefield's funeral on November 18, 1770 gave him the opportunity to re-affirm his and Charles' firm commitment to the same message that their former Oxford colleague had so eloquently preached. Speaking first of Whitefield then of the "Methodists" at Oxford, Wesley observed:

> His fundamental point was: give God all the glory of whatever is good in man…Their grand principle was: there is no power (by nature) and no merit in man. They insisted, all power to think, speak, or act right is in and from the Spirit of Christ; and all merit is (not in man, how high soever in grace, but merely) in the blood of Christ.[164]

With such clear teaching on the supremacy of grace as the enabling principle for all spiritual life, other factors besides those theological may have been involved in the ensuing debate between Wesley, the Countess of Huntingdon and other Calvinists.[165] On the other hand, Kenneth Collins has suggested that part of the confusion arose because of unfamiliarity with the complexities of Wesley's doctrine of prevenient grace.[166] In any case, Wesley distanced himself from the accusation that he was a Papist in disguise.

As the Minutes controversy took on a life of its own, John Wesley continued to dialogue with those who took an interest in the outcome. In the 1772 *Remarks on Mr. Hill's Review*, Wesley responded to the charge that he and John Fletcher held differing positions on the question of free-will: "But, indeed, both Mr. F. and Mr. W. absolutely deny natural free-will. We both steadily assert that the will of man is by nature free only to evil. Yet we both believe that every man has a measure of free-will restored to him by grace."[167] Furthermore, in a November 21, 1776 letter to John Mason, Wesley rejected the notion that some are utterly dead spiritually:

> One of Mr. Fletcher's Checks considers at large the Calvinist supposition "that a natural man is as dead as a stone"; and shows the utter falseness and absurdity of it, seeing no man living is without some preventing grace, and every degree of grace is a degree of life.[168]

John Wesley also pondered the relationship between God's sovereign grace and the preaching of the gospel. The clearest expression of this appeared in the sermon, *The General Spread of the Gospel* (1783).[169] Having drawn a negative estimate of the condition of the unbelieving world, Wesley continued by extolling the positive activity of grace in the soul of his readers:

> You know how God wrought in your own soul when he first enabled you to say, "The life I now live, I live by faith in the Son of God, who loved me, and gave himself for me." He did not take away your understanding but enlightened and strengthened it. He did not destroy any of your affections, rather they were more vigorous than before. Least of all did he take away your liberty, your power of choosing good or evil; he did not force you; but being assisted by his grace you, like Mary, chose the better part. Just so has he assisted five in one house to make the happy choice, fifty or five hundred in one city, and many thousands in a nation, without depriving any of them of that liberty which is essential to a moral agent.[170]

Albert Outler has noted in reference to this passage that this is the work of prevenient grace, and not "unaided human initiative."[171]

Another question addressed in *The General Spread of the Gospel* was the relationship between preaching and the activity of God's grace among the unconverted. John Wesley seemed prepared to accept that God *could* work irresistibly around the globe: "...(God) *can* undoubtedly convert whole nations, or the whole world. And it is as easy to him to convert a world as one individual soul."[172] But saying that God *could* work irresistibly was not the same thing as claiming he *does*.[173] Importantly, Wesley's sermon avoided hypothetical discussion of how God *might* work; rather, he recounted the way in which God had *already chosen* to work for the past fifty to sixty years, first in England, then in distant places like New York, Pennsylvania, or Newfoundland. All of this began because of the ministry of "a few young men in the University of Oxford."[174] For Wesley, human instrumentality was not a denial of divine sovereignty, but an expression of it, and the highest form of that instrumentality was preaching. Quoting Romans 10:14-15, Wesley pursued his theme:

> There are very many heathen nations in the world that have no intercourse either by trade or any other means with Christians of any kind. Such are the inhabitants of the numerous islands in the South Sea, and probably in all large branches of the ocean. Now what shall be done for these poor outcasts of men? "How shall they believe," saith the Apostle, "in him of whom they have not heard? And how shall they hear without a preacher?"[175]

Having earlier in the sermon taught the assistance of the Holy Spirit in wooing the unbeliever to Christ (i.e. prevenient grace), he now moved to the climax with an eloquent appeal for preaching in parts of the world yet untouched by the Christian message. Though never explicitly stated in the sermon, Wesley's manner of organizing the sermon left the implication that the action of prevenient grace was heightened by preaching. Preaching, wherever it took place, was a means of grace.[176]

While knowledge of Christ depended upon preaching, John Wesley was willing to allow for other means of discovering God's existence and attributes. This became apparent in the sermon, *The Imperfection of Human Knowledge* (1784).[177] Wesley's question was simple: Is the idea of God in some way inherent to human nature? This he rejected:

> But the truth is, no man ever did, or does now find any such idea stamped upon his soul. The little which we do know of God (except what we receive by the inspiration of the Holy One) we do not gather from an inward impression, but gradually acquire from without. "The invisible things of God," if they are known at all, "are known from the things that are made"; not from what God hath written in our hearts, but from what he hath written in his works.[178]

Wesley was not denying that the atonement had provided a basis for the re-inscription of the law upon the human heart.[179] Rather, he was affirming a cosmological basis for the knowledge of God as supplementary to the application by the Holy Spirit of the work of Christ.

In *On Charity*, a 1784 sermon, John Wesley emphasized the necessity of love of God and neighbor.[180] Wesley also asked if "the whole heathen world" was excluded from salvation. After all, one might reason that such a love could only spring from knowledge of the Son of God mediated by preaching (Romans 10:9-10). Surprisingly in view of his high estimate of preaching, Wesley remained agnostic about their fate, and this precisely because all have some measure of "light":

> St. Paul's words, spoken on another occasion, are applicable to this: "What the law speaketh, it speaketh to them that are under the law." Accordingly that sentence, "He that believeth not shall be damned," is spoken to them to whom the gospel is preached. Others it does not concern; and we are not required to determine anything touching their final state. How it will please God, the Judge of all, to deal with them, we may leave to God himself. But this we know, that he is not the God of the Christians only, but the God of the heathens also; that he is "rich in mercy to all that call upon him," "according to the light they have"; and that "in every nation he that feareth God and worketh righteousness is accepted of him."[181]

For those who might criticize Wesley for his seeming overdependence on John 1:9 to support his doctrine of prevenient grace, it is significant that he broadened his appeal to Scripture by citing Peter's words in Acts 10:35, the occasion of the conversion of Cornelius and his household.[182] Furthermore, Wesley was careful by his remarks not to disparage preaching, which he regarded as a normative evangelistic tool. Nonetheless, it is clear that all rules had exceptions, and concerning the fate of the unevangelised, Wesley's doctrine of prevenient grace and catholic spirit together combined to put a question mark where others might have placed a period.[183]

One year after pondering the destiny of those who have not heard the gospel message, John Wesley published the sermon, *On Working Out Our Own Salvation* (1785).[184] Herbert McGonigle called it "his most definitive sermon on scriptural salvation" and "his fullest and most mature interpretation of prevenient grace."[185] Discussing his text, Phil. 2:13, Wesley explained the seeming contradiction between Paul's claim that God works salvation in us and his prior exhortation to "work out your own salvation." The theme was summarized at the close of the sermon: "For, first, God works; therefore you *can* work. Secondly, God works; therefore you *must* work."[186]

At the outset of *Our Own Salvation*, John Wesley addressed prevenient grace. He spoke of traces of the "great truths," which included God's being and attributes as well as a sense of "moral good and evil."[187] These were found in some measure among all nations. Citing John 1:9, he credited Christ as the source of this light that "enlightened everyone coming into the world." In the same paragraph, Wesley mentioned the law being written in their hearts "by the same hand which wrote the tables of stone." Finally, he finished the thought by speaking of the universality of conscience, though he acknowledged some paid no attention to it.[188]

John Wesley was careful to locate the source of "the very first motion of good" in God and not the individual. From Wesley's viewpoint, human ability was better described as human *disability*: "If we know and feel that the very first motion of good is from above, as well as the power which conducts it to the end – if it is God that not only infuses every good desire, but that accompanies and follows it, else it vanishes away – then it evidently follows that 'he who glorieth must glory in the Lord.'"[189] To this point in the sermon, Wesley stood squarely in the tradition of the Reformers, emphasizing human inability to contribute to one's salvation.[190] How then did salvation begin?

> Salvation begins with what is usually termed (and very properly) "preventing grace"; including the first wish to please God, the first dawn of light concerning his will, and the first slight, transient conviction of having sinned against him. All these imply some tendency toward life, some degree of salvation, the beginning of a deliverance from a blind, unfeeling heart, quite insensible of God and the things of God.[191]

It is significant that Wesley again employed the metaphor of light. However, the conviction it produced was qualified as "slight" and "transient." He was careful not to attribute to prevenient grace what properly was credited to sanctification, which begins the moment an individual is justified. Nevertheless, prevenient grace – though preparatory – was rightly considered soteriologically since it implied, in Wesley's words, "some tendency toward life, some degree of salvation."

If salvation came only from God, could one excuse sinning by claiming to not be a recipient of salvation? John Wesley disallowed this response:

> For allowing that all the souls of men are dead in sin by nature, this excuses none, seeing there is no man that is in a state of mere nature; there is no man, unless he has quenched the Spirit, that is wholly void of what is vulgarly called "natural conscience." But this is not natural; it is more properly termed "preventing grace." Every man has a greater or less measure of this, which waiteth not for the call of man. Everyone has sooner or later good desires, although the generality of men stifle them before they can strike deep root or produce any considerable fruit. Everyone has some measure of that light, some faint glimmering ray, which sooner or later, more or less, enlightens every man that comes into the world. And everyone, unless he be one of the small number whose conscience is seared as with a hot iron, feels more or less uneasy when he acts contrary to the light of his own conscience. So that no man sins because he has not grace, but because he does not use the grace which he hath.[192]

In contrast to some who have maintained that only the elect are recipients of God's prevenient and saving grace,[193] Wesley argued that prevenient grace was for "everyone," was universal. Habitual sinning was no proof that one was not elect, only that an individual had chosen to "stifle" the light that he or she had received, though Wesley does not develop the meaning of the phrase "unless he has quenched the Spirit." Regardless of one's subsequent response, all receive grace at the outset, and it is from this reality that human responsibility is derived. Because such a person "does not use the grace which he hath," God cannot be held responsible for sin. Colin Williams rightly credited Wesley's doctrine of prevenient grace with two important consequences: 1) it "broke the chain of logical necessity by which the Calvinist doctrine of predestination seems to flow from the doctrine of original sin," and 2) it "gave great impetus to the evangelistic appeal of (Wesley's) message."[194]

On the other hand, it is not apparent in *Our Own Salvation* exactly what the relationship was between prevenient grace and conscience. In the early part of the paragraph, John Wesley disdained the expression "natural conscience," speaking instead of "preventing grace." Preventing grace was a "light" that could be stifled. Likewise, "conscience" was also a "light" and might be "seared as with a hot iron." Were there two lights operative within the human individual, that of conscience *and* prevenient grace, or was there a single light that Wesley was describing in two different ways? Based on this sermon alone, it is not possible to resolve the issue. It is necessary to turn elsewhere in his writings to gain more clarity.

In 1788, John Wesley turned his attention to the "threefold office" of conscience in his sermon, *On Conscience*.[195] The sermon quoted his grandfather Samuel Annesley's homily, *How we may be universally and exactly conscientious*.[196] Wesley maintained that the role of conscience was three-fold: 1) It was a *"witness*, testifying what we have done, in thought, word, and action"; 2) It was a *"judge*, passing sentence on what we have done, that is good or evil"; and 3) It also "in some sort *executes* the sentence, by occasioning a degree of complacency in him that does well, and a degree of uneasiness in him that does evil."[197] Earlier in the sermon, Wesley defined "conscience" as a "kind of silent reasoning of the mind" that approved of what was right but disapproved of what was wrong.[198] It was a "faculty" that makes us sensitive to the "merit or demerit" of thoughts, words, and actions.[199]

The question remains: What was the relationship between conscience and prevenient grace? As he maintained in *Our Own Salvation* – that no one is devoid of prevenient grace – so in *On Conscience*, Wesley affirmed that conscience was "found in every man born into the world."[200] Furthermore, Wesley's *Christian Library* abridgement of *Universal Conscientiousness* inserted four new words: "or rather preventing grace." Missing from his grandfather's original sermon, these words were Wesley's explanation of the meaning of Annesley's phrase, the "light of nature."[201] Both agreed that this light included "those common notions which are written in the hearts of men, which (as a brand plucked out of the common burning) were the relics of the image of God after the Fall," i.e. conscience.[202] On the contrary, in *On Conscience*, Wesley described conscience as "a supernatural gift of God, above all his natural endowments."[203] Though he favorably cited Frances Hutcheson's *Essay on the Nature and Conduct of the Passions and Affections*, agreeing with this expansion of the five senses to include a "public sense" and a "moral sense,"[204] Wesley could not agree with Hutcheson that these two senses were "natural" to the individual: "Whatever may have been the case at first, while man was in a state of innocence, both the one and the other is now a *branch of that supernatural gift of God which we usually style 'preventing grace.'*"[205] By calling conscience a "branch" of preventing grace, Wesley came the closest he would to equating the two concepts.

Having so closely related conscience and prevenient grace, John Wesley surprisingly nuanced his position just a few paragraphs later. What was the conscience "in the Christian sense"? In an apparent reversal from earlier, where he denied conscience as being "natural," he now calls it "a faculty of the soul," *but* one that needs "the assistance of the grace of God."[206] Discerning the nature of our actions and how they square with the rule that directs us was "not possible for him to do without the assistance of the Spirit of God."[207] This qualification came directly on the heels of Wesley's mention of God's grace, demonstrating yet again the close connection in his thought between prevenient grace and the work of the Holy Spirit. Indeed, the "unction of the Holy One" was indispensable "in all the offices of conscience."[208]

What may we conclude? Albert Outler characterized John Wesley's understanding of conscience as "a constant work of prevenience and, therefore, supernatural."[209] Charles Rogers concurred, concluding that "earlier and more fully developed treatments of the notion of conscience make it clear that Wesley viewed conscience as a supernatural gift of prevenient grace."[210] Rather than taking an "either/or" position, it is reasonable to maintain that Wesley – when examining conscience – allowed for an anthropological element (traces of the *imago Dei*), but emphasized the pneumatological component, namely, prevenient grace.[211] In either case, credit was given to God, whether through how humanity was initially created or by the later activity of the Holy Spirit.

The same year that John Wesley published *On Conscience*, he also preached *Walking by Sight and Walking by Faith* (1788).[212] This sermon, based on 2 Cor. 5:7, spoke first of those who live without faith, those who know only the five physical senses. Despite their deplorable condition, Wesley believed that they were not beyond the reach of spiritual light:

> But is there no help? Must they remain in total darkness concerning the invisible and eternal world? We cannot affirm this: even the heathens did not remain in total darkness concerning them. Some few rays of light have in all ages and nations gleamed through the shade.[213]

What were the sources of this light, or to use Wesley's terminology, what were the "various fountains"? 1) The "firmament," i.e. creation allowed one to discern the existence of a "Maker"; 2) Noah, through his posterity, has passed down "traces of knowledge" – weakened though they were by various fables – that were "streaks of light," preventing total darkness, and 3) a witness in the human heart, a knowledge reinforced by the blessings of rain and harvest. All of these fountains testified to the one who was the "true light that still, in some degree, 'englighteneth every man that cometh into the world.'"[214] Wesley was quick to point out, however, that the combined force of these anthropological and cosmological sources still amounted to no more than a "faint twilight." It could not result in a settled conviction about the invisible world.[215] Prevenient grace, though universal, was notable in this sermon for its weakness and limitations.

The last sermon John Wesley wrote was on Hebrews 11:1 and entitled *On Faith* (1791).[216] What is faith? Wesley gave two definitions: 1) a divine conviction of God and of the things of God, and 2) a divine conviction of the invisible and eternal world.[217] The sermon was largely eschatological, speaking of Hades, disembodied spirits, but also the work of angels. These are topics that required revelation in order to understand. But what if Scripture had not come? Wesley replied:

> But how exceedingly little do we now know concerning the invisible (world)? And we should have known still less of it had it not pleased the Author of both worlds to give us more than natural light, to give us "his word to be a lantern to our feet, and light in all our paths." And holy men of old, being assisted by his Spirit, have discovered many particulars of which otherwise we would have no conception.[218]

The "wisest of men" apart from revelation had "little certainty of invisible things." Why was this so? Because they only received "small glimmerings of light." Wesley described these "glimmerings" as "conjectural." They were "only a faint, dim twilight, delivered from uncertain tradition; and so obscured by heathen fables that it was but one degree better than utter darkness."[219] Such obscurity was replaced eventually with clear revelation, what Wesley called "the light of the glory of Jesus Christ."[220] In both *Walking by Sight and Walking by Faith* and *On Faith*, Wesley was of one mind. The light of prevenient grace, though a step in the right direction, could not be compared to the brightness of the revelation of Christ that came through the Word of God both in its written and – by extension – preached forms.

Nothing in the 1791 version of John Wesley's *On Faith* contradicted what he had written in a 1788 sermon of the same title.[221] However, the earlier sermon speculated on what Wesley called the "faith of heathens."[222] He viewed this as superior to the faith of deists since the former enjoyed less light:

> When one asked Chicali, an old Indian chief, "Why do not you red men know as much as white men" he readily answered, "Because you have the Great Word and we have not." It cannot be doubted but this plea will avail for millions of modern "heathens." Inasumuch as to them little is given, of them little will be required...No more, therefore, will be expected of them than the living up to the light they had. But many of them, especially in the civilized nations, we have great reason to hope, although they lived among heathens, yet were quite of another spirit; being taught by God, by his inward voice, all the essentials of true religion.[223]

This passage is significant in that it retained the language of "light" but also expanded it to include an "inward voice." Yet even here there was a note of speculation in what Wesley wrote, claiming only that "we have great reason to hope." While this might be termed the language of *optimism*, it could not be called the language of *certainty*. As far as it went, prevenient grace was always looking beyond itself to the proclamation of pardon, justifying faith provided through the sacrifice of Christ.

Summary

Having examined the references to prevenient grace from the later period of John Wesley's life, the following summary statements are in order:

1. All good in humanity was ascribed to God and was indicative of the enabling activity of prevenient grace;
2. As a benefit of the atonement, the law was re-inscribed on the human heart by means of prevenient grace;
3. Prevenient grace restored a measure of free-will that was forfeited due to the fall and resultant depravity;
4. Though sometimes portrayed in Trinitarian terms, prevenient grace more often was referenced in relation to the work of Christ and the Holy Spirit;
5. The means of grace (prayer, Scripture, and the Lord's Supper) were the ordinary means by which prevenient grace was conveyed, but the Holy Spirit may act in extraordinary ways to directly convey prevenient grace to humanity;
6. Prevenient grace – provided by the atonement – was therefore available to all, i.e. universal in scope;
7. Prevenient grace was capable of being resisted;
8. Grace unresisted led to the reception of more grace;
9. Prevenient grace was sufficient to bring one to Christ but no further, until one was justified.

Of special importance theologically was John Wesley's insistence that prevenient grace restores a measure of free will. Herbert McGonigle put this in perspective:

> How could he hold, on the one hand, a doctrine of man's total inability to save himself, and, on the other hand, a doctrine of human freedom that made man's salvation or damnation rest on his free choice, without falling into Pelagian notions of fallen man's ability to co-operate with God? His answer was to argue an understanding of grace that restored to fallen man a measure of freedom, a spiritual capacity by which sinful man could accept or refuse all subsequent grace.[224]

John Wesley in the later period further developed the notion of prevenient grace re-inscribing the law upon the heart, though he supplemented the language of Christology (the atonement) with Holy Spirit language when speaking of this restoration of the moral sense. Wesley attempted to decipher the relationship between conscience and prevenient grace, though Charles Rogers concluded that the "precise structure of the unity of grace and nature Wesley does not attempt to make explicit."[225]

Conclusion

What was the practical result of John Wesley's refinement of the doctrine of prevenient grace over the course of more than fifty years? Wesley drew upon a lesser known doctrine, appropriating it as a viable soteriological *via media* between determinism on the one hand and moralism on the other. Conversant with Scripture as well as his Puritan and Church of England theological heritage, he grounded prevenient grace both Christologically and pneumatologically, teaching its universality as a consequence of both the atonement and the unbounded ministry of the Holy Spirit. The theological value of the prevenient grace concept was captured by Kenneth Collins: "Wesley's doctrine of prevenient grace allows him to hold together, without any contradiction, the four motifs of total depravity, salvation by grace, human responsibility, and the offer of salvation to all."[226] Yet John Wesley was not alone in teaching prevenient grace. His brother, Charles, also expounded the doctrine in memorable ways. It is to his understanding of prevenient grace that this study now turns its attention.

Notes

1. For a survey of many of the moralistic theologians in late 17th century England, see C. Fitzsimons Allison, *The Rise of Moralism: The Proclamation of the Gospel from Hooker to Baxter* (Vancouver: Regent College Publishing, 1966). Wesley was particularly influenced by the writings of Jeremy Taylor (see Chapter 1 of this investigation), but his moralistic tendencies may be traced to his early childhood at Epworth. The interested reader should consult John A. Newton, *Susanna Wesley and the Puritan Tradition in Methodism* (2nd ed.; London: Epworth Press, 2002).

2. For further development of this theme, see Chapters 1 and 2.

3. An insightful work structured around the major theological controversies in which John Wesley participated is Allan Coppedge, *Shaping the Wesleyan Message: John Wesley in Theological Debate* (1987; repr., Nappanee, Illinois: Francis Asbury Press/Evangel Pub. House, n.d.). Also very helpful is Albert Brown-Lawson, *John Wesley and the Anglican Evangelicals of the Eighteenth Century* (Edinburgh, Cambridge, and Durham: The Pentland Press, 1994).

4. *Works* [BE], 1:62, 63, "Preface."

5. Randy L. Maddox, *Responsible Grace: John Wesley's Practical Theology* (Abingdon/Kingswood Books, 1994), 20. See also p. 259 (fn. 30) in Maddox for a critique of some of the possible abuses of this methodology.

6. Richard Heitzenrater, "The Current State of Wesley Studies," *Methodist History* Vol. 22, No. 4 (July 1984), 229. Concurring with this methodology, Umphree Lee observed that the student of Wesley "must make up his mind whether he calls the theology which Wesley held in 1733, or that which he held in 1738, or that which he held in 1770, 'Wesley's theology'…the changes must not be exaggerated; but they must be recognized. It is therefore necessary to trace their development in order to explain his mature views." In Umphrey Lee, *John Wesley and Modern Religion* (Nashville: Cokesbury Press, 1936), 111.

7. This is consistent with the methodology of Charles Rogers in chapter 2 of his thesis. See Charles Allen Rogers, "The Concept of Prevenient Grace in the Theology of John Wesley" (Ph.D. thesis, Duke University, 1967).

8. *The Works of John Wesley*, Bi-Centennial edition (Frank Baker, ed. 35 vols. projected. Nashville: Abingdon Press, 1984 to present), 4:295; hereafter *Works* [BE].

9. *Works* [BE], 4:293.
10. *Works* [BE], 4:294.
11. *Works* [BE], 4:294-295
12. *Works* [BE], 4:295.
13. Wesley speculated that the forbidden fruit may have contained a deadly "juice." *Works* [BE] 4:297.
14. *Works* [BE], 4:298.
15. *Works* [BE], 4:299. In the third section of the sermon, Wesley proposed humility and charity as the only means of gradually expelling the "seeds of spiritual death" and delivering the person from the "bondage of corruption." See 4:301. This 1730 sermon lacked a doctrine of justification and regeneration. For a 1782 re-write of the sermon, see *On the Fall of Man*, in *Works* [BE], 2:400-412.
16. In *Works* [BE], 2:186-201.
17. *Works* [BE], 2:188. For a discussion of Wesley's hesitancy to use the word "reason" in connection with the natural image, see Theodore Runyon, *The New Creation: John Wesley's Theology Today* (Nashville: Abingdon Press, 1998), 14-16.
18. *Works* [BE], 2:188. David Rainey saw similarity between Wesley's three-fold image and that presented by Isaac Watts in his 1740 *The Ruin and Recovery of Mankind*, where Watts spoke of the "natural powers," including knowledge, reason, judgment, and immortality, "moral perfection," entailing humanity's love and service of God, and the "political image," referring to human governance of the lower creation. See David Rainey, "John Wesley's Doctrine of Salvation in Relation to His Doctrine of God (Ph.D. thesis, King's College/University of London, 2006), 67-68.
19. *Works* [BE], 2:189.
20. *Works* [BE], 2:190.
21. *Works* [BE], 2:189.
22. *Works* [BE], 2:190.
23. *Works* [BE], 2:194. Stephen Long noted: "For Wesley, Christ restores the human creature to the natural and moral image of God. The natural image of God is a healing of understanding, will, and liberty. The moral image of God is a recovery of our intended righteousness and holiness." In D. Stephen Long, *John Wesley's Moral Theology: The Quest for God and Goodness* (Kingswood Books/Abingdon Press, 2005), 175. There is no mention by Wesley of how the lost political image may be restored.
24. *Works* [BE], 2:436-50.
25. *Works* [BE], 2:438.
26. Later in the sermon, Wesley remarked that even after the fall, there remains a "degree" of liberty in every living creature. See 2:440-41. In his 1785 *On Working Out Our Own Salvation* (*Works* [BE], 3:199-209), Wesley attributed the ability to respond to God to gracious causes.
27. *Works* [BE], 2:441. Only humans and not beasts are "capable of God."
28. *Works* [BE], 2:440.
29. *Works* [BE], 2:471-484.
30. "For this purpose was the Son of God manifested, that he might destroy the works of the devil" (KJV).
31. *Works* [BE], 2:482-483.
32. *Works* [BE], 2:474.
33. *Works* [BE], 2:474.
34. *Works* [BE], 2:477.
35. *Works* [BE], 2:482.
36. *Works* [BE], 2:481; italics added.
37. *Works* [BE], 2:481.

38. *Works* [BE], 2:475.
39. John Allan Knight, "Aspects of Wesley's Theology After 1770," in *Methodist History* (Lake Junaluska, North Carolina: Commission on Archives and History, The United Methodist Church, 1968), 33.
40. *Works* [BE], 161-67.
41. *Works*, 4:163. Wesley made the same point in his 1780 *Spiritual Worship*, in *Works* [BE], 3:92. See also discussion below of Wesley's 1783 sermon, *The General Spread of the Gospel*.
42. Rogers, 157.
43. *Works* [BE], 4:24.
44. *Works* [BE], 4:24.
45. Maddox, *Responsible Grace*, 69-70.
46. Maddox, 70.
47. Harald Lindström, *Wesley and Sanctification* (London: Epworth Press, 1950; reprint, Nappanee, Indiana: Francis Asbury Press/Evangel Publishing House, 1996), 31.
48. Herbert Boyd McGonigle, *Sufficient Saving Grace: John Wesley's Evangelical Arminianism* (Carlisle, Cumbria, and Waynesboro, Georgia: Paternoster Press, 2001), 324.
49. See John Telford, ed., *The Letters of the Rev. John Wesley, A.M.*(8 vols.; 1931; reprint, London: The Epworth Press, 1960), 4:146.
50. Telford, 4:237.
51. The full treatise appeared in *The Works of John Wesley*, 3rd ed., 14 vols. (1872; reprint, Kansas City, Missouri: Beacon Hill Press, 1978), 9:196-464. For Taylor's original 1739-40 work, see John Taylor, *The Scripture Doctrine of Original Sin Proposed to a Free and Candid Examination*, 4th ed. (London: J. Wilson, 1767). In a December 9, 1758 letter to Augustus Montague Toplady, Wesley wrote: "I verily believe no single person since Mahomet has given such a wound to Christianity as Dr. Taylor. They are his books, chiefly that upon Original Sin, which have poisoned so many of the clergy, and indeed the fountains themselves – the Universities in England, Scotland, Holland, and Germany." In Telford, 4:48. Herbert McGonigle wrote: "Wesley saw Taylor's arguments as a Deistic denial of the biblical and Reformed doctrine of the total corruption of the natural man." *Sufficient Saving Grace*, 159.
52. Lindström, 31-32.
53. Cary Balzer, "John Wesley's Developing Soteriology and the Influence of the Caroline Divines" (Ph.D. thesis, University of Manchester, England, 2005), 84-85.
54. McGonigle discerned this interest in Wesley as early as 1730. Wesley expressed disappointment in William King's *De Origine Mali* since it contained no account of the effect of Adam's sin upon the human race. See Herbert McGonigle, "Arminius and Wesley on Original Sin," *European Explorations in Christian Holiness* Issue 2 (Summer, 2001), 101.
55. *Works* [BE], 1:181-99.
56. *Works* [BE], 1:184.
57. *Works* [BE], 1:185. Here, Wesley appeared to espouse the Federal Head theory of the transmission of original sin. For further discussion of this view, see William Ragsdale Cannon, *The Theology of John Wesley* (New York and Nashville: Abingdon/Cokesbury Press, 1946), 198-200. Kenneth Collins noted that while Wesley sometimes professed not to care how original sin was transmitted, by 1762, he had adopted traducianism, i.e. the belief that original sin is passed on through procreation. See Collins, *Scripture Way*, 32-34; also *The Theology of John Wesley: Holy Love and the Shape of Grace* (Nashville, Tennessee: Abingdon Press, 2007), 68.
58. *Works* [BE], 1:187.
59. *Works* [BE], 1:200-16.

60. *Works* [BE], 1:217-32.
61. *Works* [BE], 1:204-07.
62. *Works* [BE], 1:212; italics added.
63. *Works* [BE], 1:225-26.
64. *Works* [BE], 1:226.
65. Wesley had a doctrine of "inbred sin," sin that remained in the heart even of the justified and that was a lingering consequence of Adam's sin. For this condition, God reserved the remedy of entire sanctification. The nature of this second work of grace became most apparent elsewhere in Wesley's sermons, c.f. *The Repentance of Believers* (1767*)*, in *Works* [BE], 1:335-352, esp. I.20, and *The Scripture Way of Salvation* (1765), in *Works* [BE], 2:153-69.
66. *Works* [BE], 1:227.
67. *Works* [BE], 2:172-85.
68. In *Works*, 9:191-464.
69. Wesley wrote: "As we know that there is an emperor of China, whom yet we do not know, so we know there was a King of all the earth; but yet we knew him not. Indeed we could not, by any of our natural faculties." *Works* [BE], 2:177. Herbert McGonigle noted: "He (Wesley) rejected any notion that fallen man had innate ideas of God, or that there was some lingering trace of the *imago Dei* by which sinful man perceived the existence of God." *Sufficient Saving Grace*, 328.
70. *Works* [BE], 2:183.
71. *Works* [BE], 2:182-183.
72. *Works* [BE], 2:183-184.
73. *Works* [BE], 2:185.
74. *Works* [BE], 2:185.
75. *Works* [BE], 2:186-201.
76. *Works* [BE], 2:190.
77. *Works* [BE], 2:190.
78. *Works*, 8:277.
79. Telford, 4:67. Chris Lohrstorfer viewed the controversy with John Taylor as the third of four distinct stages in the development of John Wesley's doctrine of original sin. The first stage may be dated in 1730, where Wesley preferred biological language to speak of the doctrine, stemming from his study of Peter Browne (1614-1735), the Irish philosopher, theologian, and bishop. The second stage may be traced to three years later, when Wesley adopted Augustinian and Macarian disease language to describe sin. After the controversy with Taylor (the third stage), the fourth stage was when – after reading the writings of the obscure Henry Woolner – Wesley opted for a doctrine of traducianism to explain original sin's transmission. See Chris Lohrstorfer, "Know Your Disease, Know Your Cure" (Ph.D. thesis, University of Manchester, England, 2006), 9.
80. Collins, *Scripture Way*, 38.
81. Umphrey Lee, *John Wesley and Modern Religion* (Nashville: Cokesbury Press, 1936), 124-25.
82. John L. Peters, *Christian Perfection and American Methodism* (Nashville: Pierce & Washabaugh, 1956; repr., Grand Rapids: Francis Asbury Press/Zondervan Publishing Company, 1985), 43.
83. Ron Benefiel, "John Wesley's Doctrine of Original Sin," unpublished paper, Nazarene Theological College, Manchester, England, May 29, 2002.
84. Collins, *Scripture Way*, 34-35.
85. For example, H. Ray Dunning's systematic theology listed prevenient grace in the index under 11 different headings, including free will, epistemology, repentance, and the

universal atonement. See *Grace, Faith, and Holiness* (Kansas City, Missouri: Beacon Hill Press, 1988), 655.

86. *Works* [BE], 1:35.
87. *Works* [BE], 1:401-414.
88. *Works* [BE], 1:402-403.
89. *Works* [BE], 1:403-404.
90. *Works* [BE], 1:411, italics added. Herbert McGonigle noted that this "seems to be the first explicit use in Wesley's writings of the term 'prevent' in relation to God's grace." See Herbert Boyd McGonigle, *John Wesley's Doctrine of Prevenient Grace* (Derbys: Wesley Fellowship/Mooreley's Print and Publishing, 1995), 8.
91. A discussion of the events surrounding the so-called "free grace controversy" is found in Coppedge, 31-98. Also helpful is Kenneth J. Collins, *John Wesley: A Theological Journey* (Nashville: Abingdon Press, 2003), 114-17. For a critique of Wesley's view of divine foreknowledge vs. human merit, see David Bennett, "How Arminian was John Wesley?" *The Evangelical Quarterly* Vol. 72, No. 3 (July 2000), 238-39. An irenic account of the 1741 split between Whitefield and Wesley is in John Pollock, *Whitefield the Evangelist* (Eastbourne: Kingsway Publications, 2000), 181-86.
92. *Works* [BE], 3:544-563. Whitefield's reply to Wesley's controversial sermon was published and widely distributed under the title: "A Letter from the Reverend Mr. George Whitefield to the Reverend Mr. John Wesley in Answer to his Sermon entitled 'Free Grace'" (London: Printed by G. Rogers, for S. Kneeland and T. Green, Cornhill, 1740).
93. *Works* [BE], 3:544.
94. *Works* [BE], 3:545.
95. *Works* [BE], 3:545.
96. Rogers, 26.
97. Kenneth Collins remarked that for John Wesley, prevenient grace was "based upon the salvific work of Christ." See Kenneth J. Collins, *The Theology of John Wesley: Holy Love and the Shape of Grace* (Nashville: Abingdon Press, 2007), 74.
98. *Works*, 14:211-14.
99. *Works*, 14:212; italics added.
100. On Barclay, see Chapter 2 of this investigation.
101. *Works* [BE], 9:47-66. This treatise was a reply to Josiah Tucker's *The Principles of Methodism*, where the popular Vicar of All Saints, Bristol, accused Wesley of overdependence on the ideas of William Law and the Moravians. See Albert Outler's introduction in *Works* [BE], 9:47-48.
102. *Works* [BE], 9:64.
103. *Works*, 8:277-78.
104. On Barclay's use of "seed," see Chapter 2 of this inquiry. The metaphor of light showed up again in the 1744 sermon, *Scriptural Christianity*, where Wesley quoted Ephesians 5:14 ("Awake though that sleepest…arise from the dead, and Christ shall give thee light") as an appropriate text to preach to "those who lay unconcerned in darkness and in the shadow of death." See *Works* [BE], 1:166.
105. This debate flared up again in 1756 between John Wesley and James Hervey. The latter had argued in his *Theron and Aspasio* that God's "grand end" is to "demonstrate the sovereignty of His grace." To this, Wesley replied by letter on October 5: "Not so: to impart happiness to His creatures is His grand end herein. Barely to demonstrate His sovereignty is a principle of action fit for the great Turk, not the Most High God." Telford, 3:387-88.
106. *Works*, 8:285.
107. The later controversy over the carelessly edited Minutes of 1770 was eloquent testimony to the pitfalls of addressing theological topics in this way.

108. From a Calvinistic perspective, "common grace" restrains evil in the world and preserves it from destruction, but unlike prevenient grace, it has no soteriological significance. See Dunning, *Grace, Faith, and Holiness*, 296. For further comparison of prevenient grace and common grace, see Chapter 6 of the present investigation.

109. *Works*, 8:283.

110. *Works* [BE], 1:248-266.

111. This depiction of the "natural man" seems at-odds with Wesley's claim in the 1785 sermon, *On Working Out Our Own Salvation*, that "there is no man that is in a state of mere nature," i.e. that is devoid of "preventing grace," unless he or she has "quenched the Spirit." See *Works* [BE], 3:207.

112. *Works* [BE], 1:254.

113. *Works* [BE], 1:255. In this passage, "horrid light" became a metaphor for prevenient grace.

114. Albert Outler observed a shift in Wesley's thinking between this sermon and *On Working Out Our Own Salvation* (1785). In the latter sermon, there was no person – not even the so-called "natural man" – who was devoid of some measure of prevenient grace. See Outler in *Works* [BE], 1:248.

115. *Works* [BE], 1:299-313.

116. *Works* [BE], 1:309.

117. *Works* [BE], 1:310.

118. *Works* [BE], 1:378-397. The historical context of this sermon was the 1739-41 controversy over quietism – exacerbated by the Moravian Philipp Molther – that rocked the Fetter Lane Society. Also known as the "stillness" teaching, those seeking salvation were discouraged from praying, fasting, reading Scripture, taking Communion, or observing other helpful practices traditionally promoted by the Church. Instead, one had to remain "still" and wait for God to sovereignly act salvifically in the Lord's own timing. John and Charles Wesley strenuously objected to this unorthodox teaching, and eventually led a split over the issue. For a brief discussion of this episode, see Stephen Tomkins, *John Wesley: A Biography* (Grand Rapids: Wm. B. Eerdmans, 2003), 84-94.

119. *Works* [BE], 1:381. The emphasis was Wesley's. Earlier, in the 1745 "Answer to Mr. Church's Remarks," he had described the Lord's Supper as "ordained by God to be a *means of conveying* to men either *preventing*, or *justifying*, or sanctifying grace, according to their several necessities..." The only requirement for communicating was an acknowledgement of one's spiritual need. See *Works* [BE], 9:112. Ole Borgen cautions: "Likewise, since Wesley, in describing the grace conveyed through the means of grace, uses the same terminology as when he speaks of the *ordo salutis* in general, it follows that 'sacramental grace' must be thought of as nothing different in kind." See Ole E. Borgen, *John Wesley on the Sacraments: A Theological Study* (1972; repr.,Eugene, Oregon: Wipf and Stock Publishers, 2000), 46-47.

120. *Works* [BE], 1:382. It is doubtful that Wesley's intent was to limit the means of grace to these three. We know, for example, that members of the Holy Club at Oxford visited prisoners as a way of fortifying their own faith. See Kenneth Collins, *Theological Journey*, 45. Likewise, in *Upon the Lord's Sermon on the Mount, VII*, Wesley called fasting a means of grace, a "means which God himself has ordained; and in which therefore, when it is duly used, he will surely give us his blessing." In *Works* [BE], 1:594.

Ole Borgen (pp. 126-27) discerned no connection in Wesley's theology between the conveyance of prevenient grace and infant baptism, since infants already benefit from the cancelling of Adam's sin by the atonement. Conceding this point, Rob Staples ventured: "Prevenient grace is not conveyed by infant baptism, but it is *proclaimed* by it." See Rob L. Staples, *Outward Sign and Inward Grace: The Place of the Sacraments in Wesleyan Spirituality* (Kansas City, Missouri: Beacon Hill Press, 1991), 179.

121. *Works* [BE], 1:393-394. The phrase "God comes upon him unawares," Albert Outler (in his fn. 77) interprets as "preveniently."
122. *Works* [BE], 1:394.
123. *Works* [BE], 1:394. Despite his opposition to quietism, Wesley would not rule out the possibility that God *can* operate apart from the means of grace, though he would consider this exceptional.
124. *Works* [BE], 1:510-530.
125. *Works* [BE], 1:526.
126. *Works* [BE], 1:526, fn. 125.
127. Telford, 2:118; italics added.
128. Telford, 2:118. Wesley substituted the word "grace" for Barclay's terms, "seed and light."
129. *Works*, 10:204-59. For information on Wesley's writings on predestination and related doctrines from 1749-1765, see Coppedge, 101-118. William Greathouse and Ray Dunning noted that "*unconditional election and absolute predestination* served for the Reformers as the final and decisive bulwark against and rejection of the Catholic doctrine of salvation by good works." In William M. Greathouse and H. Ray Dunning, *An Introduction to Wesleyan Theology* (Kansas City, Missouri: Beacon Hill Press, 1989), 72.
130. *Works*, 10:229-230.
131. *Works*, 10:230.
132. *Works*, 10:230.
133. *Works*, 10:231.
134. *Works*, 10:232; see also 206.
135. McGonigle, *Prevenient Grace*, 14.
136. *Works* [BE], 2:61-78.
137. *Works* [BE], 2:68.
138. *Works* [BE], 2:138-151.
139. *Works* [BE], 2:140.
140. *Works* [BE], 2:151.
141. *Works* [BE], 2:151, fn. 118.
142. *Works*, 9:191-464.
143. *Works*, 9:268.
144. *Works*, 9:268. The "if" in this sentence should not be taken to mean that some received this assistance while others did not. This became clear as Wesley developed his argument.
145. *Works*, 9:273; italics added.
146. *Works*, 9:273.
147. The edition cited here is: John Wesley, *Explanatory Notes Upon the New Testament* (London: Wesleyan-Methodist Book Room, n.d.).; hereafter, *New Testament Notes*.
148. *Works* [BE], 2:7. Albert Outler remarked: "This notion of 're-inscription' is crucial for Wesley's doctrine of the human *in se* as a divine gift (exceeding 'nature') and of 'prevenient grace.'" See 2:7, fn. 10.
149. *Works* [BE], 2:170-185. See discussion of original sin earlier in this chapter.
150. *Works* [BE], 2:185.
151. *Works* [BE], 2:180.
152. *Works* [BE], 2:180.
153. Earlier in the sermon, Wesley alluded to the "good motions put into their hearts" and that "the spirit of God did then also 'strive with man, if haply he might repent…' " (2:175). These asides went undeveloped, since they were outside Wesley's purpose: "We are not here to consider what the grace of God might occasionally work in his soul."

(Ibid). Albert Outler considered this a reference to prevenient grace. See *Works* [BE], 2:175, fn. 21.

154. This is consistent with Wesley's November 17, 1759 letter to John Downes, Rector of St. Michael's, where he defined "grace" as "that power of God which worketh in us both to will and do of His good pleasure." Telford, 4:332.

155. Telford, 4:293; italics added.

156. *Works* [BE], 2:153-169.

157. *Works* [BE], 2:154.

158. *Works* [BE], 2:156-157.

159. Telford, 5:200.

160. Telford, 5:292-293; see also 6:89, 7:195.

161. For analysis of Fletcher's use of the talents metaphor, see Mark Powell Royster, "John Wesley's Doctrine of Prevenient Grace in Missiological Perspective" (D. Miss. dissertation, Asbury Theological Seminary, 1989), 63-72.

162. See Collins, *Theological Journey*, 221-27.

163. For an overview of Wesley's doctrine of justification, see James Gregory Crofford, *Justification in John Calvin and John Wesley: A Comparative Study* (M.A. dissertation, University of Manchester, U.K., 2005), 27-52; also Colin W. Williams, *John Wesley's Theology Today* (New York and Nashville: Abingdon Press, 1960), 57-73.

164. *Works* [BE], 2:341-42.

165. These apparently entailed a letter from Wesley to the Countess including passages that many interpreted as overly critical. See Coppedge, 169.

166. Collins, *Theological Journey*, 222.

167. *Works*, 10:392.

168. Telford, 6:239.

169. *Works* [BE], 2:485-499. The use of the term "heathen," now unacceptable, was common parlance in Wesley's time. Albert Outler noted that the sermon "is drawn from seventeenth and eighteenth-century sources and reflects their general estimates of non-European lands and peoples." 2:485.

170. *Works* [BE], 2:489.

171. *Works* [BE], 2:489, fn. 26.

172. *Works* [BE], 2:490.

173. Wesley later conceded that God *at times* can work irresistibly but never at *all* times. Resisting the Holy Spirit remained a common occurrence. See I.12. Wesley reiterated the possibility of resistance as a function of human liberty in his 1784 sermon, *The Wisdom of God's Counsels*: "Here evil men and spirits continually oppose the divine will and create numberless irregularities...But (God's) wisdom is shown by saving man in such a manner as not to destroy his nature, nor to take away the liberty which he has given him." In *Works* [BE], 2:553.

174. *Works* [BE], 2:490.

175. *Works* [BE], 2:498.

176. It is true that Wesley believed prevenient grace *may* operate independently of proclamation, yet maintained – both in doctrine and practice – a high view of preaching. On the other hand, he argued that the doctrine of unconditional election rendered preaching useless. In his sermon, *Free Grace* (1739), Wesley observed: "But if this (predestination) be so, then is all preaching vain. It is needless to them that are elected. For they, whether with preaching or without, will infallibly be saved. Therefore the end of preaching, 'to save souls,' is void with regard to them." *Works* [BE], 4:547. A Reformed response to Wesley's critique is James I. Packer, *Evangelism and the Sovereignty of God* (London: InterVarsity Fellowship, 1961). Packer argued that

preaching and evangelism are performed in obedience to God's commandment, regardless of one's position on predestination (pp. 96ff).

177. *Works* [BE], 2:567-586; hereafter *Human Knowledge*.

178. *Works* [BE], 2:571.

179. See the 1750 sermon, *The Original Nature, Property, and Use of the Law*, where Wesley wrote: "And yet God did not despise the work of his own hands; but being reconciled to man through the Son of his love, he in some measure re-inscribed the law on the heart of his dark, sinful creature." In *Works* [BE], 2:7.

180. *Works* [BE], 3:290-307.

181. *Works* [BE], 2:295-96. In this context, "light" may be understood as a reference to prevenient grace.

182. See Minutes of August 1, 1745, in *Works*, 8:283, where Wesley refused to call Cornelius' righteous works "splendid sins," since they were not performed "without the grace of Christ."

183. A brief but thoughtful treatment of this theme is Eric Manchester, "Why is Evangelism Important if One Can Be Saved Without the Gospel?," *Wesleyan Theological Journal* Vol. 37, No. 1 (Spring 2002), 158-70.

184. *Works* [BE], 3:199-209; hereafter, *Our Own Salvation*

185. McGonigle, *Prevenient Grace*, 28. Albert Outler frequently appealed to *Our Own Salvation* in his critical commentary on Wesley's sermons contained in vols. 1-4 of the Bi-Centennial edition of *Works*. Many surveys of Wesley's theology prominently feature *Our Own Salvation* under the discussion of prevenient grace. Cf. Collins, *Scripture Way*, 39; Williams, *Wesley's Theology*, 43; Runyon, *New Creation*, 28. This sermon is rightly considered the *locus classicus* for Wesley's understanding of prevenient grace.

186. *Works* [BE], 3:206.

187. *Works* [BE], 3:199.

188. *Works* [BE], 3:199.

189. *Works* [BE], 3:203.

190. Greathouse and Dunning noted this solidarity between Wesley and theologians in the Augustinian tradition regarding original sin and the resultant "totally depraved condition of the human race." However, Wesley's understanding of prevenient grace – particularly its universality – was a crucial difference between them. See *Wesleyan Theology*, 72.

191. *Works* [BE], 3:203-204. Albert Outler commented that the words "preventing" and "prevenient" are synonymous, and denote "the Holy Spirit's activity in moving or drawing the will in advance of any conscious resolve." See 3:203, fn. 24. In the rest of the paragraph, Wesley presented the remainder of the *via salutis*, including repentance, justification, and sanctification.

192. *Works* [BE], 3:207.

193. This position was advanced by Neil R. Livingston, "A Calvinistic Concept of Prevenient Grace" (M.Th. dissertation, Dallas Theological Seminary, 1961), 3-4: "By the very nature of the Calvinistic definition it is evident that prevenient grace pertains only to those who come to salvation, that is, the elect." The same framework was evident in Davis Huckabee, who called prevenient grace "that special favor which God has had for His elect from eternity past." In Davis W. Huckabee, "Studies on Strong Doctrine, Chapter One: Prevenient Grace," n.p. [cited June 2, 2002]. Online: http:/ pbsministries. org/ baptists.htm.

194. Williams, 44.

195. *Works* [BE], 3:479-490.

196. Samuel Annesley, ed., *The Morning Exercises at Cripplegate, or, Several Cases of Conscience Practically Resolved, by Sundry Ministers* (London: T. Milbourn and

Joshua Johnson, 1671), 1-32. Wesley abridged and published the sermon as part of the Felix Farley edition of the *Christian Library* (Bristol: Felix Farley and Son, 1751-1755), 38:297-338; hereafter, *CL* [FE]. See Chapter 1of this inquiry for analysis of Annesley's sermon.

197. *Works* [BE], 3:483.
198. *Works* [BE], 3:481.
199. *Works* [BE], 3:481.
200. *Works* [BE], 3:481.
201. For further explanation of this gloss and its significance, see Chapter 1.
202. *CL* [FE], 38:302.
203. *Works* [BE], 3:482.
204. See Albert Outler, *Works* [BE], 3:483, fn. 15. Wesley explains that the "public sense" allows us to feel pain at the suffering of another, while the "moral sense" is the means by which one approves kindness and disapproves of cruelty.
205. *Works* [BE], 3:484; italics added.
206. *Works* [BE], 3:485.
207. *Works* [BE], 3:485.
208. *Works* [BE], 3:485.
209. *Works* [BE], 3:480, fn. 2.
210. Rogers, *Prevenient Grace*, 184, fn. 4.
211. Wesley seemed torn between an anthropological and a pneumatological interpretation of prevenient grace as related to conscience. His position at times resembled that of Robert South, a Church of England clergyman, who allowed for both the internal light of conscience *and* external, gracious influences from God. A single sermon from South's *Twelve Sermons* was abridged by Wesley and included in his *Christian Library*. See Wesley, John, ed. *A Christian Library* (50 vols.; Bristol: Felix Farley and Son, 1751-1755), 43:150-77. For further details on Robert South and his understanding of conscience, see Chapter 1 of this inquiry.
212. *Works* [BE], 4:48-59.
213. *Works* [BE], 4:51.
214. *Works* [BE], 4:52.
215. *Works* [BE], 4:52.
216. *Works* [BE], 4:187-200.
217. *Works* [BE], 4:188.
218. *Works* [BE], 4:198.
219. *Works* [BE], 4:198.
220. *Works* [BE], 4:199.
221. *Works* [BE], 3:491-501.
222. The term "heathens" is unfortunate, but consistent with the parlance of Wesley's day.
223. *Works* [BE], 3:494.
224. McGonigle, *Sufficient Saving Grace*, 319.
225. Rogers, "Prevenient Grace," 164.
226. Collins, *Scripture Way*, 45. He reached the same conclusion in *The Theology of John Wesley: Holy Love and the Shape of Grace* (Nashville: Abingdon Press, 2007), 82.

Chapter Four

Charles Wesley: Preliminary Considerations

Introduction

This inquiry has examined in detail some of the sources that influenced John Wesley's formulation of the doctrine of prevenient grace. In addition, an analysis of primary sources from Wesley that elucidate his own thinking was undertaken. However, no study to-date has evaluated what – if anything – Charles Wesley (1707-88) contributed to the prevenient grace concept. This is all the more surprising since Charles, no less than his brother John, was instrumental to the rise of Methodism. Before turning in Chapter 5 to a detailed study of that contribution, it is necessary in the present chapter to provide both a biographical and theological context in which what he said about prevenient grace can be interpreted. Therefore, Chapter 4 will address a number of preliminary issues foundational to a study of any aspect of the thought of Charles Wesley.

Charles Wesley has remained in his brother's shadow, as evidenced by the far lesser attention paid to him by biographers[1] and theologians.[2] Kenneth Newport has called attention to this neglect: "Relatively little information regarding (Charles') life and works is as yet fully in the public domain and even when attention is given to him, it is most often in his role as the brother of John."[3] Theophilus Gregory concurred, observing: "Even Methodists have given but little study to his (Charles') biography. The history of the Revival is the history of John, whose life is precisely minuted and richly documented."[4] Part of this neglect by Methodism may be due to the souring of the relationship between the Wesley brothers. Gareth Lloyd – in a reappraisal of the dynamics between the two brothers, particularly after Charles scuttled John's engagement to Grace Murray – presented a largely negative assessment:

> Founded on blood kinship and mutual faith, their partnership was one of the driving forces of the Revival for nearly twenty years. Yet by the end of their lives their relationship was characterized by disillusion and hostility. They came to stand for different ideals and Charles' reputation and achievements fell victim to the hero-worship accorded his brother.[5]

Frank Baker explained Methodism's slighting of Charles in a more traditional way: "The main reason for the comparative neglect of Charles

Wesley is, of course, John Wesley. John has completely overshadowed his younger brother."[6] This "overshadowing" was in part Charles' doing, since he chose to cease itinerating in 1756 to give more attention to his fragile health and growing family.[7] Admittedly, the careers of the brothers overlapped sufficiently that it is difficult to write the story of one without making allusion to the other. Mabel Brailsford in *A Tale of Two Brothers: John and Charles Wesley* realized this vital connection and profited from it to paint a joint portrait.[8]

In view of the close working relationship between the Wesley brothers – though strained in later years – is anything new gained by an examination of prevenient grace in the writings of Charles Wesley? Ernest Rattenbury's *The Evangelical Doctrines of Charles Wesley's Hymns* included a broad treatment of Wesley's soteriology.[9] Nevertheless, it may be questioned whether Rattenbury's research on Charles Wesley's theology plumbed the depths of the latter's voluminous writings. Brian Beck addressed this issue:

> Comparatively little seems to have been done in detail on the theology of the hymns since then. Much more attention has been devoted to their literary and poetic aspects. That may well be a tribute to the thoroughness of Rattenbury's work, but it is at least worth asking whether the last word has been spoken or whether more work ought to be done.[10]

This chapter and the next examine Kenneth Newport's critical edition of Charles Wesley's *Sermons* and, where appropriate, will reference S.T. Kimbrough, Jr.'s and Kenneth Newport's newly expanded edition of the *Journal*.[11] Greater attention is paid to the thirteen volumes of G. Osborn's *The Poetical Works of John and Charles Wesley*, the three volumes of *The Unpublished Poetry of Charles Wesley*, and the on-line critical edition of Charles Wesley's published verse.[12] After consideration in Chapter 4 of relevant introductory themes – such as in what sense Charles Wesley is a "theologian" and the meaning of "nature" and "image" in Wesley's anthropology – Chapter 5 sharpens the focus, explicating his thinking on prevenient grace.

Critical Issues in the Study of Charles Wesley's Theology

Analysis of the literature reveals three *foci* helpful to our investigation: 1) Charles Wesley as theologian; 2) challenges with primary source materials, and 3) Wesley's spiritual biography, especially in relation to the *via salutis* in which prevenient grace is situated.

A. Charles Wesley, Poet *and* Theologian?

What is the nature of Charles Wesley's contribution? This is a question of the first order, since any study of his doctrine of prevenient grace presupposes that he has something of theological value to say. Upon Charles' death in 1788, his brother, John, wrote a cursory obituary in the Conference Minutes for July 29, where Charles appeared as the fifth in a list of seven Methodist preachers who had passed away that year:

5. Mr. Charles Wesley, who, after spending fourscore years with much sorrow and pain, quietly retired into Abraham's bosom. He had no disease; but after a gradual decay of some months, "The weary wheels of life stood still at last.' His least praise was his talent for Poetry: although Dr. Watts did not scruple to say, that 'that single poem Wrestling Jacob, was worth all the verses he himself had written."[13]

John's recognition of his brother's muse was hardly isolated. S.T. Kimbrough, Jr. and Oliver Beckerlegge described Charles Wesley as "indubitably one of the important literary figures of the eighteenth century and one of the most outstanding Christian poets in English history."[14] In-depth analysis classifying Wesley among the poets of his time and studies of technical issues such as rhyme and meter have been undertaken, a tribute to his skill as a craftsman of words.[15]

The issue of his poetic brilliance aside, the question remains: In what sense was Charles Wesley a theologian? Any consideration of this question rightfully begins with Ernest Rattenbury's *The Evangelical Doctrines of Charles Wesley's Hymns*. In a chapter entitled "Charles Wesley, Theologian," Rattenbury was content neither with the title "poet" nor that of "theologian." Rather, Wesley was a "witness" and an "evangelist."[16] Nevertheless, having thus qualified his view, Rattenbury recognized the theological value of Wesley's hymns as both cognitive and affective:

> His teaching was of the head as well as of the heart; he was a highly cultivated eighteenth-century scholar, well-instructed in formal theology. Beneath all his hymns, however emotional, lay the substratum of sound and well-digested doctrine, which gave them a strength they would otherwise have lacked. They were not merely emotional effusions, but, on account of their theological substance, songs of abiding value.[17]

Noting Wesley's "restricted intellectual interest," Rattenbury called his theology "that born of the spiritual travail of a poet with an intuitive mind, not of a rationalist."[18]

After Rattenbury, the next theologian to take significant interest in Charles Wesley's theology was John Tyson. In his *Charles Wesley on Sanctification: A Biographical and Theological Study*, Tyson documented divergences in Charles' doctrine of Christian perfection from that of his brother, John.[19] In his massive thesis on Wesley's theology of the cross, Tyson conceded that Charles' hymns were "generally more pastoral than formally theological."[20] Nonetheless, they were a "marriage of theological doctrine and living religious experience."[21] This assessment was consistent with that of John Wesley himself, who in the preface to the 1780 *A Collection of Hymns for the Use of The People Called Methodists* described the hymnal as both "speculative" and "practical."[22]

A significant advance in the study of Charles Wesley's theology was made by Teresa Berger.[23] Calling the 1780 hymnal a "Methodist Manifesto,"[24] she traced the emphases apparent in selected hymns, including soteriological universalism, the individual experience of salvation, the imagery of "blood" as related to the atonement, and the assurance of salvation.[25] Additional sections devoted to salvation as realized eschatology and to what Berger terms the "struggle for Christian perfection" made it clear that there is genuine theological depth to the hymns of Charles Wesley. She was careful, however, to caution against the misuse of such "doxological texts":

> The application of theological methodology to doxological texts (hymnbooks, for example) is, one could say, "inappropriate." The hymns (whether devotional or liturgical in character) were not written for theological study but for the praise of God. They find their true being in the Christian community's sung praise of God and not as printed words on a page for theological analysis. After all, theological interpretation as text analysis is only made privy to a small act of praise: the written word alone.[26]

Berger later clarified that "doxology" is "neither *from* nor *about* God. Rather, it is directed *to* God."[27] This is in contradistinction to theology, where affirmations *about* God are commonplace. Furthermore, doxology is more than the "doxological text," or words written on a page. Doxology, as worship, is an event. According to Berger, to interpret doxology apart from its worship context is like reading a single musician's score while never hearing the symphony.[28] Despite Berger's important caveats, it is telling that she ultimately did not reject theological analysis of hymns:

> But can theology actually appropriate doxology as a *locus theologicus*? That is a very different matter. Theological interpretation, the subject matter considered, and its appropriateness as a *locus theologicus* are three distinctly different categories that should not be confused. Still, the possible appropriateness of doxology as a source for theology does not have to be denied altogether.[29]

Wilma Jean Quantrille more enthusiastically embraced the investigation of theological themes in Charles Wesley's hymns, especially his hymns on the Trinity.[30] Though she recognized that the "primary intent of Charles Wesley was not to produce systematic theology," she praised the "comprehensive nature of the hymns, which touch upon all areas of Christian faith and life, (and) lend themselves to such exploration."[31]

A more recent impetus to the rediscovery of Charles Wesley's thought was *Charles Wesley: Poet and Theologian*.[32] It is significant that in the title the word "poet" appeared before "theologian," for nowhere in this edited volume was an argument advanced that Charles was first and foremost a theologian. To the contrary, in an assessment by Thomas Langford, he appeared to be damned by faint praise:

> Charles Wesley is certainly a theologian in the same sense that anyone who thinks, sings, paints, or dances about God is a theologian; namely, every expression about God, every interpretation of Divine presence possesses implicit and inescapable theological belief and commitments...It seems safe to attribute to John the primary role as theologian of the Methodist movement. Charles served a supportive, encouraging, and propagandizing role to and for John.[33]

More positive about the theological contribution of Charles Wesley were essays by S.T. Kimbrough, Jr. and Laurence Hull Stookey. While acknowledging Charles' extensive use of allegorizing in hymns inspired by specific Scriptural texts, Kimbrough saw convergences between Wesley's method and that of "narrative theology."[34] For his part, Stookey followed-up on the Eucharistic themes first explored by Ernest Rattenbury.[35] Besides the question of Eucharistic theology, he also briefly examined Wesley's contribution through the hymns to a proper understanding of ecclesiology and biblical preaching. All three emphases form part of liturgical renewal, and as such, have implications for pastoral theology.[36]

The most recent publication fostering an appreciation of Charles Wesley was the collection of essays, *Charles Wesley: Life, Literature, and Legacy*.[37] Geoffrey Wainwright underscored the important role Charles played during the first Calvinistic controversy (1739-1741).[38] That John Wesley recognized the theological merit of his brother's poetry was evidenced when he appended Charles' hymn, "Universal Redemption," to his own controversial 1739 sermon, *Free Grace*. Speaking of God's "boundless grace" and "universal love," the hymn's 36 four line stanzas made repeated use of the word "all" to combat the Calvinistic concept of limited atonement. Likewise, when Howel Harris preached before the Bristol Methodist Society on June 27, 1741, Charles immediately responded to Harris' unwelcome preaching of Calvinistic doctrines by booming out a selection from the *Hymns on God's Everlasting Love*.[39] These are two examples of how acumen as a hymn-writer coupled with theological depth inoculated young Methodist societies against Calvinistic teaching.

In addition to Wainwright, Ted Campbell in the same collection attempted to move beyond the debate over whether Charles was a "theologian" by applying to both him and his brother the label *theologos*, one who gives us "words" (*logoi*) about "God." (*theos*).[40] Campbell clarified:

> While this may indeed be the original meaning of the term "theologian," using the term theologos here seems more appropriate since by doing so we will avoid the connotations that the word "theologian" now has, namely one who is associated with the second-order work (*theologia secunda*) of critical reflection on religious teachings or religious practices. Theologos allows us to claim more explicitly Charles Wesley's first-order work (*theologia prima*) of giving words by which we can speak of God and indeed by which we can speak to God.[41]

How was the work of a *theologos* manifested in Charles Wesley's hymns? In addition to explicating what Campbell calls "historic Christian teachings" including the divinity of Christ and the Trinity, Wesley was the *theologos* of the Wesleyan "way of salvation." Through the use of terms like "repentance," "awakened," "justified" and "sanctified," Charles Wesley "gave us profound words that express the depth and the complexity of the Christian pilgrimage empowered by divine grace."[42]

Returning to the original question, one may ask: *In what sense was Charles Wesley a theologian?* Like his brother, John, Charles was not "systematic" in that he never set out to write a systematic theology in the contemporary sense of the term. Nonetheless, his hymns, and to a lesser extent, his sermons, were a secondary explication of the "Wesleyan way of salvation." Whether as a theologian or – to use Campbell's terms, a *theologos* – Charles' extensive poetry provided nuance to Wesleyan soteriology, including the doctrine of prevenient grace.

B. Challenges with Source Materials

Beyond the question of whether Charles Wesley should be considered a theologian lies a second *locus* of problematic issues. These deal with the nature and availability of primary sources. Any scholar of Charles Wesley must come to grips with several hurdles that make interpreting his theology more difficult, but not impossible.[43] Following is a summary of materials that have a bearing on any biographical or theological investigation of the younger Wesley:

Charles Wesley's *Journal* – This covered the period from 1736 to 1756, where it abruptly stopped.[44] Unfortunately, many sections from the original manuscripts did not appear in the heretofore published editions of the *Journal*. This was due in large part to the use by Charles of a shorthand system, ostensibly to keep prying eyes from violating the privacy of the writer, but also to encode material of a more sensitive nature.[45] For this investigation, Newport's and Kimbrough's new critical edition of Wesley's *Journal* will usually be cited.[46] This edition includes translations of shorthand sections of the *Journal* that have never been published and occasional paragraphs of a sensitive nature excised by earlier editors.

Charles Wesley's *Letters* – Several hundred unpublished letters from Charles Wesley's correspondence are contained in the Methodist Archives housed at the John Rylands Library of the University of Manchester.[47] Almost half of these letters were written between Charles and his wife, Sarah, both prior to and after their 1749 wedding.[48] The only published effort to unlock the contents of these letters was Frank Baker's excellent but brief *Charles Wesley As Revealed by His Letters*.[49] Baker identified some of the challenges inherent in any study of Wesley's letters, including Charles' penchant for not signing his name or dating the letters, plus his use of shorthand, Latin, and Greek.[50] Despite these obstacles, *Charles Wesley Revealed* provided clues about some key episodes in his life. As more recent work on the *Letters* advances, it is hoped that new light can be shed on Wesley's life and work.[51]

Charles Wesley's *Sermons* – Students of John Wesley accustomed to volumes of prose materials including logically organized sermons may be surprised by the relative paucity of extant sermons by Charles.[52] This is due in no small degree to Wesley's October 1738 abandonment of manuscript preaching in favour of an *extempore* style.[53] The only attempt at publishing Wesley's written homilies had been in 1816, when a slim volume containing twelve sermons attributed to him was published.[54] Thomas Albin and Oliver Beckerlegge transcribed six manuscript sermons in 1987, all six of which appeared in the 2001 Oxford edition of Charles Wesley's *Sermons*. On the basis of these sermons, Kenneth Newport concluded: "Charles was a theologian of not insignificant ability, and his attempts to explain both the plight of the human condition and what he perceived to be the divine answer to it deserve careful attention."[55] However, of the twenty-three sermons included by Newport, he conceded that only the first thirteen could be shown with certainty to have been composed by Charles, and so only these are evaluated here for their contribution to the Wesleyan doctrine of prevenient grace.

Charles Wesley's hymns – By far, the most fecund Charles Wesley source for theological inquiry is his thousands of hymns.[56] The precise number of hymns has been variously estimated. Ernest Rattenbury maintained that 4,480 hymns were published during Wesley's lifetime, with 2,840 left behind in manuscript form.[57] Neville Shepherd gave a hymn total of 8,900, a figure approximating the estimate of 9,000 concluded by Frank Baker, which encompasses 27,000 stanzas and 180,000 lines.[58] On the other hand, S.T. Kimbrough, Jr. and Oliver Beckerlegge judged even the more conservative figure of 6,500 hymns to be a "myth," insisting that many of the poems Charles wrote were never intended for public worship.[59] Whatever the exact number of hymns, all agreed that this literary output is astounding:

> This is something like three times the output of one of our most prolific poets, William Wordsworth, and even more than that of the redoubtable Robert Browning. Moreover, unlike both these poets, Charles Wesley's verse consists almost solely of lyrics in stanzaic form – a mere 7,500 lines are extant in various couplet forms. Taking the average – and it must be stressed that this is an average, not a description of normal practice – Charles Wesley wrote ten lines of verse every day for 50 years, completing an extant poem every other day.[60]

A large portion of these hymns appeared in hymnals jointly published beginning in 1739 by John and Charles Wesley or, in some cases, published independently by Charles.[61] Nonetheless, the most extensive effort to publish the quasi-totality of the poetic output of the brothers appeared between 1868 and 1872 as *The Poetical Works of John and Charles Wesley*.[62] Though impressive in their own right, the *Poetical Works* were not perfect. Beckerlegge and Kimbrough called Osborn's principle of selection obscure, noting that in many instances he printed only part of a hymn or poem. This is rectified – and poems omitted by Osborn were gathered up – in the three volume *The Unpublished Poetry of Charles Wesley*.[63] In addition, the newly released on-line critical edition of Charles Wesley's published verse is considered.[64] An examination of these sources helps determine the nature and scope of Charles Wesley's contribution to the doctrine of prevenient grace.

A final preliminary question to address is what Frank Baker has termed "the vexed problem of the joint authorship of the Wesley poetry."[65] Frank Baker acknowledged that between 1739 and 1745, five volumes were published as joint authors, but after this date, John wrote almost no verse.[66] Baker cited Henry Bett's attribution to John of all 33 poems translated from the German, as well as a handful from Spanish. Bett also identified fifteen stylistic criteria by which John's poems could be deciphered, including the tendency by John to elaborate and repeat a thought, plus his more frequent use of couplets.[67] Having weighed the technical issues surrounding this thorny question, John Lawson concluded:

> It is not in every case possible to be certain what work is by John Wesley, and what is by Charles, because their earlier publications, which contain the greater

part of their most valuable work, were issued jointly without statement of the respective contributions. In general, however, the masterly translations from the German are the work of John Wesley, though he did compose a few early hymns in English, whereas the bulk of the work composed in English is from the prolific pen of Charles Wesley.[68]

Neville Shepherd reached a similar conclusion, noting that "the scholar is likely to acquire a feel for the difference between the two writers, even if this cannot be reduced to precise criteria."[69] Though John Wesley had editorial control of the earlier hymn collections, this did not negate the fact that ninety percent or more of the material contained in the *Poetical Works* was original work stemming from Charles' pen.[70] On this basis, it is possible to decipher Charles Wesley's position on any number of theological topics. In addition to the scholarly publications by John Tyson, Teresa Berger, and others already alluded to above, doctoral level explorations conducted on facets of the younger Wesley's theology and the confident use they have made of the Wesley hymns are a testament to the accepted practice of employing his hymns in theological research.[71]

C. Soteriological Shift in Charles Wesley

A final preliminary consideration is determining the nature of Charles Wesley's understanding of salvation. Integral to this exploration are the religious influences and experiences that shaped his soteriology. Ernest Rattenbury recognized the close connection between Charles' theology and spiritual development: "So much was his doctrine conceived and expressed as personal experience that if many of his theological verses are to be truly weighed and assessed the man must be considered in his psychological development, which implies, of course, biographical study."[72] There is precedent in more recent Wesleyan studies for such an experiential methodology. Kenneth Collins' *John Wesley: A Theological Journey* intertwined the life narrative of the older brother with the significant theological development that occurred at key junctures in that journey. In a similar manner, the younger brother's soteriology underwent modification based upon his religious experience. For both John and Charles, the most obvious example is what is sometimes called their "evangelical conversion" that transpired in May 1738.[73] Yet to immediately focus one's attention on this narrow time reference too lightly brushes aside the early influence of his mother, Susanna, on Charles Wesley's religious worldview.

Epworth: the Inculcation of Moralism Pre-1738

The details of Charles Wesley's early childhood have been frequently outlined. In his preface to Wesley's early *Journal*, John Telford set out key dates from his life, including his birth on December 18, 1707 and his 1716 entrance to Westminster school.[74] With the exception of a brief period following the rectory fire of February 8, 1709 when the Wesley children were scattered to other homes, the primary parental influence in their religious education was their mother, Susanna Wesley.[75] Herself of Puritan ancestry, Susanna inculcated in Charles and her other offspring a strict sense of right and wrong, the fear of God, and a commitment to piety. This rigor in all things spiritual breathed through the letters compiled by Charles Wallace in *Susanna Wesley: The Complete Writings*.[76] In an March 11, 1704 letter to her son, Samuel Jr. – who would later for several years become a *de facto* surrogate parent to the young Charles upon his entry to Westminster school in London – Susanna compared nature's laws with divine rules for human conduct:

> And if God has taken such care of natural agents to prepare a law for them and to secure their obedience to it, we may conclude that he would not suffer man to be without law, since, if he were, he must be the most miserable of all beings in the world. It's therefore plain and undeniable that God has also given a law to mankind because their nature requires it. He has a right to do it as creator, wisdom and goodness to direct our actions to what is best, and power to enforce his laws by rewards and punishments of infinite weight and duration.[77]

The moralistic bent of Susanna's mind was also evidenced in "principal rules" of childrearing set down in a July 27, 1732 letter to her son, John. After briefly describing household regulations concerning the taking of meals, punishment for wrongdoing, and various other aspects of proper parenting, Mrs. Wesley gave not a psychological but a theological rationale: "As self-will is the root of all sin and misery, so whatever cherishes this in children ensures their after-wretchedness and irreligion; whatever checks and mortifies it promotes their future happiness and piety."[78]

Beyond childrearing, in an illuminating December 6, 1738 letter to Charles, Susanna Wesley explained her understanding of justification:

> My notion of justifying faith is the same with yours, for that trusting in Jesus Christ or the promises made in him is that special act of faith to which our justification or acceptance is so frequently ascribed in the gospel. This faith is certainly the gift of God wrought in the mind of man by his Holy Spirit. But then, as the Gospel promises are conditional, I can't believe that the Spirit of Holiness will give that faith to any but such as sincerely desire and endeavor to perform the conditions of the gospel covenant required on their part.[79]

To this letter, Charles appended a note: "My mother (not clear) of faith Dec. 6. 1738."[80] The same rigor apparent in the raising of children manifested itself in the spiritual realm as strict obedience to divine principles. A sense of human striving to live up to God's standards was never far beneath the surface. Importantly, this same sense of striving appears to have been passed on to Charles, as evidenced in pre-May 1738 sermons that have survived.[81]

Especially insightful is the July 1738 sermon, *The Threefold State*. Written two months after his evangelical conversion, it may be understood as a retrospective describing Charles Wesley's spiritual journey to that point. The three states examined were: 1) "rest and acquiescence in sin"; 2) a "state of contention" against sin, and 3) a "state of victory."[82] The first two states "cannot qualify a man for pardon," though at least the second state has "something of life and righteousness in it."[83] It is this second state which would seem to be a description of Charles' own condition prior to May 1738:

> In the beginning of this state, they are generally full of delight; God does not let them serve Him for nought, but draws them on with sensible comforts, and leads them in the ways of pleasantness. They seem to taste the good word of God and the powers of the world to come in the witness of sensible devotion. Nor is there any temper of a real inward Christian which they do not in some sort anticipate. They will often have peace with God, even the peace which passes all understanding, and sometimes rejoice with joy unspeakable. Nay, the love of Christ seems to constrain them, and they long to do great things for Him.[84]

The words of this sermon appear to re-trace the steps of Charles Wesley in his Oxford days. That Charles during his time at Oxford had a "first state" (of nature, or following after sin) is implied in a description of his brother during this period, later written by John: "He pursued his studies diligently, and led a regular, harmless life; but if I spoke to him about religion he would warmly answer, 'What! would you have me be a saint all at once?' and would hear no more."[85] Yet this soon turned to a seriousness in religion (the "second state") as reflected in a January 22, 1729 letter to John. After lamenting his brother's absence, and the good effect his presence had upon him spiritually, Charles observed:

> I verily think, dear brother, I shall never quarrel with you again till I do with my religion, and that I may never do that I am not ashamed to desire your prayers. 'Tis owing in great measure to somebody's (my mother's, most likely) that I am come to think as I do, for I can't tell myself how or when I first awoke out of my lethargy – only that 'twas not long after you went away.[86]

The "third state" Wesley described through a veritable panoply of Scripture references. This was the true child of God, one who had "received the atonement."[87] It was this state that depicted Wesley's own spiritual condition as of May 21, 1738, and it is to this crucial soteriological shift that this investigation now turns its attention.

London, May 21, 1738: Charles Wesley's "Pentecost"

In the closing paragraph of a chapter describing the evangelical conversions of John and Charles Wesley, Mabel Brailsford concluded that the events of May 1738 transformed the brothers Wesley into persons who were no longer "ego-centric" but "theo-centric."[88] In an attempt to capture the essence of a key life passage, Brailsford may have overstated her case. After all, any objective reading of either brother's *Journal* shows the numerous ways in which the young clergymen served God through acts of charity toward others. Yet never far below the surface was the egocentric motive of meriting one's salvation through righteous acts.

Charles Wesley's *Journal* opened in March 1736 in the outpost of Frederica, where Charles served as secretary to General Oglethorpe, the governor of Georgia. Apart from detailed descriptions of intrigue among the residents of the tiny colony, including an attempt to force out Charles over charges of sexual impropriety, the *Journal* was notable for its gaps. Often up to a week elapsed between entries. When no news was forthcoming of the safe return of Oglethorpe from a scouting trip that had already lasted several days, Charles wryly observed on Easter Sunday, April 25: "Though I expected every hour that the Spaniards would bring us the news of Mr. Oglethorpe's death, yet I was insensible to fear, and careless of the consequence. *But my indifference arose from stupidity rather than faith.* There was nothing I cared for in life, and therefore the loss of it appeared a trifle."[89]

Ill-suited to the drudgery and long hours of secretarial work, and weakened by the harsh conditions of pioneer life and inadequate provisions, on July 25, 1736 Charles submitted his resignation to Oglethorpe. After convincing Charles to remain as his secretary for a time by returning with dispatches to the Trustees in London, the governor gave him advice: "On many accounts I should recommend to you marriage, rather than celibacy. You are of a social temper, and *would find in a married state the difficulties of working out your* salvation *exceedingly lessened, and your helps as much increased.*"[90] It is significant at this vital juncture that Charles made no commentary on the theology behind the governor's words. His silence may be interpreted as a tacit admission that his own good works were indeed an attempt to merit salvation.

Barrie Tabraham culled from the *Journal* key entries made over the next 22 months, selections that depicted a young man in search of spiritual peace.[91] Important episodes included a meeting in late August 1737 back in England with William Law, the ascetic author of *On Christian Perfection* and *A Serious Call to a Devout and Holy Life*, as well as correspondence in November of the same year with Count Nicolaus von Zinzendorf, leader of the Moravians.[92] Around the same time, Charles seems to have been impressed by the preaching of his old friend and fellow Holy Club member, George Whitefield, who spoke with great certainty and effect, and whose sermon on the new birth had been printed and widely circulated.[93] Only one day after Whitefield sailed for Georgia in late January 1738, John Wesley returned to England and the brothers quickly became associated with the Society in Fetter Lane.[94]

Charles' *Journal* recorded repeated contact with Peter Böhler, the Moravian missionary who taught at Fetter Lane in London.[95] On February 24, bedfast and suffering from a severe toothache, Charles received Böhler's visit. The exchange was significant, revealing the marrow of Wesley's moralistic soteriology:

> Soon after Peter Böhler came to my beside. I asked him to pray for me. He seemed unwilling at first, but, beginning very faintly, he raised his voice by degrees, and prayed for my recovery with strange confidence. Then he took me by the hand, and calmly said, "You will not die now." I thought within myself, "I cannot hold out in this pain till morning. If it abates before, I believe I may recover." He asked me, "Do you hope to be saved?" "Yes." "For what reason do you hope it?" "Because I have used my best endeavours to serve God." He shook his head, and said no more. I thought him very uncharitable, saying in my heart, "What, are not my endeavours a sufficient ground of hope? Would he rob me of my endeavours? I have nothing else to trust to."[96]

Another illness in late April was the occasion of a second bedside visit by Böhler, whom Wesley believed "God had detained in England for my good."[97] Following Böhler's prayer for him, Charles noted: "I immediately thought it might be that I should again consider Böhler's doctrine of faith; examine myself whether I was in the faith; and if I was not, never cease longing after it till I attained it."[98] This "longing" continued throughout May, and included study of Martin Luther's commentary on Galatians. As if encountering the doctrine of *sola fide* for the first time, Charles questioned the neglect of this soteriological tenet by his beloved Church of England:

> Who would believe our Church has been founded on this important article of justification by faith alone? I am astonished I should ever think this a new doctrine; especially when our Articles and Homilies stand unrepealed, and the key of knowledge is not yet taken away. From this time I endeavoured to ground as many of our friends as came in this fundamental truth, salvation by faith alone, not an idle, dead faith, but a faith which works by love, and is necessarily productive of all good works and all holiness.[99]

The details of May 21, 1738 are well-rehearsed by Charles Wesley's biographers. This appears justified, since his *Journal* set off that day with a large heading in upper-case letters, "THE DAY OF PENTECOST." Again recuperating in bed, Charles heard the words: "In the name of Jesus of Nazareth, arise, believe, and thou shalt be healed of all thy infirmities." He recounted at-length the investigation that determined the words to have been reluctantly spoken outside his door by Mrs. Turner, the servant who had been tending the sick clergyman. Whatever the source, the words had the desired effect. Wesley noted: "I said, yet feared to say, 'I believe! I believe!'"[100]

Two days later, Charles Wesley composed a hymn that was sung on May 24, the occasion of his brother John's own evangelical conversion. There is some dispute regarding the identity of this hymn,[101] but Frederick Gill and Barrie Tabraham concur that it was "Where shall my wondering soul begin," a vivid description of salvation:

> Where shall my wond'ring soul begin?
> How shall I all to heaven aspire?
>   A slave redeemed from death and sin,
>   A brand plucked from eternal fire,
> How shall I equal triumphs raise,
> Or sing my great Deliverer's praise?
>
> O how shall I the goodness tell,
> Father, which thou to me hast showed?
>   That I, a child of wrath and hell,
>   I should be called a child of God!
> Should know, should feel my sins forgiven,
> Blest with this antepast of heaven![102]

Clearly, something momentous had happened on the spiritual journey of Charles Wesley. Interestingly, in the May 24 entry of his *Journal*, Charles spoke of receiving correspondence from the colonies: "I was farther comforted by an excellent letter from my namesake in Georgia, persecuted for Christ's sake; on the highest step, I trust, of the legal state."[103] This early mention of the "legal state" was evidence of a shift in Wesley's soteriology.[104] In months to come, the early *Journal* recorded repeated instances where in private correspondence and conversation, he preached justification by faith.[105] Though there were periods of spiritual deadness,[106] no longer apparent was the note of intense striving for salvation by works. Like his brother John, Charles had come to a new and seemingly revolutionary understanding. Whereas before they performed good works in the hope of being justified before God, i.e. sanctification *preceding* justification, they now believed that *justification* precedes sanctification, a divine cause producing an effect, namely, holiness of heart and life.

A further evidence of this crucial soteriological shift appeared in Charles Wesley's *Journal* for Friday, August 10, 1739. While visiting William Law, the renowned author of the 1729 *A Serious Call to a Devout and Holy Life*,[107] Wesley had an extended conversation about the nature of faith. Citing Galatians 3:24, he called Law his "schoolmaster to bring him to Christ," but tellingly observed that "the reason why I did not come sooner to him was *my seeking to be sanctified before I was justified.* I disclaimed all expectation of becoming someone great."[108]

What impact would this Copernican Revolution have on the productivity of Charles Wesley, poet and hymn writer? Teresa Berger cautiously noted:

> The widespread (pious) assumption that his conversion first freed the creative spirit within him birthing the poet, Charles Wesley, is false. It is clear, however, that with his experience of conversion, a whole new theme for his poetry appeared and with the growing Methodist renewal movement an entirely new audience began to emerge. This fact, both as cause and incentive, may account for Wesley's incredible productivity...[109]

This evangelical understanding would launch him into years of fruitful ministry, initially itinerating as a Methodist preacher and overseer, then through his distinctive contribution to the Revival, namely, the composition of hymns extolling faith that works through love.

Charles Wesley's Anthropology: On "Nature" and "Image"

Having considered several preliminary issues germane to the study of any aspect of Charles Wesley's theology, this inquiry now addresses his anthropology. Such a study is helpful since it clarifies the theological context in which his doctrine of prevenient grace may be understood. From Wesley's perspective, what was the deep problem that merited a radical solution? In other words, what do the sermons and hymns tell us regarding the human condition apart from grace? To answer these questions, a study of two key concepts is undertaken.

These two concepts – under which other relevant topics like original sin can be grouped – are "nature" and "image."

A. The Characteristics of "Nature"

The *Compact Oxford English Dictionary* defined "nature" as "the physical world, including plants, animals, the landscape, and natural phenomena, as opposed to humans or human creations."[110] To superimpose this modern understanding of the word onto Charles Wesley's writings, however, is to misconstrue his meaning. For Wesley, "nature" was rarely a cosmological term; rather, it was anthropological, a convenient poetic shorthand for human nature.[111] Calling the word "nature" a "key to (Charles') mind, and perhaps to the mind of his age," George Findlay explained:

> The essence of his Gospel, the motif running through all his hymns, is that, though (human) nature is bad, it can most gloriously be changed to unthinkable good. If there is a nature within us which is the enemy of God, there is also a Divine nature available for us in Christ, if only we sufficiently want it.[112]

By Findlay's account, roughly two-thirds of Wesley's references to "nature" in his hymns spoke of it as fallen, while one-third spoke of its divine transformation. In Charles' vision, this transformation was far from simple, as Findlay noted: "Only the miraculous power of the grace of God could bind the strong man or spoil his goods. Nature is in complete possession, and from its citadel within sullenly defies the Divine summons."[113]

Having analyzed three hundred Charles Wesley hymns, Gilbert Morris grouped them under four headings: 1) the nature of God; 2) the nature of man, i.e. humanity; 3) the conversion experience; and 4) the pilgrim experience.[114] The pervasiveness of "nature" as a crucial category for Wesley was thereby confirmed.

Shortly after his 1738 conversion, Charles Wesley began penning hymns in an attempt to describe the radical change he had undergone. His theological anthropology was delineated via descriptions of human nature as asleep, enslaved, and blindly dwelling in darkness. These images permeated a 1739 hymn on John 15:18-19, including the first two verses, appearing in *Hymns and Sacred Poems*:

> Where has my slumbering spirit been,
>   So late emerging into light?
> So imperceptible, within,
>   The weight of this *Egyptian* night!
>
> Where have they hid the WORLD so long,
>   So late presented to my view?
> Wretch! though myself increased the throng,
>   Myself a part I never knew.[115]

Included in the same collection was a hymn entitled "Free Grace," more commonly known today under the title "And Can it Be?" The fourth stanza presented a self-portrait of Charles Wesley prior to his "Pentecost" experience:

> Long my imprison'd spirit lay,
>   Fast bound in sin and nature's night:
> Thine eyes diffused a quickening ray;
>   I woke; the dungeon flamed with light;
> My chains fell off, my heart was free,
>   I rose, went forth, and follow'd Thee.[116]

Charles pursued the motif of "nature's night" in an interesting allusion to the Holy Spirit. In a poem simply entitled "Another," a two stanza invocation was followed by a third:

> Expand Thy wings, prolific Dove,
>   Brood o'er our nature's night;
> On our discorder'ed spirits move,
>   And let there now be light.[117]

The same phrase "nature's night" appeared in "A Morning Hymn." At dawn the light of the sun overcame the "remains of night"; in verses two and three, the light of Christ attended our "second birth" –

> Burst we then the bands of death,
> Raised by His all quickening breath;
> Long we to be loosed from earth,
> Struggling into second birth.
> Spent at length is nature's night;
> Christ attends to give us Light…
>
> Turn, O turn us, Lord, again,
> Raiser Thou of fallen man!
> Sin destroy and nature's boast,
> Saviour Thou of Spirits lost!…[118]

In addition to the darkness of nature (representing sinfulness), Wesley added the adjective "fallen." Likewise, in verse one of a hymn entitled "The Fifty-Fifth Chapter of Isaiah," he made an appeal –

> Ho! every one that thirsts, draw nigh
>   ('Tis God invites the fallen race:)
> Mercy and free salvation buy
>   Buy wine, and milk, and Gospel grace.[119]

The hymn "Christ our Wisdom" had the same interest, juxtaposing in the opening two stanzas the light/darkness metaphor with the adjective "fallen":

> MADE unto me, O Lord, my God,
>   Wisdom Divine Thou art:
> Thy light, which first my darkness show'd,
>   Still searches out my heart.
>
> Thy Spirit, breathing in the word,
>   Gave me myself to see,
> Fallen, till by Thy grace restored,
> And lost, till found in Thee.[120]

Since we are fallen, we cannot be called in any sense "good." The first and fifth stanza of the hymn "Why should our parents call us good" accentuated this human reality:

> Why should our parents call us good,
> And poison us with praise,
> When born in sin by nature proud,
> And void we are of grace?...
>
> Glory to God, if we receive
> The smallest spark of grace;
> He only doth our goodness give,
> And His be all the praise.[121]

Akin to the absence of goodness was the alienation from the life of God characteristic of human nature. In the hymn "Weary, why should I farther go," stanza three evoked images of a lost Eden:

> My paradise is lost and gone,
> Distress'd, disconsolate, alone,
> A banish'd man I rove,
> I faint beneath my nature's load,
> An alien from the life of God,
> A stranger to His love.[122]

A further metaphor describing human nature is sickness or disease. Charles Wesley in "Jesus, the fame Of Thy great name" called upon "Thee my Physician" to bring healing to his "forlorn estate," a "sin-sick soul" characterized by "palsy," "leprosy" and the "fever" of "pride" and "fierce desire." As if these ailments are not enough, in the sixth stanza, he added "dropsy" to the list:

> Of creature bliss My nature is
> Rapacious above measure:
> Heal this dropsical disease,
> This thirst of praise and pleasure.[123]

Charles suffered more physical ailments than his brother, John, so it is fascinating to see him draw upon his experiences of physical illness to describe the spiritual realm.

Beyond disease, an integral component of our fallen condition is an insensitivity to all things spiritual. In verses one and six of a "Hymn for the Kingswood Colliers," Charles Wesley used picturesque terms to depict their spiritual condition before and after conversion:

> GLORY to God, whose sovereign grace
> Hath animated senseless stones,
> Call'd us to stand before His face,
> And raised us into *Abraham's* sons…
>
> For this, no longer sons of night,
> To Thee our thanks and hearts we give;
> To Thee who call'd us into light,
> To Thee we die, to Thee we live.[124]

In a poem entitled "Misery," the seventh verse portrayed the spiritual deadness of the individual in his or her natural condition:

> Man cannot serve Thee: all his care,
> Engross'd by groveling appetite,
> Is fix'd on earth; his treasure there,
> His portion, and his base delight:
> He starts from Virtue's thorny road,
> Alive to sin, but dead to God![125]

This insensitivity to things spiritual was portrayed elsewhere through the metaphor of sleep. In an eighteen stanza hymn, "For the Anniversary of One's Conversion," the first stanza depicted the pre-conversion state:

> Awake from guilty nature's sleep,
> And Christ shall give you light,
> Cast all your sins into the deep,
> And wash the *Ethiop* white.[126]

Likewise, in the 1742 "An Elegy on the Death of Robert Jones, Esq," a poetic tribute to a friend of the Methodist Revival, Charles described Jones' new birth:

> Who then the gracious wonder shall explain,
> How could a man of sin be born again?
> Roused from his *sleep of death*, he never knew
> To fix the point from which the Spirit blew,
> So imperceptibly the stroke was given,
> The stroke divine that turn'd his face to heaven.[127]

Intriguingly, the hymn "For an unconverted husband" would not call positive character traits splendid sins, but attributed them to divine activity. The believing wife prayed:

> Thy goodness form'd, and turn'd his mind,
> Thou mad'st him generous, just, and kind;
> Yet O, incarnate God,
> Through Thee escaped the gulf of vice,
> *In nature's deadly sleep he lies*,
> Nor pants to feel Thy blood.[128]

Despite the recognition of the positive character traits divinely instilled, yet the husband was spiritually asleep. Wesley saw in this description no contradiction, only an acknowledgment of fact.

The spiritual slumber characteristic of nature was a theme not only in Wesley's hymns and poems but also in his April 4, 1742 sermon, *Awake, Thou That Sleepest*, preached before the university of Oxford.[129] Based on Paul's words in Ephesians 5:14, Wesley began by defining what he means by "sleep":

> By sleep is signified the natural state of man: that deep sleep of the soul into which the sin of Adam hath cast all who spring from his loins; that supineness, indolence, and stupidity, that insensibility of his real condition, wherein every man comes into the world, and continues till the voice of God awakes him.[130]

Such an individual was in a "state of utter darkness," a "sinner satisfied in his sins" and "contented to remain in his fallen state." Though gravely diseased, he thought he was in perfect health.[131]

The emphasis upon the spiritual slumber apparent in *Awake, Thou That Sleepest* was not a new theme for Charles Wesley. He had already preached upon it repeatedly throughout 1738 and 1739 using a sermon on 1 John 3:14.[132] Given the title *The Threefold State* by Thomas Albin and Oliver Beckerlegge,[133] the sermon began by describing the first state, which was characterized by the dreadful results of Adam's sin for humankind:

> In the midst of life these are in death, even that spiritual death which Adam tasted together with the forbidden fruit. God, who cannot lie, had plainly told him, 'in the day that thou eatest thereof, thou shalt surely die." The sentence was accordingly executed. The union of his soul with God (in which spiritual life consisted, like as the natural life stands in the conjunction of the soul with the body) this union, I say, was dissolved. His soul was separated from God, and in the day that he ate, he spiritually died.[134]

Such an individual was likened to a "dead body" that could not appreciate music or dancing. His or her will was in a "natural state." As such, one can neither understand the things of God nor be subject to God's law.[135] Likewise, in a sermon on Romans 3:23-24, Wesley asserted that we "are all by nature sold under sin, and enemies to God; and consequently children of wrath and heirs of hell."[136] Expounding the same passage, he affirmed in a second, longer sermon that the human being had inherited from Adam a "miserable, corrupt and sinful nature." Wesley continued:

> All the powers of man are totally depraved. The whole head is sick, and the whole heart faint. From the sole of his foot even unto the head there is no soundness in him, but wounds and bruises and putrefying sores: his understanding is darkened, his will perverse, his affections set on earthly things. Pride and concupiscence make up his wretched composition; and if you take away that spark of God which was restored to him at his redemption, there remains in him nothing but pure beast and devil.[137]

Quoting the ninth Article of the Church of England, Wesley called this condition "original sin," describing it both as an "infection of nature" and "two opposite principles, inclining him to good and evil." Importantly, these were found in both the unregenerate and the regenerate.[138]

In the examples seen thus far, "nature" was presented in categorically negative terms. Importantly, it was only divine initiative that could remedy the situation. This seems to be a change from Charles Wesley's earlier position. In a November 20, 1735 sermon based on 1 Kings 18:21 and preached on the Isle of Wight, Wesley called his listeners to "an entire devotion of yourselves to God."[139] In moralistic language similar to that of the other two extant sermons from the pre-May 1738 period,[140] he exhorted:

> Be strong therefore and quit yourselves like men. Be bold to assert your liberty; to vindicate the dignity of your nature, to shake off the bondage of corruption; and to behave yourselves as becometh the children of God, and inheritors of the kingdom of heaven...but his mercy is pleased in consideration of our weakness, and of the poor corrupted state of our nature, to content himself with such services as we are able to do for him.[141]

While Charles appears to have assumed a converted audience, his mixed characterization of nature was striking. It possessed "dignity" yet was "corrupted." It was not divine action that intervened to make change possible; rather, one had to be "bold to assert your liberty." This was at variance with his post-May 1738 preference for metaphors of enslavement, such as the one who in the hymn "Free Grace" was portrayed as "fast-bound in sin and nature's night."[142] The later Wesley was clear that Adam's sin had abrogated the liberty humanity once had to choose God. In stanzas five and six of the hymn "The Cry of a Reprobate," the picture was of one who – caught up in the current of original sin – added the offence of actual sins:

> I *cannot* from destruction turn,
> Nor wish it might from me depart;

> Down the *swift stream of nature borne*,
> I sin with all my wretchless heart.
> My greedy soul knows no remorse,
> (While conscience sear'd no longer cries,)
> Impetuous as the headlong horse
> Rushes into the fight, and dies.[143]

The word "cannot" was essential to Wesley's understanding of original sin. There was no power naturally resident in the post-fall human being enabling him or her to turn to God. Nature was "impotent," analogous to the lame who need the healing touch of Christ, the "kind physician."[144] To attribute to nature the inherent power to turn to God would for Wesley have precluded the necessity of divine grace generally, and prevenient grace specifically.[145] Yet to the individual incapable of things spiritual, God offered the assistance of grace.

Blind, fallen, sleep, night, stones, diseased, death, corrupted, fast bound, alienated from God – these are words that evoked the legacy of Adam's sin to his posterity, characteristics of what George Findlay called "unredeemed human nature."[146] It is noteworthy that even in the handful of post-May 1738 quotations cited thus far, the language of grace and of the Spirit was present. In the soteriology of Charles Wesley, these were closely intertwined as concomitants of the divine response to the problem of sin. No matter how corrupt human nature may be, there was in Wesley a hope of divine transformation as the fruit of grace:

> Transform my nature into Thine,
> Let all my powers Thine impress feel,
> Let all my soul become Divine,
> And stamp me with Thy Spirit's seal.[147]

Before examining that question in greater depth in Chapter 5, this chapter turns its attention from "nature" to a second important word in Wesley's anthropology, namely, "image."

B. Renewal in *Imago Dei*

Parallel with the affirmation that human nature had been corrupted was the confidence that the *imago Dei* might be divinely restored. The terms "nature" and "image" – though they can appear in close proximity – are not to be confounded. For Charles Wesley, the first term ("nature") referred primarily to the problem of human depravity, whereas the second term ("image") looked forward to the solution provided by God in Christ. This solution is a divine restoration, a renewal in holiness, i.e. the *moral* image of God. In a "Hymn for Christmas Day," Charles Wesley in ten stanzas extolled the magnificence of the incarnation. Stanzas eight and nine specifically identified the *telos* of Christ's coming:

> Now display Thy saving power
> Ruin'd *nature* now restore.
> Now in mystic union join
> Thine to ours and ours to Thine.
>
> Adam's likeness, Lord, efface,
> Stamp Thy *image* in its place;
> Second Adam from above
> Reinstate us in Thy love.[148]

In "God of Love, incline Thine ear," Charles Wesley recorded a prayer for salvation. The poem opened with the supplicant imploring:

> God of Love, incline Thine ear!
> Christ my King, Haste and bring
> Thy salvation near.[149]

And what was this "salvation"? It could not be distinguished from renewal in the image of God. The tenth (and final) stanza crowned a poem that earlier had expressed a desire for cleansing from a heart filled with impure thoughts. The divine agency for this cleansing was none other than *love*:

> Love, thine image Love, restore:
> Let me love, Hence remove,
> And be seen no more.[150]

How was the *imago Dei* forfeited? Charles Wesley touched upon this subject in a lengthy sermon on Romans 3:23-25.[151] Describing his condition prior to the fall and afterward, Wesley observed:

> God created man in his own image, after his likeness. He made him perfect, but a little lower than the angels, one in heart and mind with himself, a real partaker of the divine nature. But man soon fell from that original dignity. He sinned by eating of the forbidden fruit, and in the day that he ate spiritually died. The life of his soul, consisting in its union with God (like as the natural life consists in the union of soul and body) his spiritual life, I say, was extinguished. The glory immediately departed from him, and he knew that he was naked; naked of God, stripped of his divine image; a motley mixture of beast and devil.[152]

Curiously, having spoken of the loss of the image of God, Charles spoke little in the remainder of the sermon of its restoration. Instead, he examined the nature of justification by faith, which was his preoccupation in 1739 when the sermon was delivered at Oxford.

The limitations of the Oxford sermon were remedied in part by a frequently preached sermon on John 3:14.[153] There, Wesley presented three "states" that together represented the totality of humanity. The first state included those who were "dead in trespasses and sins." However, this was not always the case. At the time of baptism – even when it took place in infancy – the *imago Dei* was restored, but subsequently was defaced again:

> It is true, at the moment of our baptism, our second birth, that image was restored to us, a principle of divine life infused, and the child of wrath became a child of God. But alas, the soul of most of us soon lost that second life: again was that image wholly impaired and diffused; and the image of the world so strongly graven on it, that God's is no more discernible there.[154]

The end result – as affirmed by Wesley in a separate sermon on Ephesians 5:14 – was that the sinner lived and died without the image of God.[155]

There appear to be no explicit references in Charles Wesley's poetical works to the loss of the *imago Dei*. This loss, however, was implied by frequent allusion to its restoration. Often, this yearning appeared in the context of sanctifying grace. In a poem based on Isaiah 45:22, Wesley began with the reality of the fall:

> Sinners, your Saviour see!
> O, look ye unto Me!
> Lift your eyes, ye *fallen* race!
> I, the gracious God and true,
> I am full of truth and grace,
> Full of truth and grace for you![156]

As the poem progressed, the pilgrim moved along the *via salutis*. It was believers who awaited the restoration of the *imago Dei*:

> On Thee we fix our eyes,
> And wait for fresh supplies
> Justified, we ask for more,
> Give the' abiding Spirit, give;
> Lord, *Thine image here restore*,
> Fully in Thy members live.
>
> Author of Faith, appear!
> Be Thou its Finisher.
> Upward still for This we gaze,
> Till we feel the stamp Divine,
> Thee behold with open face,
> Bright in all Thy glory shine.[157]

The same motif of renewal in the image of God appeared in other poems, including *Moriar ut te videam!* (Let me die, that I may see Thee!). The final stanza summarized the thrust of the preceding six verses:

> Die all of self to live no more,
> Die the old man no more to rise;
> Me to Thine image here restore,
> Receive me to Thy paradise,
> (Whence I may never more remove,)
> The paradise of perfect love.[158]

In a poem based on Revelation 3:17, Charles Wesley spoke of the lukewarm believer in whom the *imago Dei* must be renewed and restored. Such a restoration was necessitated because of original sin, as affirmed in verses two and five:

> Who my misery can relate,
> My depth of woe reveal?
> I have left my first estate,
> In hapless Adam fell;
> Driven out of my abode,
> I now have lost my perfect bliss,
> Fallen, fallen out of God,
> And banish'd paradise...
>
> Naked of thine image, Lord,
> Forsaken and alone,
> Unrenew'd and unrestored
> I have not Thee put on:
> Over me Thy mantle spread,
> Send down Thy likeness from above,
> Let Thy goodness be display'd,
> And wrap me in Thy love.[159]

The longing for renewal in the moral image of God was a recurrent theme for the younger Wesley. In a poem entitled "Restoring Grace," the hymn writer portrayed the ardent desire of the backslider to be freed from the grip of sin. In the sixth (and final) stanza, the prayer reached a suitable climax:

> For this only thing I pray,
> And this will I require,
> Take the power of sin away,
> Fill me with chaste desire;
>
> Perfect me in holiness;
> Thine image to my soul restore:
> Love me freely, seal my peace,
> And bid me sin no more.[160]

In verse one of "Come Father, Son, and Holy Ghost," the location in the *via salutis* of the restoration of the *imago Dei* was broadened beyond sanctifying grace:

> Come, Father, Son, and Holy Ghost,
> Whom One all-perfect God we own,
> Restorer of Thine image lost,
> Thy various offices make known,
> Display, our fallen souls to raise,
> Thy *whole economy of grace*.[161]

The *imago Dei* was retrievable through the working of grace. Wesley affirmed this again in stanzas two and three of "The great Invisible, unknown," a hymn on John 14:6:

> Author of our salvation, Thee
> Author of faith our hearts confess,
> Through Thy atonement on the tree
> Bold we approach the throne of grace,
> And find Thy name to sinners given
> Saves us from hell, and lifts to heaven.
>
> Thy Father's mind through Thee we know,
> *His image with His grace retrieve*
> To Him we in Thy footsteps go
> His hidden life in Thee we live,
> And led by Thy good Spirit we move
> To see His open face above.[162]

These references are significant, for they point to what will become more apparent in Chapter 5, namely, the role of grace in the renewal of the natural image of God in humanity, especially as related to a partial restoration of the capacity to choose.

That being said, for all the varied references to the word "image" in Charles Wesley's hymns, it is not through this word that his understanding of the debilitating effects of original sin upon one's ability to choose God would become apparent. For Wesley, the word "image" denoted the *moral* image.[163] What John Wesley called the "natural image" and the "political image" are terms that never fell from Charles' pen.[164] The reason for this may be that Charles understood these aspects of the *imago Dei* would not be restored on earth, but only eschatologically. The hymn "Whom Christ His brethren owns" implied this truth:

> Whom Christ His brethren owns,
> Are God's adopted sons:
> Jesus with His brethren shares

All that God to Him hath given;
Join'd with Him, the sons are heirs,
Heirs to pompous thrones in heaven.

'Tis then we soon shall find
The joy for us design'd,
That inheritance receive
Purchased by our Brother's blood,
All His image bear, and live,
One with Christ, as Christ with God.[165]

The same dichotomy of earthly renewal of the moral image followed by heavenly restoration of all that was lost in Eden appeared in "God of eternal truth and grace," a short poem on Micah 7:20:

God of eternal truth and grace,
Thy faithful promise seal,
Thy word, Thy oath to Abraham's race
In us, even us fulfil:
Let us to perfect love restored
Thine *image here retrieve*,
And in the presence of our Lord
The life of angels live.[166]

Again in "Lord, we long to see thy glory," a hymn on Zechariah 13:43, Wesley pulled back the veil of the *eschaton*:

Lord, we long to see Thy glory
Made eternally our own,
Long with all Thy saints to' adore Thee,
Bright as the meridian sun:
　Come, Redeemer,
Rap us to Thy Father's throne!

In Thy Father's presence own us
Faithful witnesses of Thine,
Put Thy majesty upon us,
Let us in Thy lustre shine,
Bear Thine image
All immortal, all Divine.[167]

No longer was "image" limited to the moral image. Indeed, it appeared to surpass even what was lost in Eden. In language that borders on the mystical, Wesley – referencing the assembly of the saints around the Father's throne – envisaged an eschatological attenuation of the *imago Dei* to include attributes hitherto reserved for God alone. The means to achieving this end was succinctly stated in Wesley's prayer: "Nature yield, and stronger grace / Wax stronger every hour."[168] The whole economy of grace – ending with sanctifying grace, but beginning with grace prevenient – was the secret to restoration in the image of God.

Conclusion

Theologians mining the writings of Charles Wesley are faced with several challenges, not the least of which is understanding the nature of his contribution to theological discourse. Nonetheless, it is possible to appreciate Wesley on his own terms, as a *theologos* who gave us words about God. These words – though rationally construed and cognitive – were also artistically depicted and affective. An appreciation of his spiritual journey from a driven man "fast bound in sin and nature's night" to an able communicator of justification by faith and the subsequent faith that works by love is the interpretive key to a *corpus* of literature that only now is becoming readily accessible. The frequent references to "nature" and "image" in his writing set the stage for a doctrine of grace that permeated his thinking and lifted it out of the despair of moralism. It is to the doctrine of grace – specifically, preventing grace – that this inquiry now turns.

Notes

1. For a recitation of the merits and deficiencies of Charles Wesley biographies, see Gareth Lloyd, "Charles Wesley: A New Evaluation of His Life and Ministry" (Ph.D. thesis, University of Liverpool, 2002): 4-37. The most recent biography, appearing in the *Exploring Methodism* series, is both accessible and attractively formatted, but covers familiar ground and is marred by a misquote (p. 7) of the death bed words of Samuel Wesley, Sr. to Charles, saying that religion in England would "survive" rather than "revive." See Barrie W. Tabraham, *Brother Charles* (Vol. 6 in the *Exploring Methodism* series; Peterborough: Epworth Press, 2003). Lloyd has called for a fresh biography to be written that takes into account the Kenneth Newport critical editions of the *Journal* (Abingdon, 2007) and the forthcoming *Letters* (Oxford, 2010 projected).

2. An example of this relative neglect is the infrequent attention paid to his ideas in the *Wesleyan Theological Journal*. Over the past forty years, only five articles have appeared addressing various aspects of his theology.

3. Kenneth G.C. Newport, *The Sermons of Charles Wesley: A Critical Edition with Introduction and Notes* (Oxford: Oxford University Press, 2001), 5; hereafter, *Sermons* [OE].

4. Theophilus S. Gregory, "Charles Wesley's Hymns and Poems," *London Quarterly and Holborn Review* Vol. 182 (October 1957): 253-262.

5. Lloyd, 5-6. Gareth Lloyd's conclusion appears unduly pessimistic, and ignores the depth of feeling evidenced by John shortly following his brother's death. See Frederick C. Gill, *Charles Wesley: the first Methodist* (London: Lutterworth Press, 1964), 225.

6. Frank Baker, *Charles Wesley as Revealed by His Letters* (London: The Epworth Press, 1948), 1.

7. *Charles Wesley Revealed*, 1.

8. Mabel Richmond Brailsford, *A Tale of Two Brothers: John and Charles Wesley* (New York: Oxford University Press, 1954).

9. J. Ernest Rattenbury, *The Evangelical Doctrines of Charles Wesley's Hymns* (London: The Epworth Press, 1941).

10. Brian Beck, "Rattenbury Revisited: The Theology of Charles Wesley's Hymns," *Epworth Review* Vol. 26, No. 2 (April 1999):71.

11. S.T. Kimbrough, Jr., and Kenneth G.C. Newport, eds., *The Manuscript Journal of the Reverend Charles Wesley, M.A.* (2 vols.; Nashville: Kingswood Books/Abingdon Press, 2008).

12. G. Osborn, ed., *The Poetical Works of John and Charles Wesley: Reprinted from the Originals, with the Last Corrections of the Authors; Together with the Poems of Charles Wesley not before Published* (13 vols.; London: Wesleyan-Methodist Conference Office, 1868-1872); hereafter, *Poetical Works*. See also Oliver A. Beckerlegge and S.T. Kimbrough, Jr., eds., *The Unpublished Poetry of Charles Wesley* (3 vols.; Nashville: Kingswood Books/Abingdon Press, 1988); hereafter, *Unpublished Poetry*. The critical edition of Charles Wesley's verse may be accessed online: http: //www.divinity.duke.edu/wesleyan/texts/cw_published_ verse.html.

13. *Minutes of the Methodist Conferences from the First, held in London, by the Late Rev. John Wesley, A.M., in the year 1744* (London: Thomas Cordeaux/Conference Office, 1812), 201.

14. *Unpublished Poetry*, 1:11.

15. These questions are beyond the scope of the present investigation. The interested reader should consult Frank Baker, *Charles Wesley's Verse: An Introduction* (2nd ed.; London: The Epworth Press, 1988). By the same author and equally useful is *Representative Verse of Charles Wesley* (London: The Epworth Press, 1962). See also Mark A. Noll, "Romanticism and the Hymns of Charles Wesley," *The Evangelical Quarterly* Vol. XLVI, No. 4 (Oct.-Dec. 1974): 195-223, and James Dale, "The Theological and Literary Qualities of the Poetry of Charles Wesley in Relation to the Standards of His Age" (Ph.D. thesis, University of Cambridge, 1960).

16. Rattenbury, *Evangelical Doctrines*, 89.

17. *Evangelical Doctrines*, 89-90.

18. *Evangelical Doctrines*, 93, 95. In distinction from his brother, John, who was something of a "universal man" with broad-ranging interests in fields outside divinity, including medicine, Charles was never an academic. In a revealing letter to John, written during his Oxford days, Charles confessed: "I'm very *desirous* of knowledge, but can't *bear* the drudgery of coming at it near so well as you could. In reading anything difficult, I'm bewildered in a much shorter time than I believe you used to be at your first setting out. My head will by no means keep pace with my heart, and I'm afraid I shan't reconcile it in haste to the extraordinary business of thinking." In *Charles Wesley Revealed*, 12-13. For a listing of the books contained in Charles Wesley's personal library, see Randy L. Maddox, "The Collection of Books Owned by the Charles Wesley Family," *Wesleyan Theological Journal*, Vol. 38, No. 2 (Fall 2003):175-216.

19. See especially Chapter 5, "Love perfected" (pp. 157-79) where Charles was shown to have believed that Christian perfection is granted at death, whereas John argued that believers could be entirely sanctified earlier. Ken Collins has recently underscored John's pastoral concession that many only experienced entire sanctification just prior to death, though he taught that the blessing could be granted sooner. See Kenneth J. Collins, *The Theology of John Wesley: Holy Love and the Shape of Grace* (Nashville: Abingdon Press, 2007), 304-07. Tyson was justified in observing: "Charles could take an independent course in theological matters as well; we see evidence of this in the Wesleyan revival, as he battled the forces that sought to separate the Methodists from their mother church, the Church of England." In John Tyson, *Charles Wesley on*

Sanctification: A Biographical and Theological Study (Grand Rapids: Zondervan Publishing House/Francis Asbury Press, 1986), 18-19.

20. John Rodger Tyson, "Charles Wesley's Theology of the Cross: An Examination of the Theology and Method of Charles Wesley as Seen in His Doctrine of the Atonement" (Ph.D. thesis, Drew University, 1983), 22.

21. Tyson, "Theology of the Cross," 80.

22. Frank Baker, ed., *The Works of John Wesley* (Bi-Centennial Edition; 35 vols. projected; Nashville: Abingdon Press, 1984 to present), 7:74; hereafter, *Works* [BE]. In his introduction to the collection of hymns as it appears in volume 7, Oliver Beckerlegge (p. 2) referenced hymns 231 and 232 on the attributes of God as examples of what is "speculative." However, in a hymn book containing more than 500 hymns, this was a small fraction.

23. Teresa Berger, *Theology in Hymns? A Study of the Relationship of Doxology and Theology According to* A Collection of the Hymns for the Use of The People Called Methodists [1780] (trans. Timothy E. Kimbrough; Nashville: Kingswood Books/Abingdon Press, 1995).

24. Berger, *Theology in Hymns*, 68. Though not a Methodist, Bernard Manning was effusive in his praise of the 1780 hymnbook: "This little book – some 750 hymns – ranks in Christian literature with the Psalms, the Book of Common Prayer, the Canon of the Mass. In its own way, it is perfect, unapproachable, elemental in its perfection. You cannot alter it except to mar it; it is a work of supreme devotional art by a religious genius." In Bernard Manning, *The Hymns of Wesley and Watts: Five Informal Papers* (London: Epworth Press, 1942), 14.

25. *Theology in Hymns*, 108-32. The use of the term "universalism" by Berger should not be construed to mean that all will be saved, regardless of their response to the offer of salvation. Rather, it is a reference to Christ's death, the merits of which *may* be freely appropriated by all.

26. *Theology in Hymns*, 154.

27. *Theology in Hymns*, 158.

28. *Theology in Hymns*, 173.

29. *Theology*, 174.

30. Wilma Jean Quantrille, "The Triune God in the Hymns of Charles Wesley" (Ph.D. thesis, Drew University, 1989).

31. Quantrille, 1.

32. S.T. Kimbrough, Jr., ed., *Charles Wesley: Poet and Theologian* (Nashville: Kingswood Books/Abingdon Press, 1992).

33. Kimbrough, *Poet and Theologian*, 98-100.

34. *Poet and Theologian*, 134-136. Kimbrough noted (p. 134): "He (Wesley) shares the view of those narrative theologians who view the entire Bible as a commentary on God's redemptive work in Christ."

35. See J. Ernest Rattenbury, *The Eucharistic Hymns of John and Charles Wesley* (London: Epworth Press, 1948; repr., 2nd American edition, Akron, Ohio: OSL Publications, 1996).

36. Laurence Hull Stookey, "Mentor and Contributor to Liturgical Renewal," in *Poet and Theologian*, 137-154.

37. Kenneth G.C. Newport and Ted A. Campbell, eds., *Charles Wesley: Life, Literature, and Legacy* (Werrington, Peterborough: Epworth Press, 2007).

38. Geoffrey Wainwright, "Charles Wesley and Calvinism," in *Life, Literature and Legacy*, 184-203.

39. Wainwright, 194.

40. Ted A. Campbell, "Charles Wesley, *Theologos*," in *Life, Literature and Legacy*, 265.

41. Campbell, 265.
42. Campbell, 272-273.
43. More extant material has been published in the last ten years thanks to the efforts of Kenneth G.C. Newport, S.T. Kimbrough, Jr., and Gareth Lloyd.
44. See *The Journal of Charles Wesley* (2 vols.; Staffordshire: Tentmaker Publications, 2002). A single volume journal covering 1736-1739 is available through on-line booksellers. These include *The Journal of the Rev. Charles Wesley, M.A., Sometime Student of Christ Church, Oxford, The Early Journal, 1736-1739* (new edition; Taylors, South Carolina: Methodist Reprint Society, 1977).
45. Kenneth G.C. Newport, "Charles Wesley, 'Warts and All": the Evidence of the Prose Works," in *Proceedings of the Wesley Historical Society* 56:4 (February 2008): 178-79.
46. S.T. Kimbrough, Jr., and Kenneth G.C. Newport, eds., *The Manuscript Journal of the Rev. Charles Wesley, M.A.* (2 vols.; Nashville: Kingswood Books/Abingdon Press, 2007), hereafter, *Manuscript Journal*.
47. A limited number of the letters appeared in the two volumes of 1849 edition of the *Journal*, edited by Thomas Jackson, and reprinted in 2002 by Tentmaker Publications. See endnote 44 above.
48. Kenneth Newport, NTC lecture; see also Baker, *Charles Wesley Revealed*, 3.
49. For bibliographic information, see endnote 6 in this chapter.
50. *Charles Wesley Revealed*, 1-6.
51. A foray into the remaining unpublished letters (many written in shorthand) is being undertaken by Kenneth Newport and Duke University. No publication date has been announced.
52. Of value in assessing the authenticity of sermons ascribed to Charles is Thomas R. Albin, "Charles Wesley's Other Prose Writings," in *Charles Wesley: Poet and Theologian*, 85-94.
53. See Kenneth G.C. Newport, *Sermons* [OE], 35-38.
54. It is likely that only five of the twelve sermons in this volume were actually written by Charles, the others having been copied from John. For a full discussion, see *Sermons* [OE], 71-90.
55. *Sermons* [OE], 48.
56. John Tyson made extensive references to the hymns in his research on Wesley, including in his *Charles Wesley: A Reader* (Oxford: Oxford University Press, 1989).
57. Rattenbury, *Evangelical Doctrines*, 20.
58. Neville Thomas Shepherd, "Charles Wesley and the Doctrine of the Atonement" (Ph.D. thesis, University of Bristol, 1999), 2. See also Frank Baker, *Representative Verse of Charles Wesley* (London: The Epworth Press, 1962), xi. The disagreement over the number of hymns composed stems from how one defines the word "hymn." Baker used "hymn" and "poem" synonymously. Likewise, Shepherd (p. 18) saw little difference between Charles Wesley's own use of the words. This investigation uses the terms interchangeably.
59. *Unpublished Poetry*, 1:11-12.
60. Baker, *Representative Verse*, xi.
61. A listing of these collections appears in Shepherd, 18-19. Though not the final hymnbook published by John Wesley, the 1780 *A Collection of Hymns for The Use of the the People Called Methodists* would prove to be of the most enduring value. To access .pdf versions of the Duke critical edition of the original Charles Wesley collections, see the internet address in endnote 12 (Chapter 4).
62. G. Osborn, *The Poetical Works of John and Charles Wesley: Reprinted from the Originals with the Last Corrections of the Authors; Together with the Poems of Charles*

Wesley not before Published (13 vols.; London: The Wesleyan-Methodist Conference Office, 1868-1872); hereafter, *Poetical Works.*

63. For bibliographic information, see endnote 12.

64. See internet address in endnote 12.

65. *Representative Verse*, lviii.

66. *Representative Verse*, lviii.

67. Cited by Frank Baker, *Representative Verse*, lix. For further discussion, see also John Tyson, "Theology of the Cross," 66-74.

68. John Lawson, *The Wesley Hymns as a Guide to Scriptural Teaching* (Grand Rapids: Zondervan/Francis Asbury Press, 1987), 20.

69. Shepherd, 20.

70. Of the thirteen volumes of the *Poetical Works*, all hymn translations from John or hymns by other authors, such as Watts, would barely fill one volume. The Duke University website hosting the on-line critical edition of Charles Wesley's published verse concluded: "The challenge of distinguishing between the two brothers dissipates by 1749, as Charles Wesley turned to publishing most of his verse independent of his brother's editorial hand." See http://www.divinity.duke.edu/wesleyan/texts/authorship.html.

71. Many theses, like the present inquiry, have examined Charles' theology as part of its overall topic. However, others have studied an aspect of Charles Wesley's theology, with no extended separate treatment of John. For examples, see section 3 of the bibliography.

72. *Evangelical Doctrines*, 88. Paul Ellingsworth acknowledged the strong note of personal experience in Charles' hymns, but also discerns *corporate* experience expressed by the pronoun "we." See Paul Ellingsworth, " 'I' and 'we' in Charles Wesley's Hymns," *The London Quarterly and Holborn Review* Vol. 188 (April 1963), 160-161.

73. The meaning for John Wesley of the events of May 24, 1738 has been debated extensively. Representative of this discussion is Umphrey Lee, *John Wesley and Modern Religion* (Nashville: Cokesbury Press, 1936), 83-109, and Albert C. Outler, ed., *John Wesley* (New York: Oxford University Press, 1964), 7-14. Comparatively little debate has centered around the meaning of May 21, 1738, the date of Charles Wesley's "Pentecost."

74. See *Early Journal*, 5-6.

75. A popularly written but useful biography of Susanna Wesley is Kathy McReynolds, *Susanna Wesley* (Minneapolis: Bethany House Publishers, 1998).

76. Charles Wallace, Jr., ed., *Susanna Wesley: The Complete Writings* (New York and Oxford: Oxford University Press, 1997).

77. Wallace, *Complete Writings*, 41.

78. *Complete Writings*, 370.

79. *Complete Writings*, 175-176.

80. *Complete Writings*, 175. Charles' note was appended after having received assurance of his own salvation in May of the same year. On the other hand, Susanna Wesley appears to have experienced the assurance of her salvation during an August 1739 communion service officiated by her son-in-law. See John Wesley's *Journal* entry for September 3, 1739, in *Works* [BE], 19:93-94. For a brief discussion of the meaning of this event in the context of her life-long service to God, see John A. Newton, *Susanna Wesley and the Puritan Tradition in Methodism* (2nd ed.; London: Epworth Press, 2002), 197-200.

81. For example, see Charles Wesley's sermon on Phil. 3:13-15, in *Sermons* [OE], 95-106.

82. Thomas R. Albin and Oliver A. Beckerlegge, *Charles Wesley's Earliest Evangelical Sermons: Six Shorthand Sermons now for the first time Transcribed from the Original* (Clayhall, Ilford: Wesley Historical Society, 1987), 9.

83. Albin and Beckerlegge, *Evangelical Sermons*, 10.
84. *Evangelical Sermons*, 13.
85. *Charles Wesley Revealed*, 10.
86. *Charles Wesley Revealed*, 11.
87. *Evangelical Sermons*, 21.
88. Brailsford, 116.
89. *Manuscript Journal*, 1:28; italics added.
90. *Manuscript Journal*, 1:46; italics added.
91. See Chapter 4, "Wrestling Jacob," in Tabraham, *Brother Charles*, 32-43.
92. Tabraham, 33-35. The Moravians had early on impressed the Wesleys en route to Georgia with their calm in the midst of a severe storm. See John Wesley's entry for January 25, 1735 in *Works* [BE], 18:142-143.
93. Tabraham, 35; also *Early Journal*, 130.
94. Arnold Dallimore, *A Heart Set Free: The Life of Charles Wesley, Evangelist, Hymn-writer, and Poet* (Welwyn, Hertfordshire: Evangelical Press, 1988), 58.
95. The first entry (Saturday February 18, 1738) mentioned Böhler as one in addition to a group of scholars with whom Wesley prayed. On February 20, he wrote: "I began teaching Peter Böhler English." *Manuscript Journal*, 1:97.
96. *Manuscript Journal*, 1:97.
97. *Manuscript Journal*, 1:100.
98. *Manuscript Journal*, 1:100.
99. Entry for May 17, 1738, in *Manuscript Journal*, 1:104.
100. *Manuscript Journal*, 1:106.
101. Arnold Dallimore argues that it was the now familiar "And Can it Be?" See Dallimore, 61-63.
102. From Hymn # 29, in *A Collection of Hymns for the Use of The People Called Methodists*, in *Works* [BE], 7:116.
103. *Manuscript Journal*, 1:111. It is unclear to precisely what "namesake" Charles is referring.
104. See above discussion of the sermon, *The Threefold State*.
105. The first instance appears to be on Thursday May 25: "In the evening I broke through my own great unwillingness, and at last preached faith in Christ to an accidental visitor." *Manuscript Journal*, 1:112. Entries for May 31, and June 7 and 11 are merely representative of numerous instances where the zealous evangelist testifies to his newfound conception of faith.
106. On June 1, for example, Charles confessed: "I was troubled today that I could not pray, being utterly dead at the sacrament," and the following day, he reported being "full of a cowardly desire of death." *Manuscript Journal*, 1:114.
107. See William Law, *A Serious Call to a Devout and Holy Life, Adapted to the State and Condition of All Orders of Christians* (London: William Innys, 1729). It is also available on-line: http://www.ccel.org/ ccel/law/ serious_call.html . Mabel Brailsford noted that the Holy Club at Oxford, of which Charles was a part, studied the book, and that "it became the companion of his walks, the main subject of his conversation and the book from which he read aloud to his hosts, in homes as far apart as London and New York." In Brailsford, 67. Wesley himself on October 17, 1736 – prior to his 1738 Pentecost experience – gladly accepted one's comparison of him to Law: "Glad I was and surprised to hear that good man mentioned, and confessed all I knew of religion was through him." *Manuscript Journal*, 1:58.
108. *Manuscript Journal*, 2:184; italics added.
109. *Theology in Hymns?*, 66.

110. *Compact Oxford English Dictionary*, "nature," n.p. [cited October 11, 2007]. Online: http://www.askoxford.com/concise_oed/nature?view=uk.

111. In an extended treatment of Isaiah 40, Wesley employed "nature" as a more general reference to the heavens and the created order, alluding to "nature's light." See *Poetical Works*, 2:54. This cosmological usage, however, was infrequent.

112. George H. Findlay, *Christ's Standard Bearer: A Study in the Hymns of Charles Wesley as they are contained in the last edition (1876) of* A Collection of Hymns for the Use of the People Called Methodists, *by the Rev. John Wesley, A.M.* (London: The Epworth Press, 1956), 47-48.

113. Findlay, 49.

114. Gilbert Leslie Morris, "Imagery in the Hymns of Charles Wesley" (Ph.D. thesis, University of Arkansas, 1969), 212.

115. From the collection, *Hymns and Sacred Poems* (London: William Strahan, 1739); in *Poetical Works*, 1:23. Unless otherwise noted, all italics are those of Charles Wesley.

116. *Poetical Works*, 1:105. The motif of enslavement in "nature's night" also appeared in poems portraying a believer's longing for deliverance from the "old man" and perfection in love. See the poem *Moriar ut te videam!* (Let me die that I may see Thee!) in *Poetical Works*, 2:68-69. For an interesting reversal of the enslavement metaphor, see the children's hymn "Giver of Nature's Every Gift," in *Unpublished Poetry* 3:287, where it is Satan who is "in chains."

117. From *Hymns and Sacred Poems* (London: W. Strahan, 1740), 43; hereafter, *HSP* [1740]; in *Poetical Works*, 1:239. This is one of two poems bearing the title "Another," following the poem "Before Reading the Scriptures" (1:237).

118. *Poetical Works*, 1:158-159. Other instances of "night" as a metaphor of nature include 2:68, 3:128, 137;

119. *HSP* [1740], 1; in *Poetical Works*, 1:205.

120. *Poetical Works*, 1:282.

121. Hymn LVIII, in *Poetical Works* (digital edition), 6:425-26; hereafter, *Poetical Works* [DE]. Unlike the Osborn edition, the digital edition does not include italics or indenting of alternate lines. Otherwise, the content is identical.

122. Hymn CXI, in *Poetical Works* [DE], 7:134.

123. *Poetical Works* [DE], 7:186-87.

124. *Poetical Works*, 1:287-88.

125. *Poetical Works*, 1:60.

126. *Poetical Works*, 1:301. The "guilt" would appear to be the result of one's own acts of sin. Wesley's reference to the "Ethiop" seems racially biased to the modern reader.

127. *Poetical Works*, 3:110-11; italics added.

128. *Poetical Works* [DE], 7:152; italics added.

129. *Sermons* [OE], 211-24; also in John Wesley's *Works* [BE], 1:142-58.

130. *Sermons* [OE], 213; *Works* [BE], 1:142.

131. *Sermons* [OE], 212-13; *Works* [BE], 1:142-43.

132. *Sermons* [OE], 130-51. A note of dates and places transcribed upon the manuscripts indicates that Wesley preached this untitled sermon twenty-one times. See Newport's introductory comment, 130-31.

133. See *Evangelical Sermons*, 7.

134. *Sermons* [OE], 135.

135. *Sermons* [OE], 137.

136. *Sermons* [OE], 169.

137. *Sermons* [OE], 188. Similar language appeared at the beginning of a sermon on Luke 18:9-14, where Wesley asserted that all "by nature" are like either the Pharisee or

the publican, i.e. desperately sick but "utterly senseless of his disease." See *Sermons* [OE], 270.

138. *Sermons* [OE], 189. This sermon was Wesley's clearest prose statement on the nature of original sin and the consequences of the fall. On the question of original sin remaining in believers, Wesley was in agreement with the broader stream of Wesleyan theology, where the divine work of sanctification was seen to address the problem of remaining sin. See John Wesley, *The Scripture Way of Salvation*, in *Works* [BE], 2:153-69 and *On Sin in Believers*, *Works* [BE], 1:314-34.

139. *Sermons* [OE], 119.

140. See Sermon 1 (Phil. 3:13-14) and Sermon 3 (Psalm 126:7) in *Sermons* [OE], 93-106, and 123-29.

141. *Sermons* [OE], 120; italics added.

142. *Poetical Works*, 1:105.

143. Hymn XI, in *Poetical Works* [DE], 3:24; italics added.

144. Poem on Acts 8:7, in *Unpublished Poetry*, 2:318.

145. See Hymn XVI, "Free Grace," in *Poetical Works* [DE], 3:93-94: "By nature only free to ill, / We never had one motion known / Of good, hads't Thou not given the will, / And wrought it by Thy grace alone."

146. *Christ's Standard Bearer*, 49.

147. *Poetical Works* [DE], 2:196. See also Hymn LXXXVII, in *Poetical Works* [DE], 3:278: "To Thy foul and helpless creature / Come, and cleanse All my sins; / Come, and change my nature." Examples of other instances in Wesley's hymns of the anthropological use of the word "nature" include 4:319, 466; 5:114, 251, 314; 6:425-26, 432, 437; 7:33, 60, 73; 8:29, 392; 10:23, 183, 352; 11:14, 79, 427; 12:158, 209, 333; 13:11, 17, 57.

148. *Poetical Works* [DE], 1:184.

149. *Poetical Works* [DE], 1:223.

150. *Poetical Works* [DE], 1:224.

151. *Sermons* [OE], 183-210.

152. *Sermons* [OE], 188.

153. See *Sermons* [OE], 130-151. Thomas Albin and Oliver Beckerlegge titled the sermon "The Threefold State." See *Evangelical Sermons*, 7-25. Kenneth Newport, following Charles Wesley, left the sermon untitled.

154. *Sermons* [OE], 135.

155. *Sermons* [OE], 214.

156. *Poetical Works* [DE], 1:336-37; italics added.

157. *Poetical Works* [DE], 1:337-38; italics added.

158. *Poetical Works* [DE], 2:68-69.

159. *Poetical Works* [DE], 2:92-93.

160. *Poetical Works* [DE], 2:120.

161. *Poetical Works* [DE], 7:310; italics added.

162. *Poetical Works* [DE], 12:7-8; italics added. Occasionally, hymns spoke of both regaining God's favour and image, obvious references to justification and sanctification. See for example the hymns "The God of all grace" and "The Unspeakable Grace" in *Poetical Works* [DE], 12:167-68 and 12:284-85, respectively.

163. The *Poetical Works* frequently employed the term "image," most referring to the *imago Dei* and its restoration as the *telos* of sanctification. While exhaustive treatment of this theme is outside the scope of this thesis, all thirteen volumes of the *Poetical Works* contain allusions to the restoration of the *imago Dei*. Representative poems include: 2:129, 280; 3:19, 92; 4:114, 309; 5:15, 308; 6:80, 380; 7:292, 389; 8:27, 116; 9:2, 57; 10:28, 100; 11:32, 47; 12:

164. These terms appeared in John Wesley's 1760 sermon, *The New Birth*, in *Works* [BE], 2:186-201.

165. *Poetical Works* [DE], 10:439.

166. *Poetical Works* [DE], 10:100; italics added. Even renewal in the moral image of God seemed to occur just prior to our translation to heaven: "I seek the kingdom first,/ The gracious joy and peace,/ Thou know'st, I hunger, Lord, and thirst/ After Thy righteousness; / My chief, and sole desire / Thine image to regain, / And then to join Thine heavenly choir, / And with Thine ancients reign." From the hymn "I seek the kingdom first," in *Poetical Works* [DE], 10:190.

167. Hymn # 347, in *Poetical Works* [DE], 10:275-76.

168. Hymn # 511, in *Poetical Works* [DE], 9:164.

Chapter Five

Prevenient Grace in Charles Wesley: The Contours of a Doctrine

Introduction

In what sense was Charles Wesley a theologian? What was the *imago Dei* as conceived by Charles Wesley? In his view, how had the sin of our first parents affected humanity, particularly in the arena of volition? These questions were addressed in Chapter 4 of this investigation. The current chapter builds upon this anthropological foundation, examining a cluster of themes that emerges from a study of prevenient grace in the primary sources, with an emphasis on the *Poetical Works* and the on-line Duke collection of Charles Wesley writings as important touchstones for that investigation.[1]

The Language of Preceding Grace

What is grace? Ray Dunning identified two historical definitions of this word so pervasive in Wesleyan theology. Prior to the Reformation, the emphasis was upon grace as an "ontological substance of a spiritual nature."[2] It was power for healing and good works channeled through the ecclesiastical administration of the sacraments. Martin Luther, on the other hand, emphasized grace as the divine attitude of forgiveness. John and Charles Wesley taught that justification preceded sanctification, explicating grace as both pardon and divine enablement.[3]

The dual role of grace appears in the writings of Charles Wesley. A poem on Romans 1:16 mentioned grace as pardon, but then spoke of "saving power":

> Whoe'er the joyful news believes,
> Pardon'd through instantaneous grace,
>   The saving power Divine receives;
> And while on Christ his soul he stays,
> He gains at last the perfect love,
> And mingles with the saints above.[4]

In a treatment of Romans 2:13, only grace as forgiveness appeared at first to be indicated:

> Not all that hear the word,
> But who through faith obey,
> Shall stand before their glorious Lord,
> Acquitted in that day:
>
> Who freely saved by grace,
> Their pardon here receive,
> And live the life of holiness,
> They shall for ever live.[5]

Salvation by grace was presented in close conjunction with sanctification, since the reception of pardon was followed by the "life of holiness." These two selections from Wesley are representative of his concern to hold together both understandings of grace, i.e. pardon and empowerment. Nevertheless, as he developed the idea of grace's prevenience, the notion of empowerment predominated.

Beyond a rudimentary understanding of the word "grace" in Charles Wesley's writings, one must consider the signification of "prevenient" or – as Wesley preferred – "preventing," especially as the word evolved throughout the 18th century. The *Compact Oxford English Dictionary* defined "prevent" as "to keep from happening or arising."[6] This modern derivation of the Latin *praevenire* was known by Wesley. Indeed, he used it repeatedly in his hymns and poems. In the January 1756 "A Hymn for the English in America," Wesley wrote in the seventh stanza:

> But O! *prevent* the misery;
> The ills we tremble to foresee,
> In mercy, Lord, avert.
> Our foes, when ready to devour,
> Disarm; and chase the lust of power
> From every human heart.[7]

More frequent in his writings was the older use of "prevent," meaning to go before, which is used in the King James Version (1611) for 1 Thessaalonians 4:15, where those "which are alive and remain unto the coming of the Lord shall not prevent them which are asleep." Likewise, in his 1753 short dictionary, John

Wesley defined "prevent" as "to come or go before."[8] Charles Wesley's hymn, "Meet and right it is to praise," is one example of this preponderant usage of "prevent":

> Meet and right it is to praise
> God the Giver of all grace,
> God whose mercies are bestow'd
> On the evil and the good:
> He *prevents* the creature's call,
> Kind and merciful to all,
> Makes His sun on sinners rise,
> Showers His blessings from the skies.[9]

Besides this verbal form is the adjective "prevenient." "Prevenient" appeared just twice from Charles Wesley. The first occurrence was a pneumatological reference in "May we not grant our God's request," a 1762 poem based on Deuteronomy 10:12:

> May we not grant our God's request,
> And serve Thee with an heart sincere,
> With Thy *prevenient Spirit* bless'd,
> Inspired with Thy ingenuous fear,
> And strengthen'd by sufficient grace
> To walk in all Thy righteous ways![10]

The second instance was found in a lengthy poem, "On the Death of Mrs. Mary Horton, May 4, 1786, Aged Thirty-Four":

> Her piety with life begun,
> Worshipper of the God unknown,
> She trembled and adored;
> Kept, by her parents' hallow'd cares,
> From sin, the world, and Satan's snares,
> And nurtured for the Lord.
>
> Allured by His *prevenient grace*,
> Even she walk'd in pleasant ways,
> Far from the thoughtless crowd;
> A stranger to their hopes and fears,
> Remembering, in her tenderest years,
> Her Maker and her God.[11]

Rather than the modern "prevenient," Charles Wesley preferred the traditional "preventing" when describing the activity of preceding grace. Though far from frequent, "preventing grace" appeared occasionally in Wesley's poems.[12] However, he refused to be confined to the phrase itself; instead, the contours of the doctrine of preventing grace took shape through the use of biblical metaphor in conjunction with the word "grace." These metaphors included "seed," "talent," and "light." Also, Wesley's copious poems on Scripture gave him ample opportunity to explicate prevenient grace in unexpected places, such as the star of Bethlehem, the parable of the prodigal son, and select passages from the Acts of the Apostles. Finally, it is in response to the first predestinarian controversy beginning in the late 1730s that Charles Wesley – in conjunction with his brother, John – began to formulate a crucial *via media* between moralism and deterministic theology.

Christ's Atonement: Source of Universal Prevenient Grace

For Charles Wesley, the doctrine of prevenient grace was related to the doctrine of the atonement of Christ.[13] More specifically, it was a corollary to the question of the atonement's *extent*. Was the sacrifice of Christ salvific for all regardless of their response? This was universalism. On the other hand, was Jesus' death only on behalf of the elect, i.e. those predestined by God to eternal life? This was the position espoused in Wesley's day by George Whitefield. Neither John nor Charles Wesley were satisfied with either possibility. Instead, they taught that the atonement was for all, but salvation depended upon personal response either to proclamation or – in special circumstances – to the "light" of truth one received through nature, this "light" sometimes called preventing grace.

Albert Brown-Lawson pointed to the 1739 sermon, *Free Grace*, as "the bone of contention that lead to the temporary estrangement between (John) Wesley and George (Whitefield)."[14] The sermon argued against a Calvinistic understanding of predestination.[15] Importantly, John Wesley appended his brother Charles' hymn, "Universal Redemption," to the back of the sermon.[16] The hymn reiterated many of the themes already raised in *Free Grace*. Among these was the universal love of God for all creation, a love expressed Christologically and to which one might respond through divine grace. The word "all" – signifying the expansive nature of the atonement's benefits – appeared ten times in thirty-six stanzas, as typified in the third and eighth stanzas:

> Thy darling attribute I praise,
> Which all alike may prove,
> The glory of thy boundless grace,
> Thy universal love...
>
> *For every man he tasted death,*
> *He suffer'd once for all,*
> He calls as many souls as breathe,
> And all *may* hear the call.[17]

The italicized "may" underscored that universal redemption should not be confused with universalism. While the offer of salvation was universally available, salvation remained a possibility contingent upon human response.[18] For Charles Wesley – in view of the consequences of the fall – such a response was feasible only through grace. Furthermore, in the context of the hymn, following as it did in the very next stanza, the ninth, this restoration of a measure of volition was a benefit of the atonement:

> A power to chuse, a will t'obey,
> Freely his grace *restores*;
> We all *may* find the living way,
> And call the Saviour ours.[19]

As the debate over predestination continued between George Whitefield and the Wesley brothers, Charles' hymns became an important tool inoculating the Methodist societies against the inroads of Calvinistic teaching. The 1741 *Hymns on God's Everlasting Love* was replete with teaching on the universal nature of divine love and grace.[20] The first two stanzas of the opening hymn, "Father, whose everlasting love," set the tone for the collection:

> Father, whose everlasting love
>   Thy only Son for sinners gave,
> Whose grace to all did freely move,
>   And sent him down a world to save;
>
> Help us thy mercy to extol,
>   Immense, unfathom'd, unconfin'd;
> To praise the Lamb who died for all,
>   The general Saviour of mankind.[21]

In fewer than fifty words, Charles Wesley laid down a marker affirming the expansive nature of Christ's atonement. As before, the word "all" encapsulated the vastness of divine mercy. This mercy was "immense, unfathom'd, unconfin'd," while "mercy" itself was synonymous to the "grace" already referenced at the close of the first stanza. Grace "freely moves" not to a predestined few, but to a "world." There could be no mistaking Wesley's intent. Jesus was the "Lamb" whose sacrificial death was on behalf of all humanity. He was the "general Saviour of mankind."[22]

As the hymn progressed, the third and fourth stanzas made the first explicit link between the atonement and prevenient grace:

> Thy undistinguishing regard
>   Was cast on Adam's fallen race:
> For all thou hast in Christ prepar'd
>   Sufficient, sovereign, saving grace.

> Jesus hath said, we all shall hope;
>   Preventing grace for all is free:
> "And I, if I be lifted up,
>   I will draw all men unto me."[23]

The final words were a reference to John 12:32. By invoking this Johannine passage, Wesley inexorably wed the universality and prevenience of grace. Grace did not precede salvation only for the elect; rather, it reached out without distinction to all humanity. As original sin impacted humankind irrespective of geographical boundaries, so the possibilities of grace must be available to all peoples.

The 1742 edition of the *Hymns on God's Everlasting Love* explicitly built upon the foundation laid in the 1741 collection. In "Free Grace," universal grace was predicated upon the atonement. The "God of everlasting love" and "God of universal grace" (stanza one) deferred (in verses two and three) to the action of that grace:

> 'Tis not by works that we have done,
>   'Twas grace alone his heart inclin'd,
> 'Twas grace that gave his only Son
>   To taste of death for all mankind.
>
> For every man he tasted death;
>   And hence we in his sight appear,
> Not lifting up our eyes beneath,
>   But publishing his mercy here.[24]

Stanza four spoke of Christ's death as "the fountain this of all our good," while the following verse alluded to the "general sin" that – thanks to the atonement – had been "wash'd away."[25] Nonetheless, divine mercy could only be embraced because of the presence of prevenient grace (stanzas six and seven):

> He worketh once to will in all,
>   Or mercy we could ne'er embrace,
> He calls with an effectual call,
>   And bids us all receive his grace.
>
> Thou drawest all men unto thee,
>   Grace doth to ev'ry soul appear,
> *Preventing grace* for all is free,
>   And brings to all salvation near.[26]

In one instance, Charles Wesley linked prevenient grace with the Eucharistic celebration of Christ's death.[27] On Easter Day, April 6, 1740, Wesley attended the Sacrament with a handful of others. Some appear to have been infected by quietism, or the Moravian stillness doctrine,[28] one calling the "comfort" they received following the Sacrament as originating from "the devil." Alluding to John 6:44, Wesley replied in his *Journal*: "I should less blasphemously have called it, the drawing of the Father, or preventing grace."[29]

It is clear that Charles Wesley understood Christ's atonement to be the source of universal grace. This grace was not circumscribed, extending only to a limited number of God's chosen. The "effectual call" was expansive, available to all.[30] It was not particular, but general.[31] The theological impact of Wesley's hymns was considerable. James Gordon aptly summarized the hymn writer's contribution to the debate of the time:

> Wesley's use of paradox and oxymoron and the pervasive use of his favourite inclusive "all," provide many of his hymns with theological bite and polemical edge...Applied positively to God's universal love and negatively in denying any limit to the availability or sufficiency of the atonement, these inclusive absolutes became verbal icons, words through which something of the essential nature of God is glimpsed.[32]

Yet if Christ's sacrificial death was the fountain of universal prevenient grace, how was this grace applied? This was the question of the *agency* of grace, a subject on which Wesley was hardly silent.

Prevenient Grace and Pneumatology

Timothy Smith observed: "In the religion of the Wesleys, creation theology and salvation theology had become one, in grace. And grace, for them, had become a synonym for the presence and action of the hallowing Spirit – in the universe and in the lives of God's children."[33] Smith's contention is ratified as the researcher analyzes the various hymn collections. It is striking how frequently the word "Spirit" and "grace" were juxtaposed. Often, the two were conjoined, resulting in the colorful phrase "Spirit of grace."[34] In one instance, Charles Wesley described the Holy Spirit as "the principle of grace."[35] Elsewhere, the "Spirit of his (the Lord's) grace" was described as extending to "all mankind."[36] This close linkage is evidence that - in Wesley's soteriology - prevenient grace was a colorful image depicting the activity of the Holy Spirit, the One whose indiscriminate drawing is an echo of God the Father's expansive love demonstrated at Calvary. By employing pneumatological language, Wesley was following in the tradition of the Puritan writers for whom such terminology to describe divine activity was frequent.[37]

In the first edition of *Hymns and Sacred Poems*, the second stanza of Charles Wesley's hymn on Psalm 117 acknowledged the gracious activity of the Holy Spirit in the life of the Christian:

> To him who reigns enthron'd on high,
> To his dear Son, who deign'd to die
>   Our guilt and errors to remove;
> To that blest Spirit who grace imparts,

> Who rules in all believing hearts,
>> Be ceaseless glory, praise and love![38]

In verse nineteen of "Hymn to Christ the Prophet," Charles Wesley asked the "Messias" to impart understanding *via* the Holy Spirit:

> Witness, within us place
>> The Spirit of his grace;
> Teach us inwardly, and guide
>> By an unction from above,
> Let it in our hearts abide,
>> Source of light, and life, and love.[39]

Likewise, this work of the Holy Spirit in the heart of the believer was typified in the poem "Stupendous mystery." The second of three verses celebrated God's gracious presence:

> Thy grace our souls receives
> And animates our lives,
> The Spirit from Thee proceeds,
> And sanctifies our deeds,
> Prevents, and with His power attends,
> And all in Thy great glory ends.[40]

Once again, "grace" and "Spirit" were depicted in close proximity, the Spirit portrayed as one who "prevents," i.e. goes before the Christian, providing empowerment resulting in God's glory.

Charles Wesley employed the language of grace not only when speaking of the believer, but also when describing those who are drifting from their faith. Part II of Charles Wesley's hymn on Isaiah 63 lamented that Israel "grieved the Spirit of His grace."[41] As grace increased for those who appropriate it, so it decreased for those who resisted the Spirit's correction. In Part III of the same hymn (stanzas six and seven), this waning of grace was pictured pneumatologically as the withdrawal of divine presence:

> Why then, O Lord, if ours thou art,
>> Why hast thou suffer'd us to rove?
> Withdrawn thy Spirit from our heart,
>> And left us to our want of love?

> Why hast thou hid thy lovely face,
>> And caus'd us from thy paths to err?
> Abandon'd by restraining grace
>> Our hearts were harden'd from thy fear.[42]

In stanza six, the Lord had "withdrawn" his Spirit, whereas the seventh stanza depicted our abandonment by "restraining grace." Wesley employed a parallelism between the language of the Spirit and grace that could appear to equate the two. A similar usage was found in "After a Relapse into Sin," a melancholy acknowledgment of the debilitating effect of disobedience. The fourth stanza lamented:

> Long did thy loving Spirit strive,
>   To win me over to my good;
> The spark of grace was kept alive,
>   For years amidst temptation's flood:
> I now have sinn'd it all away,
> And ended is my gracious day.[43]

The same interchangeability of "Spirit" and "grace" apparent when describing Christians or those fallen away remained evident as Charles Wesley considered the unconverted. The Third Person of the Trinity was depicted as a universal presence graciously drawing all humanity Godward. In the opening two stanzas of "Hymn for Whitsunday," even enemies of God were not excluded from the gracious influence of the Paraclete:

> Granted is the Saviour's prayer,
> Sent the gracious Comforter;
> Promise of our parting Lord,
> Jesus to his heav'n restor'd:
>
> Christ; who now gone up on high,
> Captive leads captivity,
> While his foes from him receive
> Grace, that God with man may live.[44]

In the same way, "Sinners, your hearts lift up" celebrated the coming of the Holy Spirit. The first verse spoke of the "Holy Ghost," while the second substituted the word "grace." This gift was available because Christ had died "for every man." In language evoking Peter's sermon in Acts 2:14-40, "gifts" rained down "from the skies" as "never-ceasing showers." As none are spared in a deluge, so none were exempt from the reach of grace. Verses five and six affirmed:

> All may from Him receive
>   A power to turn and live;
> *Grace* for every soul is free,
>   All may hear the' effectual call,
> All the light of life may see,
>   All may feel He died for all.

> Drop down in showers of love,
>   Ye heavens, from above;
> Righteousness, ye skies, pour down;
>   Open, earth, and take it in;
> Claim the Spirit for your own,
>   Sinners, and be saved from sin.[45]

In "Father, whose everlasting love" – a hymn already examined for its Christological significance – a significant pneumatological reference was interwoven. The fourth and sixth stanzas celebrated the free preventing grace provided for all by the atonement, while the fifth stanza explained how this grace is universally administered:

> Jesus hath said, we *all* shall hope;
>   Preventing grace for all is free:
> "And I, if I be lifted up,
>   I will *draw all men* unto me."
>
> What soul those drawings never knew?
>   With whom hath not thy Spirit strove?
> We all *must* own that God is true;
>   We all *may* feel, that God is love.
>
> O *all ye ends of earth* behold
>   The bleeding, all-atoning Lamb!
> *Look unto him* for sinners sold,
>   Look and *be sav'd* thro' Jesu's name.[46]

The realities of divine truth and love could be apprehended by all because of the ministry of the Spirit. The italicizing of "must" was Wesley's reminder that no one can claim never to have been exposed to divine truth, whereas the italicized "may" seems to have indicated that one experiences the love of God by appropriating the preventing grace that the Spirit proffers.

Charles Wesley celebrated the availability of grace more personally in "A Prayer for Holiness." The ten verse poem portrayed Wesley's longing to be perfected in love. In verse five, he passed in review the story of God's grace in his life, beginning before his conversion:

> Why hast thou on me bestow'd
>   Thy free, *preventing grace*?
> Why beheld me in my blood,
>   And call'd to seek thy face?
> Thou hast not my soul abhor'd,
>   But still with me thy *Spirit* strove:
> Help me, Saviour, speak the word,
>   And perfect me in love.[47]

As before, Wesley alternated between the use of "Spirit" and "grace" to describe the drawing action of God in relation to the unbeliever. It was because God the Holy Spirit had been faithful in administering prevenient and justifying grace that Wesley had hope of also receiving sanctifying grace from the same source.

A fascinating juxtaposition of the language of Spirit and prevenient grace occurred as an interpretation of the story of the Magi (Matthew 2:1-12). The two verse poem "Mine eyes have seen His orient star" likened the search by the Magi for the Christ child to the unbeliever's spiritual quest:

> Mine eyes have seen His orient star,
> And sweetly drawn I come from far,
> Leaving the world behind;
> His *Spirit* gently leads me on
> A stranger in a land unknown,
> The new-born King to find.
>
> The word of *all-preventing grace*
> Marks out the Saviour's natal place;
> And follower of the word,
> I keep His glimmering star in sight,
> Which by its sure unerring light
> Conducts me to my Lord.[48]

This composition is a prime example of the interchangeability by Charles Wesley of the language of Spirit and grace. In the first verse, it was "His Spirit" that "leads me on," allowing the "stranger" to discover the Christ child. The second verse omitted Spirit language, speaking instead of "all-preventing grace" which was symbolized in the narrative by the "orient star." As the Spirit led, so preventing grace "conducts me to my Lord." This "glimmering star" was characterized by a "sure unerring light." Though the use of light as a metaphor for prevenient grace was hardly unusual, this assessment of the intensity and reliability of that light appears to be more optimistic here than is typical for Wesley.[49] In any case, the linkage between prevenient grace and the ministry of the Holy Spirit is striking.[50]

What may be concluded regarding the pneumatology of prevenient grace? While Charles Wesley grounded the doctrine of universal grace in the atonement of Christ, it is clear that the language of "preventing grace" sometimes served as a poetic substitute for the initiative of the Holy Spirit. The parallelism employed by Wesley could even at times appear to confound grace and Spirit. In-light of the ongoing dialogue between those of Wesleyan and Pentecostal persuasion,[51] this grace/Spirit dynamic is an important point of contact that merits further investigation.

Beyond Prevenient Grace: Other Metaphors for Divine Initiative

Like John Wesley, Charles Wesley did not hesitate to explore multiple biblical metaphors that portrayed God's activity.[52] While the use of the word "prevenient" or "preventing" as an adjective describing grace was relatively rare in Wesley's hymns and poems, other words consonant with Scripture became powerful alternative metaphors for describing divine initiative. These words included "seed," "talent," and "light."[53]

A. "Seed" and "Talent"

One metaphor Charles Wesley employed for grace is "grain." Mark 4:31-32 had compared the kingdom of heaven to a mustard seed, and Wesley profited from this allusion to compose a three verse poem. Verse one affirmed:

> The principle of grace divine
> Sown in this earthly heart of mine,
> Is humble joy, and heavenly peace,
> And true, implanted righteousness:
> Though scarce discernible the *grain*,
> It doth the tree of life contain,
> The purity of saints above,
> And all the powers of perfect love.[54]

The entirety of the poem made it apparent that the "grain" of grace under consideration was sanctifying grace, not prevenient grace. Nonetheless, the language of "principle of grace" was important as it would be employed elsewhere by Wesley to describe earlier moments in the *via salutis*.[55]

The parable of the leaven in Luke 13:21 was another instance where the "heavenly principle" was active. Charles Wesley wrote:

> By silent, slow, unnotic'd means
>   The heavenly principle proceeds,
> And while its secret way it wins,
>   Its sanctifying virtue spreads,
> Thro' all we think, and speak, and do,
> And makes our life and nature new.
>
> Long in the heart of man conceal'd
>   And cover'd up the grace remains,
> But more and more diffus'd reveal'd,
>   O'er every bosom lust it reigns,
> Till all our powers its influence prove,
> And all our souls are peace and love.[56]

As in the previous poem, this composition spoke of grace in relation to sanctification. However, the opening language of the second verse appeared to trace back the origin of grace to an earlier time when the grace (like leaven) that was "concealed" or "cover'd up" rested in the heart of "man." His choice of words is instructive. The image was of humanity in general, and was not limited to believers. Similar to "grain," the image of leaven afforded Wesley the opportunity to say something about the subversive nature of prevenient grace. Grace unresisted – in the words of the poem, "more and more diffus'd" – would always lead to more grace. The first verse of a two verse poem on Luke 13:8-9 (the parable of the barren fig tree) showed the extent to which God was willing to lavish grace even on the resistant:

> Mild my Advocate replied,
>   'Grant him still a larger space,
> Till I for his cause have tried
>   All the methods of my grace;
> Let this barren soul alone,
> I have made his curse my own.'[57]

The word "seed" appeared in "A Father's Prayer for His Son." Verse two portrayed the father asking that his son be "restrain'd" and "prevented" by divine love. This set the stage for the fourth (and final) verse:

> Soon may the all-inspiring Dove
>   With brooding wings his soul o'erspread;
> The hidden principle of love
>   The pure, incorruptible seed
> Hasten into his heart to sow;
>   And when the word of power takes place,
> Let every blossom knit and grow,
>   And ripen into perfect grace.[58]

As seen earlier in this chapter, the Holy Spirit ("all-inspiring Dove") was intricately involved in the first workings of grace. This grace was a "seed," a promise of things to come, but imperfect. It only "ripens into perfect grace" when the "word of power" was introduced.[59] Though Wesley did not explain the signification of "word of power," it was likely a reference to preaching.

Another hymn that underscored the nature of grace as a "seed" was "Hymn for a New-Born Child."[60] Written at the birth of his first child, John, the second stanza implored heaven:

> Seize, O seize his tender heart
>   Beating to the vital war;
> Everlasting life impart,
>   *Sow the seed of glory there*:

> Grace be to my infant given,
> Grace the principle of heaven.[61]

In "At the Baptism of a Child," the metaphor of "seed" appears to have included prevenient grace but pointed beyond it to the broader work of salvation. The five stanzas of the hymn merit consideration in their entirety:

> God of eternal truth and love,
> Vouchsafe the promis'd grace we claim,
> Thine own great ordinance approve,
> The child baptis'd into thy name
> Partaker of thy nature make,
> And give her all thine image back.
>
> Born in the dregs of sin and time,
> These darkest, last, apostate days,
> Burthen'd with Adam's curse and crime
> Thou in thy mercy's arms embrace,
> And wash out all her guilty load,
> And quench the brand in Jesus' blood.
>
> Father, if such thy sovereign will,
> If Jesus *did* the rite injoin,
> Annex thy hallowing Spirit's seal,
> And let the grace attend the sign;
> The *seed* of endless life impart,
> Seize for thy own our infant's heart.
>
> Answer on her thy wisdom's end
> In present and eternal good,
> Whate'er thou didst for man intend,
> Whate'er thou hast on man bestow'd,
> Now to this favour'd babe be given,
> Pardon, and holiness, and heaven.
>
> In presence of thy heavenly host
> Thyself we faithfully require;
> Come Father, Son, and Holy Ghost
> By blood, by water, and by fire,
> And fill up all thy human shrine,
> And seal our souls for ever thine.[62]

In the light of other hymns already considered, the "seed of endless life" in the last portion of the third stanza may be construed as prevenient grace. However, this was overshadowed in the hymn by other concerns, including the washing away of the guilt of original sin (stanza two) and the granting of "pardon, holiness, and heaven" (stanza four). The *telos* of infant baptism was restoration of the *imago Dei*: "Partaker of thy nature make/And give her all thine image back" (stanza one). For Wesley, infant baptism seems to have included not only the conveyance of prevenient grace, but also the regeneration of the child.[63]

When referencing prevenient grace, in addition to the language of "seed," Charles Wesley employed the metaphor of "talent." The single verse poem, "The harmless inoffensive man," was a commentary on Matthew 25:26, the master's judgment on the wicked servant in the parable of the talents:

> The harmless inoffensive man
> Is cast before the bar of God,
> Cast by his own excuses vain
> For not performing what he could:
> And, burying that *preventing grace*,
> Who justly perish unforgiven,
> Shall mix'd with fiends in groans confess
> They might have sung with saints in heaven.[64]

In eight brief lines, Wesley established that prevenient grace was both a divine enablement and a reason for eschatological hope. The parable of the talents – and Wesley's poem – taught this from a negative perspective. It is precisely because the servant did *not* perform what he could that he was punished. The reverse implication is equally trenchant: Reward awaits those who – appropriating the talent of prevenient grace given – do what they can.

Charles Wesley again employed the talent metaphor in a lengthy poem inspired by Rev. 3:14.[65] In verse twelve of part two, Wesley affirmed that Christ's death had "bought the grace for all." The following two verses extrapolated upon this grace:

> What thou hast lent we all may use,
>   We all our talents may improve;
> We need not, Lord, thy grace refuse,
>   Or stop our ears against thy love.
>
> Thou hast obtain'd for us a power
>   Thy proffer'd mercy to embrace,
> And all may know their gracious hour,
>   And all may close with SAVING GRACE.[66]

Though the word "preventing" was absent from the hymn, significant elements of prevenient grace doctrine were embedded in the lyrics. These included:

1. *the universality of grace* – No one was excluded; everyone had talents.

2. *resistance or improvement* – Grace was resistible and could be refused. Those who did not reject divine love would receive more grace.
3. *the empowerment of grace* – As a "power," grace enabled the individual to "embrace" God's "proffer'd mercy." This construct allowed Wesley to avoid the twin errors of Pelagianism and determinism.
4. *the preliminary nature of prevenient grace* – Prevenient grace pointed beyond itself to saving grace. Use of the word "close" and the capitalization of "saving grace" emphasized the *telos* of prevenient grace, i.e. justification.[67]

Charles Wesley's use of the talent metaphor was not limited to prevenient grace. On at least one occasion, he utilized it as a reference to salvation itself. A poem on Titus 2:11 spoke to this effect, the first two verses affirming:

> We magnify the gift of God,
>   The common Saviour praise:
> A talent is on all bestow'd,
>   A seed of saving-grace.
>
> To every soul it comes unsought,
>   To raise him from his fall;
> To all it hath appear'd, and brought
>   Salvation unto all.[68]

The remainder of the poem made it clear that the "grace" of salvation had as its end nothing less than holiness, in Wesley's words, a "sinless life."[69] However, the opposite outcome was envisaged in "Burst, struggling soul, the bands of sin." The sixth verse of this eight verse poem lamented:

> Because I did receive the Seed,
>   Th'Immortal Seed of God in vain;
> The Talent of my Lord I hid,
>   And did not other Talent gain,
> I would not live, I would rebel,
> And thus from Saving Grace I fell.[70]

In his interpretation of the parable of the talents, Wesley showed a fluidity that allowed him to adapt the talent metaphor to the need of the moment. In one instance, it was prevenient grace, in another, saving grace. Where both Charles and John Wesley were consistent was in viewing the image of talent as representative of grace, wherever it may fall in the *via salutis*.

B. "Light"

Besides the metaphors of seed and talent, a third metaphor of grace employed by Charles Wesley was light.[71] In "Hymn to Christ the Prophet," stanzas four and five accentuated the universal light of Christ:

> Light of the world below,
>   Thee all mankind may know;
> Thou, the universal friend,
>   Into every soul hast shone:
> O that all *would* comprehend,
>   All adore the rising Sun.
>
> Thy chearing beams we bless,
>   Bright Sun of Righteousness:
> Life and immortality
>   Thou alone to light hast brought,
> Bid the new creation be,
>   Call'd the world of grace from nought.[72]

Unsurprisingly, where light was featured, grace was not far from view. It is the "Bright Sun of Righteousness" who had "call'd the world of grace from nought." As for John Wesley, so for Charles, the Johannine imagery of Christ as the light of the world provided a Christological underpinning for the doctrine of grace, particularly its universality.

Already considered for its presentation of the juxtaposition of the language of "Spirit" and "grace," the poem "Mine eyes have seen His orient star" also is significant for its correlation of light and prevenient grace. The second verse affirmed:

> The word of all-preventing grace
> Marks out the Saviour's natal place;
> And follower of the word,
> I keep His glimmering star in sight,
> Which by its sure unerring light
> Conducts me to my Lord.[73]

It is instructive to observe that "all-preventing grace" was not compared to noon-day sun, but rather to the weaker light of a "glimmering star." Nevertheless, this light – when augmented by "the word" – was "sure" and "unerring." By placing prevenient grace and "the word" in close proximity, Charles Wesley appeared to be acknowledging the former as preparation for the latter. As an evangelist, Wesley was careful not to undercut the role of proclamation.

Besides Christological images, Charles Wesley also used pneumatological word pictures in connection with "light." In "Hymn for Whitsunday," stanzas eight and nine depicted the Holy Spirit as a hovering dove, present at the new birth of a Christian in the same way the Spirit was present at Creation:

> Now descend and shake the earth,
> Wake us into second birth;

> Now thy quick'ning influence give,
> Blow—and these dry bones shall live!
>
> Brood thou o'er our nature's night,
> *Darkness kindles into light*;
> Spread thy over-shadowing wings,
> Order from confusion springs.[74]

A fascinating melding of Christological and pneumatological imagery unfolded in "Hymn for the Day of Pentecost." The first stanza of the hymn speaks of the Day of Pentecost. Reminiscent of Peter's sermon on that occasion (Acts 2:33), the plea was for Christ to pour out the Holy Spirit upon the gathered. The result of this outpouring (stanza five) was grace for all:

> All may from him receive
>   A power to turn and live
> Grace for every soul is free,
>   All may hear th' effectual call;
> All the *light of life* may see,
>   All may feel he died for all.[75]

Apart from the repetition of "may" – a concession to those who resist the grace of God – the stanza is significant for its explicit association of the vocabulary of "power" and "light." Furthermore, this enablement and enlightenment both sprung from the atonement of Christ ("all may feel he died for all"), an expiation that was universal in scope though not universally appropriated.

Having seen instances where Charles Wesley employed Christological and pneumatological terminology in connection with the metaphor of light, it should be noted that God the Father was not excluded from the equation. In the 1740 edition of *Hymns and Sacred Poems*, Wesley addressed a lengthy hymn to the "Father of all mankind." The theme of the hymn was the universal love of God, and the language was overtly Trinitarian. In the thirty-fourth stanza, Wesley implored:

> Shine in our hearts, Father of light;
>   Jesu, thy beams impart;
> Spirit of truth, our minds unite,
>   And keep us one in heart.[76]

This example serves as a reminder that the metaphor of light – while largely developed in the context of Son and Spirit – could also be treated by Wesley in a Trinitarian manner.

A further hymn where prevenient grace is analogous to light is "To the meek and gentle Lamb." Stanza three observed:

> Free as air thy mercy streams,
>   Thy universal grace
> Shines with *undistinguish'd* beams
>   On all the fallen race:
> All from thee a power receive
>   To reject, or hear thy call,
> All *may* chuse to die or live;
>   Thy grace is free for all.[77]

Though using neither "preventing" nor "prevenient," this hymn is arguably the most significant Charles Wesley composition addressing the function of prevenient grace.[78] As part of the 1741 collection, *Hymns on God's Everlasting Love*, Wesley was answering the claims of Calvinism, i.e. that God's mercy extended only to the elect.[79] The picture was of an awakened sinner questioning whether a claim may be made upon the mercy of God. Stanza two had already established that God was not "distant." Rather, it is possible to "feel thee near," the sole condition being "if I would." Stanza three (cited above) made a series of affirmations about God, humanity, and prevenient grace:

1. Humanity was fallen. Wesley was careful to present the divine remedy in the context of the human predicament. Original sin– though not overtly mentioned – was affirmed in the phrase "fallen race." The human predicament precluded ascribing merit to the individual for any response to divine initiative.[80]

2. God was merciful to all. In eight short lines, the word "all" appeared four times. As indicated by the adjective "undistinguished," no one was excluded from the universal offer of salvation. This was an important counterpoint to the particularistic understanding of his time, which understood Christ's atonement to be limited to the elect.

3. God's grace – freely available – was sufficient to enable a human response. The adjective used to describe grace was "universal." Divine mercy was "free as air," and grace was "free for all." However, returning to the metaphor of grace as light, it was hardly overpowering. Like "beams" illuminate the darkness, this "power" was received via God's grace. Such an enablement was sufficient to allow the possibility of favorable response, yet even this was not predetermined, as indicated by the italicized "all *may* chuse to die or live." Because of grace's universality and its restorative effects, responsibility for the outcome was not imputed to the Creator, but remained with the individual.

Charles Wesley employed light as a metaphor for prevenient grace and – as such – it appeared in a pre-conversion setting. Nonetheless, his usage of the metaphor was not limited to this *locus* in the *via salutis.*. On at least one occasion, the light of grace appeared in the context of a believer's longing to flee from sin. Based on 2 Timothy 4:5, the hymn "Watch in all things" included stanza twelve:

> My whole regard still may I place
>   On the faint ray of opening light,

(The sure prophetick word of grace)
    That glimmers thro' my nature's night.[81]

The flickering light of prevenient grace appeared not as a substitute for proclamation, but rather as preparation for "that sure prophetick word of grace," the preaching of the gospel.

Grace in the Gospels and Acts of the Apostles

In addition to the parables of the leaven (Luke 13:21) and the barren fig tree (Luke 13:8-9),[82] Charles Wesley discerned the workings of prevenient grace in other pericopes of the Gospels and Acts of the Apostles. A brief examination of these Scripture selections will now be made.

Luke 13:10-17 – A Crippled Woman Healed

In the poem "A sinner long possess'd by sin," it is fascinating how the author interpreted his own spiritual journey through the story of a woman long bent over due to demonic influence. The first stanza portrayed the common condition of humanity stemming from original sin:

> A sinner long possess'd by sin
> By Satan's power together bow'd,
> Is *utter impotence within*,
> Nor can lift up his soul to God;
> Carnal his unregenerate mind,
> Perverse his will, to evil prone,
> His soul is all to earth inclined:
> And such alas I find my own.[83]

Wesley was careful to demonstrate the total incapacity of the individual – left to his or her own meager devices – to turn Godward. The human will was "perverse," *ergo* the sinner was unable to "lift up his soul to God." Not until the second stanza was it apparent how one so devoid of spiritual wherewithal could begin the pursuit of things divine:

> But surely Thou hast cast on me
> *The eye of Thy preventing grace*,
> Hast seen my depth of misery,
> And undertook my desperate case.
> Even now I hear Thine inward word,
> Obedient to Thy sovereign will,
> Which draws and brings me to my Lord,
> And bids me wait Thy hand to feel.[84]

This "preventing grace" was described as an "inward word," that "draws and brings me to my Lord." While the Lord's will was portrayed as "sovereign," divine initiative is met by human responsiveness, i.e. Wesley described himself as "obedient." Furthermore, the final line called upon the sinner to actively "wait Thy hand to feel." The salvation encounter was far from monergistic; rather, it might be envisaged as a synergism of grace.[85]

Luke 19:1-10 – Jesus and Zaccheus

A second incident where Charles Wesley deciphered the movement of grace was found in the familiar story of Zaccheus. In the two stanza poem, "Allured by his Redeemer's love," Wesley employed the sycamore tree as a symbol of the divine call heavenward:

> Allured by his Redeemer's love,
> *Prevented by His secret grace,*
> He runs with eagerness, above
> All earthly things himself to raise,
> Surmounts the judgment of mankind,
> And leaves a scoffing world behind.
>
> He waits in hope to see and know
> The Lord in His appointed ways,
> Where Christ is wont to pass, and show
> Himself to those who seek His face,
> Who all behold His love reveal'd,
> And glory in their pardon seal'd.[86]

Besides the close identification between divine love and grace, the poem is significant for its consonance with "A sinner long possess'd by sin." Both poems prominently featured the drawing aspect of prevenient grace, and both called for human response. Zaccheus, having been "allured" and "prevented" (i.e. preceded) by the Redeemer's "secret grace" reacted positively by running "with eagerness, above/ all earthly things himself to raise." As Zaccheus climbed the tree, so Christ awaits a favorable response from all allured by his indiscriminate love.

Luke 15:20 – The Prodigal Son

Still working in Luke's Gospel, Charles Wesley's "With mercy's quickest eyes" developed via the image of the returning son a further depiction of prevenient grace. The first two verses envisioned a worried father mercifully running to meet his son:

> With mercy's quickest eyes
> His wretched son He sees,
> The prodigal far off espies,
> And pities his distress:

> At sight of human woe
> His yearning bowels move,
> The Father swiftly runs to show
> His warm paternal love.[87]

In the final two verses, the language of mercy was supplemented by "grace" that "prevents" the son's request, culminating in justification:

> A late-returning child,
> His mercy's arms embrace,
> His lips declare him reconciled,
> *His lips distilling grace*;
> The kiss dispels his fears,
> With balmy words applied,
> The self-condemning sinner hears,
> And seals him justified.
>
> Not one upbraiding word
> The pardon'd sinner grieves:
> In mercy rich his heavenly Lord
> Forgets when He forgives:
> He hears his heart's desire,
> *Preventing his request*,
> And recent from the swine and mire
> Receives him to His breast.[88]

While it would be unwise to read into this poem more doctrine than Wesley himself intended, it nevertheless incorporated some key elements of prevenient grace doctrine: 1) the initiative was with God, pictured as the father running to meet his son; 2) it was crafted with the language of *mercy*, an important synonym for grace in Wesley's lexicon; 3) the time-frame was pre-justification, which was the preferred (though not exclusive) context in Wesley for the activity of prevenient grace; and 4) when unresisted, prevenient grace resulted in acceptance with God, i.e. forgiveness or justification.

John 1:9 – "That was the true Light, which lighteth every man that cometh into the world."

Charles Wesley composed a four stanza hymn based on what was for his brother John a key text undergirding the doctrine of prevenient grace. The composition is notable for its Christological content and lack of pneumatological reference:

> True light of the whole world, appear,
> Answer in us thy character,
>   Thou uncreated Sun;

> Jesus, thy beams on all are shed,
> That all may by thy beams be led
> To that eternal throne.
>
> Lighten'd by thy interiour ray
> Thee every child of Adam may
> His unknown God adore,
> And following close thy secret grace
> Emerge into that glorious place
> Where darkness is no more.
>
> The universal light thou art,
> And turn'd to thee the darkest heart
> A glimmering spark may find;
> Let man reject it or embrace,
> Thou offerest once thy saving grace
> To me, and all mankind.
>
> Light of my soul, I follow thee,
> In humble faith on earth to see
> Thy perfect day of love,
> And then with all thy saints in light
> To gain the beatific sight
> Which makes their heaven above.[89]

Several observations are in order. First, this light was universal in nature. Its "beams" were shed upon "every child of Adam." Secondly, the light was anthropologically oriented. In other words, while emanating from Christ the Light, it operated inside the individual, as indicated in the poem by the phrase "lightened by thy interiour ray." Thirdly, its light was hardly overpowering; instead, it was feeble, a mere "spark" that was "glimmering." As a corollary of the third point, fourthly, this light may be resisted, as suggested by the words "let man reject it or embrace." Finally, when followed, this gracious light led to higher levels of grace, in Wesley's poetic turn-of-phrase, "Thy perfect day of love" or the "beatific sight." With great brevity, Wesley enumerated key elements of prevenient grace doctrine that would receive further elaboration in other hymns and poems.

John 6:44 – The Drawing of the Father

In his *Explanatory Notes Upon the New Testament*, John Wesley commented regarding this passage: "No man can believe in Christ, unless God give him power. He draws us first by good desires, not by compulsion, not by laying the will under any necessity; but by the strong and sweet, yet still resistible, motions of his heavenly grace."[90] Charles Wesley appeared to agree with his brother's interpretation, as evidenced by his poem, "Father Thou hast our hearts inclined." The first verse extolled these "powerful drawings":

> Father Thou hast our hearts inclined,
> Or we had never sought Thy Son
> We still Thy powerful drawings find,
> And cannot rest in grace begun;
> Till Thou Thine own desires fulfil,
> And Jesus in our hearts reveal.[91]

In the second verse, the role of prevenient grace was introduced:

> To this, O God, Thou hast us wrought,
> That now we might Thy Son confess;
> Led by *preventing grace* and taught,
> Add us to Jesu's witnesses;
> Command the light of faith to shine,
> And fear gives place to love Divine.[92]

For the younger Wesley, "preventing grace" was a word picture describing divine initiative, a depiction of God's desire to lead and to teach. This leading was equivalent to the "drawings" already referenced in the poem's first verse, and the object to whom one was led was Jesus himself. The individual drawn to Christ already received a rudimentary instruction. That all of this occurred prior to conversion was intimated by the phrase "command the light of faith to shine".[93] Furthermore, the "powerful drawings" originating from the Father had to be met by the response of the individual, as implied by the phrase "cannot rest in grace begun." For Wesley, God graciously empowered, but did not overwhelm; God enabled yet did not coerce.[94]

John 12:32 – Christ Is Lifted Up

In volume two of the 1762 *Short Hymns on Select Passages of the Holy Scriptures,* Charles Wesley included a single verse poem that sees in the atoning work of Christ a universal guarantee of "all-attracting grace":

> The promise made our fallen race,
>   And by the blood of Jesus seal'd,
> The word of all-attracting grace,
>   I find ten thousand times fulfill'd:
> But, Lord, I want *the sight* above,
>   The grace to saints triumphant given;
> Draw by the cords of perfect love,
>   And draw me to thyself in heaven.[95]

It is significant that the promise of "all-attracting grace" was intricately linked with the language of love, a "perfect love" that like "cords" drew individuals to heaven. Love and grace for Wesley were two closely related concepts; where one is found, the other was never far away.

Acts 9:3 – Saul on the Road to Damascus

In "At the conversion of Saul," Charles Wesley came as close as he would to making grace a *force majeure* that negated personal response. In this poem just two verses in length, Wesley observed:

> He doth not seek the light,
> Or labour or inquire,
> It shines into his deepest night
> *Preventing* his desire;
> Not waiting for his call
> It stops his mad career:
> And thus the grace which ransoms all
> Doth once to all appear.
>
> It visits us unsought
> That first *celestial ray*,
> *Preventing* every serious thought
> And every wish to pray;
> We no advances make
> To meet the God unknown,
> Till mercy doth our souls attack
> And seizes for its own.[96]

The poem began with the previously discussed metaphor of light shining into Saul's "deepest night." This "light" symbolized the "grace which ransoms all" and that appeared universally.[97] The word "preventing" (employed twice) underscored the divine initiative, while "mercy" in the second verse paralleled "grace" in the earlier section. What is most surprising is the vociferous language Wesley mustered to describe the salvation encounter, particularly the personification given to "mercy." God's grace was far from passive; it attacked and seized the hapless traveler, an individual who had made "no advances to meet the God unknown." Furthermore, the story was not particular to Saul, but applied to all humanity, as made apparent from the use of "us" and "we." Wesley clearly discerned in this narrative a soteriological paradigm for all and not an historically isolated incident. Far from being resistible, this mercy that brings salvation would appear to be irresistible.

What should be made of this poem? It should be acknowledged that Charles Wesley was not alone in his interpretation, but was in agreement with John Wesley that grace can seem irresistible. In his *Journal* for August 23, 1743, attempting to find common ground with George Whitefield and his followers, the elder Wesley wrote:

> With regard to the second, irresistible grace, I believe, that grace which brings faith and thereby salvation into the soul, is irresistible at that moment; that most believers may remember some time when God did irresistibly convince them of sin that most believers do at some times find God irresistibly acting upon their souls; Yet I believe that the grace of God both before and after those moments, may be, and hath been, resisted; and that, in general, it does not act irresistibly, but we may comply therewith or may not.[98]

Assessing the issues involved, Kenneth Collins affirmed that – while saving grace could be resisted – prevenient grace is irresistible, i.e. no individual can choose to *not* receive "graciously restored faculties."[99] Collins' interpretation, though consistent with the consensus of Wesleyan theology, neglected the *saving* nature of the grace under consideration. As such, it resolved neither the difficulties of the *Journal* selection nor those of Charles Wesley's poem. John's remarks – hedged in by qualifications – were not duplicated in other settings, and Charles only addressed the Damascus Road experience in this isolated passage. The conclusion would seem justified that these are anomalous citations, discordant with the whole tenor of the brothers' teaching on prevenient grace.

Acts 10:34-35 – The Conversion of Cornelius

Another pericope from the Acts of the Apostles that Charles Wesley viewed through the lens of grace was the story of Cornelius. The two-verse poem, "God is not partial in His love," critiqued the doctrines of reprobation and limited atonement:

> God is not partial in His love,
> Nor e'er decreed a few to' approve
> And all the rest pass by;
> Whole nations unredeem'd to leave,
> Who never can His grace receive,
> But must for ever die.
>
> The Lord to every soul is good,
> For every soul He shed His blood,
> That each might pardon find;
> His, and the common Saviour praise,
> The God of *free, unbounded grace*,
> The Friend of all mankind.[100]

This poem is significant, for it grounded the expansiveness of divine mercy not only in the atonement ("For every soul He shed His blood") but also in the very character of God. The divine nature was love without partiality; integral to this concern was the lavish grace described as both "free" and "unbounded."

Only such a grace could merit for God in Christ the exalted title of "Friend of all mankind."

A second poem inspired by the Cornelius narrative was "The everlasting gospel hear." This four verse composition grappled with some of the missiological implications of prevenient grace. Verses one and two introduced the topic:

> The everlasting gospel hear
> To neither time nor place confined,
> Whoe'er thou art thy Maker fear,
> The awful Father of mankind,
> > The great and bountiful, and wise,
> > Who made, and rules both earth and skies.
>
> The sovereign Cause and End of all,
> > Who justly claims His creature's heart,
> On Him with pious reverence call,
> From all acknowledged ill depart,
> And, *true to thy imperfect light*,
> Do what thy heart approves as right.[101]

Charles Wesley broached his subject cosmologically. God was pictured as the creator and ruler of "both earth and skies," the "Cause and End of all." The "everlasting gospel" might be discerned by the "creature." This "gospel" was limited neither by history nor geography since the reality of this "awful Father" who was "great and bountiful, and wise" could be deduced from the *cosmos*. Like Cornelius, others might live a life of "pious reverence" by remaining "true to thy imperfect light." As already discovered, "light" was a metaphor for divine initiative. Significantly, Wesley described it as "imperfect," yet even in its imperfection God's grace could guide the seeker who was sincere. The final two verses further developed this theme, but with a crucial Christological caveat:

> While thy religious actions show
> The principle of secret grace,
> Led by a Friend thou dost not know
> In all the paths of righteousness,
> Heathen, Mahometan, or Jew,
> Thy soul is safe, as God is true.
> Surely thou dost even now partake
> The grace and favour of thy God,
> Accepted for His only sake
> Who bought the nations with His blood;
> And when He makes thy pardon known,
> Thou know'st that God and Christ are one.[102]

Whereas prevenient grace was symbolized in verse two by "light," the third verse adopted the familiar language seen elsewhere, i.e. "principle of secret grace." As the adherent of non-Christian religions followed this principle, walking in "all the paths of righteousness," there could be no doubt regarding his or her destiny. Their eternal safety was guaranteed by the "Friend" whose character one may trust: "Thy soul is safe, as God is true." Nevertheless, as obedience to light would always brings more light, so prevenient grace pointed beyond itself to the "pardon" provided through the atonement of Christ. Inevitably, the God-fearing individual who received forgiveness through Christ would come to understand that "God and Christ are one." The light of prevenient grace – though imperfect – would always when unresisted lead to Christ who is the Light.

In this hymn, we have one of the clearest statements from Charles Wesley on the fate of those who have not heard the gospel message. His interpretation was consistent with his understanding of the parable of the talents (Matthew 25), as discussed earlier. Each will be judged according to the measure of "light" (or number of talents) one receives. Wesley's position accorded with that of Robert Barclay, who also was optimistic about the destiny of the righteous living in areas untouched by the Christian message.[103] Though the hymn made no mention of preaching, this was likely the way by which God "makes thy pardon known," though it was unclear to what extent the Wesley brothers took an interest in preaching missions beyond the countries immediately nearby (Scotland, Wales, and Ireland) or the colonies in North America.

Acts 13:48 – Ordained to Eternal Life

Charles Wesley did not hesitate to interpret a Scripture portion that is problematic from a Wesleyan theological standpoint: "And when the Gentiles heard this, they were glad, and glorified the word of the Lord: and as many as were ordained to eternal life believed" (Acts 13:48, KJV). In "Ordain'd, prepared, disposed," Wesley noted in the first of three verses:

> Ordain'd, prepared, disposed
> By His *preventing grace*,
> With Christ they gladly closed,
> The Friend of human race;
> Their proffer'd Saviour they received,
> And every open'd heart believed.[104]

The second and third verses continued:

> Saviour and Friend of men
> Be still benignly near,
> And us to life ordain
> Who now Thy gospel hear,
> Incline us to depart from sin,
> And thus Thy grace and glory win.

> Our broken hearts prepare
> By deepest poverty,
> And then by entering there
> Fulfil Thine own decree
> That every penitent may find
> The' eternal Life of all mankind.[105]

For Wesley, "preventing grace" metaphorically referred to the universal initiative of God, leading "every open'd heart" to believe. Because God acted first, they "gladly closed" with the "Friend of human race." It was "every penitent" who could find the "eternal life" offered to "all mankind." This hymn was a moderately successful riposte to the particularistic understanding of salvation characteristic of predestinarian theology.

Acts 17:11-12 – The Bereans Search the Scriptures

A final selection from the second part of Luke's account took place in Berea, where some searched the Scriptures and believed. Using the text as a platform, Charles Wesley's poem, "Can we in unbelievers find," gathered together some of the themes regarding prevenient grace already examined in this chapter. Containing four verses, the first verse posed a theologically pertinent question:

> Can we in unbelievers find
> That noble readiness of mind
> To hear, investigate, and prove
> The truth of Jesus' pardoning love?
> Yes, Lord; *through Thy preventing grace*,
> There are who cordially embrace
> The joyful news of sins forgiven,
> With God Himself sent down from heaven.[106]

The second verse alluded to the effect of preventing grace and the reading of Scripture, namely, one was stirred-up from the "sleep of nature," a reference to the spiritual insensitivity resulting from original sin.[107] After a distracting polemic against the Roman Catholic Church in the third verse,[108] Wesley capped the poem in verse four with an appeal:

> Turn, sinners, turn from such away,
> And rather God than man obey,
> The Scriptures search both day and night,
> And try if what ye hear be right;
> Put forth your grain of gracious power,
> (Your use of that shall bring ye more,)
> Till the true Light Himself impart,
> And breathes the Witness in your heart.[109]

When compared with the poem "Ordain'd, prepared, disposed," this composition was superior in its explication of the action of prevenient grace. It was the responsibility of the "sinner" – enabled by preventing grace – to "turn" from error. This graciously enabled response was painted in metaphorical terms as a "grain" of "gracious power." Significantly, utilization of this measure of grace resulted in the reception of additional enablement: "Your use of that shall bring you more." Changing metaphors, Wesley alluded to the "true Light" imparted by Christ. Through these metaphorical means, the poet softened a stark monergism, carefully balancing divine initiative and human response. Though marred by its unfortunate ecclesiastical prejudice, the poem succeeded in briefly and effectively summarizing several of the author's most important emphases related to the prevenient grace concept.

The Function of Prevenient Grace in Charles Wesley's Theology

Having inductively examined the raw data on prevenient grace in Charles Wesley's writings, it may be asked: *What was the function of prevenient grace in Wesley's theology?* Four responses to this question emerge:

A. Prevenient grace depicted God's restoration of a measure of volition to the individual, allowing for repentance. In the ninth stanza of "Free Grace," Charles Wesley presented the dilemma and hinted at its resolution:

> By nature only free to ill,
>   We never had one motion known
> Of good, hadst thou not given the will,
>   And wrought it by thy grace alone.[110]

As one who subscribed to the traditional understanding of original sin, Charles Wesley needed a biblical mechanism other than predestination that would provide for the possibility of conversion without ascribing merit to the individual. This "third way" was prevenient grace, which restored volition sufficient for responding to the offer of salvation:

> A power to chuse, a will t' obey,
> Freely his grace *restores*;
> We all *may* find the living way,
> And call the Saviour ours.[111]

Wesley similarly affirmed that "He worketh once to will in all,/ Or mercy we could ne'er embrace."[112] Likewise, prevenient grace received from Christ made turning away from sin a possibility:

> All may from him receive
> A power to turn and live;

> Grace for every soul is free,
>   All may hear th' effectual call;
> All the *light of life* may see,
>   All may feel he died for all.[113]

Wesley contended in another hymn that "through grace we take the purchas'd grace."[114] Elsewhere, a poem on 1 Chronicles 38:9 queried:

> Do we not all from thee receive
> The dreadful power to seek, or leave?
> The dreadful power thro' grace I use,
> And chose of God, my God I chuse:
>
> Thee will I seek while life shall last;
> Ah! Do not from thy presence cast,
> But now, e'en now be found of me,
> And let my soul be hid in thee.[115]

In every instance, grace was the prevenient power enabling one to respond to the salvation offer.

B. Non-resistance to God's prevenient activity was an invitation to further divine influence. That divine overtures could be resisted was undeniable, from Charles Wesley's vantage point. In stanza thirteen of a hymn on 1 Timothy 2:4, he advised:

> Thy mercy then takes place,
> We find that love thou art,
> When we *no more resist thy grace*,
>   And harden not our heart.
> Answer, if this be true,
>   Thy counsel now fulfil,
> On me for good some token shew,
>   O! Work in me to will.[116]

Addressing the same Scripture passage, Wesley spoke elsewhere of the possibility of grieving the Spirit and "shutting out thy light."[117] A hymn on Isaiah 6 developed this same theme in the context of idolatry. Verses twenty-three and twenty-four described the prophet's lament:

> Ye fear to use the grace ye have,
>   Ye dare not with your God comply,
> Ye will not suffer him to save,
>   But salvable resolve to die.
>
> Against the truth ye stop your ears,
>   Ye shut your eyes against the light,

> And mock your Saviour's cries and tears;
> And perish in his love's despight.[118]

Nonetheless, there are those who responded favorably to the overtures of the alluring grace of God. Stanza two of "In Doubt" was a believer's retrospective on the pre-conversion divine/human interchange:

> Allur'd by unresisted grace,
>   Thy footsteps why did I pursue?
> Why did I ever seek thy face?
>   What secret power my spirit drew
> After I knew not whom to run?
> Speak, Father; am I not thy son?[119]

The remainder of the poem showed that prevenient grace was the doorway to justifying grace, symbolized by the language of sonship. Furthermore, as established earlier during analysis of Charles Wesley's poem on the Bereans (Acts 17:11-12), use of their "gracious grain of power" precipitated more grace. For Wesley, this kind of cooperation with God's gracious activity was analogous to leaven (Luke 13:21) that works its way through the whole loaf. Positive use of grace resulting in additional divine enablement was also evident post-conversion. The fourth verse of the poem "At Parting" exhorted:

> Closer, and closer let us cleave
>   To his belov'd embrace,
> Expect his fulness to receive,
>   And *grace to answer grace*.[120]

Whether speaking of prevenient grace prior to justification or grace generally at later points in the *via salutis*, it is apparent that grace utilized was grace multiplied.

C. God preveniently restrained us from sin. This function of grace was most obvious in the third stanza of Hymn XXVI from *Hymns for the Use of Families*:

> In soft compassion mind us,
>   If e'er we go astray,
> And speak the word behind us
>   "Return, this is the way!"
> *Restrain our will* consenting
>   To sin and misery,
> And thro' thy *grace preventing*,
>   Allure us back to thee.[121]

Similarly, in the second verse of "A Father's Prayer for His Son," the language of love stood in for that of grace:

> Not yet by the commandment slain
> O may he uncorrupted live,
> His simple innocence retain,
> And dread an unknown God to grieve:
>
> *Restrain'd, prevented* by thy love
> Give him the evil to refuse,
> And feel thy drawings from above,
> And good, and life, and virtue chuse.[122]

Likewise, in "Free Grace," prevenient grace seems to be indicated in stanza fourteen:

> Grace only doth from sin restrain,
> From which our nature cannot cease,
> By grace we still thy grace retain,
> And wait to feel thy perfect peace.[123]

Prevenient grace emerged more clearly in the poem, "At sending a son to school":

> Hedge up his way with legal thorns,
> With *previous grace*, and pious fear;
> When to the right, or left he turns,
> Let him thy warning Spirit hear;
> Restrained from every outward ill,
> From all iniquity depart,
> Till Thou thy dying love reveal,
> And stamp thy Name upon his heart.[124]

A composition with a similar tone was the December 11, 1788 "A Birthday Hymn." Passing his childhood in review, Wesley reminisced in the second of four stanzas:

> In the slippery paths of youth
> Led by *all-preventing grace*,
> Govern'd by the word of truth,
> Jesus, I thy hand confess,
> Wonderful in guardian power,
> Thee with all my soul adore.[125]

Broader than God's care for individuals, Ray Dunning ascribed to prevenient grace a preserving influence in the world, akin to Calvinism's common grace.[126] This interpretation does not find strong support in Charles Wesley's writings, though the passages cited above would not preclude it.

D. God has graciously taken the initiative, preparing us for Gospel preaching. The final three stanzas of "Free Grace" juxtaposed preaching and the drawing symbolized by prevenient grace:

> He promised all mankind to draw;
>   We feel Him draw us from above,
> And preach with Him the gracious law,
>   And publish the DECREE OF LOVE.
>
> Behold the all-atoning Lamb;
>   Come, sinners, at the gospel call;
> Look, and be saved through Jesu's name;
>   We witness He hath died for all.
>
> We join with all our friends above,
>   The God of our salvation praise,
> The God of everlasting love,
>   The God of universal grace.[127]

One might expect one who emphasized God's prevenient activity to have minimized the importance of preaching. If God is drawing sinners to Christ through the ministry of the Holy Spirit, then of what use is gospel proclamation? Yet in this hymn, the preaching of the "gracious law" – a fascinating choice of words in itself – was to follow and supplement these heavenly drawings.[128] The "DECREE OF LOVE" was to be "published." As seen previously during the discussion of the seed metaphor, prevenient grace would ripen, but this depended upon the introduction of the "word of power."[129] While vital, prevenient grace was preparatory, a breaking up of the "soil" preparing it for the "seed" of *kerygma*. This was consistent with the interpretation given by Charles Wesley to biblical accounts like that of Cornelieus (Acts 10).

Conclusion

Charles Wesley – particularly in the early years of the Methodist Revival – was a powerful force as both evangelist and poet. His muse set to music important doctrines that would have remained far more obscure had only John Wesley's sermons and other writings been propagated. Among these doctrines was that of prevenient grace. With Christological and pneumatological language as an important theological backdrop, the younger Wesley was able to "paint" a tableau of grace, a metaphor for divine initiative that Wesley developed via other biblical metaphors, namely, "seed," "talent," and "light." Charles was not unique in his usage of these word pictures. As has been shown in earlier chapters of this inquiry, they were used by others, including Robert Barclay and John Wesley. Nonetheless, by composing hymns and poems on numerous Bible passages in addition to John 1:9 – his brother's preferred proof-text – Charles reinforced the biblical basis on which the prevenient grace concept could be defended. This contribution to the development of the doctrine of grace is significant, and to-date, has been overlooked.

Notes

1. See G. Osborn, *The Poetical Works of John and Charles Wesley: Reprinted from the Originals, with the Last Corrections of the Authors; Together with the Poems of Charles Wesley not before Published* (13 vols.; London: Wesleyan-Methodist Conference Office, 1868-1872); hereafter, *Poetical Works*. The Duke Collection entailing eighty Charles Wesley primary sources in .pdf format may be accessed on-line: http://www.divinity.duke.edu/ wesleyan/texts/cw_published_verse.html.

2. H. Ray Dunning, *Grace, Faith, and Holiness* (Kansas City, Missouri: Beacon Hill Press, 1988), 456.

3. John and Charles Wesley as a rule did not present grace in the pre-Reformation manner described by Dunning, though the 1746 sermon, *The Means of Grace*, employs some substantival language. See endnote 27 below. On occasion, Charles appeared to make grace a parallel entity operating in conjunction with but separately from the Holy Spirit.

4. *Poetical Works* [DE], 13:3-4;

5. *Poetical Works* [DE], 13:4-5.

6. "Prevent," in the *Compact Oxford English Dictionary* [cited November 27, 2007], Online: http://www.askoxford.com/concise_oed/prevent?view=uk.

7. In *Poetical Works* [DE], 6:50, italics added. Other modern uses of the term included 6:80, 7:52, 72, and 10:238.

8. See "prevent" in *The Complete English Dictionary, Explaining most of those Hard Words, Which are found in the Best English Writers, By a Lover of God English and Common Sense* (London: W. Strahan, 1753).

9. Charles Wesley, *Hymns for the Use of Families* (Bristol: Pine, 1767), 13; italics added; also in *Poetical Works*, 7:16. For other instances of this usage, see 6:421; 7:131, 133, 176; 10:224, 263; 12:21, 116, 234; 13:265.

10. Charles Wesley, *Short Hymns on Select Passages of the Holy Scriptures* (2 vols.; Bristol: Farley, 1762), 1:98, italics added; hereafter, *Scripture Hymns*; also, *Poetical Works*, 9:101.

11. *Poetical Works* [DE], 6:357-58. The tribute also appeared in the *Arminian Magazine* (1783), pp. 108ff.

12. See *Poetical Works*, 2:275, 3:3, 94; 9:274; 10:142, 11:218; 12:285, 333.

13. John Rutherford Renshaw observed: "The Wesleys' understanding of the application of the atonement to the life and experience of man began with what they called prevenient or preventing grace. They clearly taught that, prior to the soul's conscious experience of God's saving grace, divine grace is operating powerfully, though not irresistibly, for the true well-being of all men." In John Rutherford Renshaw, "The Atonement in the Theology of John and Charles Wesley" (Ph.D. thesis, Boston University, 1985), 150-51.

14. Albert Brown-Lawson, *John Wesley and the Anglican Evangelicals of the Eighteenth Century: A Study in Cooperation and Separation With Special reference to The Calvinistic Controversies* (Edinburgh: The Pentland Press, 1994), 163. See also Allan Coppedge, *Shaping the Wesleyan Message: John Wesley in Theological Debate* (Nappanee, Illinois: Francis Asbury Press/Evangel Publishing House, 2003), 45-67.

15. For further analysis of the sermon, see Chapter 3 of this inquiry.

16. See John and Charles Wesley, *Hymns and Sacred Poems* (London: Strahan, 1740), 136-42; hereafter, *HSP* [1740]; see also *The Works of John Wesley,* Bi-Centennial

edition (Frank Baker, ed. 35 vols. projected. Nashville: Abingdon Press, 1984 to present), 1: 559-63; hereafter, *Works* [BE]. Other editions of *Hymns and Sacred Poems* appeared in 1739 and 1742, hereafter *HSP* [1739] and *HSP* [1742].

17. *HSP* [1740], 136-37.

18. The reality of varied responses to the gospel offer was elsewhere affirmed by Charles Wesley: "Thy grace for all is free,/Tho' all accept it not,/To every sinner and to me/It hath salvation brought." In Hymn VII, *Hymns on God's Everlasting Love* (London: Strahan, 1742), 22; hereafter, *HGEL* [1742].

19. *HSP* [1740], 137.

20. See *Poetical Works*, 3:1-96; also, Charles Wesley, *Hymns on God's Everlasting Love; To Which is Added the Cry of a Reprobate and the Horrible Decree* (Bristol: Farley, 1741); hereafter, *HGEL* [1741].

21. *HGEL* [1741], 3; *Poetical Works*, 3:3.The frequent italicising was Wesley's and conveyed the sense of urgency behind his words.

22. The grace "free for all" theme also appeared in a hymn on Isa. 55, in *HSP* [1740], 1-6.

23. *HGEL* [1741], 3; *Poetical Works*, 3:3. This appears to be the first time the phrase "preventing grace" was used by Charles Wesley. See also 3:94.

24. *HGEL* [1742], 50; *Poetical Works*, 3:93

25. This seems to be a reference to the guilt of original sin.

26. *HGEL* [1742], 51; *Poetical Works*, 3:94; italics added. Note the allusion to John 12:32, already seen in the previous hymn examined. See also Hymn 9 on pp. 26-28 of the same collection, especially the final stanza: "Surely thy dying prayer is heard,/God for thy sake hath all forgiven,/Grace hath to all mankind appear'd,/And all *may* follow it to heaven."

27. This theme is surprisingly undeveloped in Charles Wesley's theology. An analysis of Ernest Rattenbury's *The Eucharistic Hymns of John and Charles Wesley* (second edition; Akron, Ohio: OSL Publications, 1990, 1996), for example, shows little connection between the celebration of the Lord's Supper and prevenient grace. Charles' remark following the April 6, 1740 taking of Sacrament was consistent with his brother John's view that the Lord's Supper was one of the "*ordinary* channels whereby he might convey to men preventing, justifying, or sanctifying grace." See *The Means of Grace* (1746), in *Works* [BE], 1:381; also discussion in Chapter 3 of this investigation.

28. Other than the ongoing conflict with predestinarians, early Methodism's clash with quietism was significant, and included the Wesley brothers' split from the Fetter Lane Society in late July 1740. See Collins, *John Wesley: A Theological Journey* (Nashville: Abingdon Press, 2003), 110-14. Reginald Ward and Richard Heitzenrater noted that Charles appears to have been tempted by quietism for a short period, but was dissuaded in part by Lady Huntingdon. From John Wesley's *Journal*, in *Works* [BE], 19:179, fn. 5. See especially John Wesley's *Journal* entries for January 22 and February 12, 1741.

29. S.T. Kimbrough, Jr., and Kenneth G.C. Newport, eds., *The Manuscript Journal of the Rev. Charles Wesley, M.A.* (2 vols.; Kingswood Books/Abingdon Press, 2007), 1:235; hereafter, *Manuscript Journal.*

30. By using "effectual call," Wesley had co-opted a Calvinistic term, reshaping it with his own meaning. For the individual application of what Wesley elsewhere calls "condescending grace," see the poem "The Resignation," in *HSP* [1740], 76-79.

31. See for example *HGEL* [1741], 32, stanza 6, where Wesley spoke of "general grace." The same phrase appeared in *HGEL* [1742], 38, 55, 57; also, *HSP* [1742], 171, 282, 283. Universal redemption also figured in his extemporaneous sermons. Having preached on John 12:32, Wesley noted in his *Journal* for May 7, 1741: "Was I to search

after the strongest Scriptures for universal redemption, I could not choose so well as Providence chooses for me." *Manuscript Journal*, 1:305.

32. James G. Gordon, "Impassive He Suffers, Immortal He Dies: Rhetoric and Polemic in Charles Wesley's Portrayal of the Atonement," *Scottish Bulletin of Evangelical Theology* Vol. 18, No. 1 (Spring 2000), 69.

33. Timothy L. Smith, "The Theology of the Wesleys' Hymns," in *A Contemporary Wesleyan Theology: Biblical, Systematic, and Practical* (2 vols.; ed. Charles W. Carter, R. Duane Thompson, and Charles R. Wilson: Grand Rapids: Zondervan/Francis Asbury Press, 1983), 2:1014.

34. See for example the fifteenth stanza of Hymn 1, in *HGEL* [1742], 6: "The Spirit of thy grace and love/ Never, no never yet subdu'd/ A more rebellious worm than me/Or gained an harder victory."

35. See stanza three of Hymn III, in John and Charles Wesley, *Hymns of Petition and Thanksgiving for the Promise of the Father* (Bristol: Farley, 1746), 5.

36. See stanza three of Hymn IX, in *Promise of the Father*, 14.

37. For further development of this theme, see Chapter 1.

38. *HSP* [1739], 139; *Poetical Works*, 1:124.

39. *HSP* [1740], 146; *Poetical Works*, 1:319. A hymn on Psalm 5:7, "Assisted by preventing grace," appears to be an anomaly, making no mention of the Holy Spirit in conjunction with prevenient grace: "Assisted by preventing grace,/ I bow me toward the holy place,/ Faintly begin my God to fear,/ His weak, external worshipper…" See Hymn # 787, in Charles Wesley, *Short Hymns on Select Passages of the Holy Scriptures* (2 vols.,; Bristol: Farley, 1762), 1:253; hereafter *Scripture Hymns;* also, *Poetical Works*, 9:274.

40. *Poetical Works*, 12:21.

41. *HSP* [1742], 11; *Poetical Works*, 2:58.

42. *HSP* [1742], 13; *Poetical Works*, 2:60.

43. *HSP* [1742], 59; *Poetical Works*, 2:109. The metaphor of a "spark" is evaluated later in this chapter.

44. *HSP* [1739], 213; *Poetical Works*, 1:189.

45. *HSP* [1742], 168; *Poetical Works*, 2:230; italics added.

46. *HGEL* [1741], 3; *Poetical Works*, 3:3-4.

47. *HSP* [1742], 220; *Poetical Works*, 2:275, italics added. The next verse of the poem spoke of the "work of faith begun," a clear reference to justification by faith. This helps situate the reference to "preventing grace" as prior to conversion.

48. *Poetical Works* [DE], 10:142, italics added.

49. For further analysis of this hymn, see discussion below of Charles Wesley's use of light as a metaphor for prevenient grace.

50. See also stanzas five and six of Hymn XVII, in Charles Wesley, *Hymns for the Nativity of our Lord* (London: Strahan, 1742), 22-23, where Christ's Spirit "glimmering in our hearts" is analogous to grace that draws from "afar," a "ray divine."

51. The 2008 meeting of the Wesleyan Theological Society, held at Duke University, explored themes of common interest to Wesleyans and Pentecostals.

52. Since "grace" itself is a metaphor of divine activity, then Wesley's use of "seed," "talent," and "light" should be considered additional ways of talking about God's initiative.

53. It is significant that these metaphors ("seed," "talent," and "light") also appeared in the *Apology* of Robert Barclay. For further discussion, refer to Chapter 2 of this inquiry.

54. Oliver A. Beckerlegge and S.T. Kimbrough, Jr., eds., *The Unpublished Poetry of Charles Wesley* (3 vols.; Nashville: Kingswood Books/Abingdon Press, 1988), 2:55-56; italics added; hereafter, *Unpublished Poetry*.

55. Elsewhere, the divine principle is called the "Gospel pearl," a reference to justification. See *HSP* [1739], 105; also, *Poetical Works*, 1:94, a poem on Romans 4:5.

56. *Unpublished Poetry*, 2:145.

57. *Unpublished Poetry*, 2:143-44.

58. Charles Wesley, *Hymns for the Use of Families* (Bristol: Pine, 1767, and London: Hawes, 1776), 118-19; hereafter, *Family Hymns*; *Poetical Works*, 7:133-34. While here the Holy Spirit was the "principle of love," elsewhere the Spirit was the "Principle, and Lord of life." See "Hymn for Whitsunday," *HSP* [1739], 213; *Poetical Works*, 1:189.

59. The same language of grace as the ripening of seeds appeared in a 1736/37 Charles Wesley sermon on Psalm 126:7. See Kenneth G.C. Newport, *The Sermons of Charles Wesley: A Critical Edition with Introduction and Notes* (Oxford: Oxford University Press, 2001), 129: "Yet a little while and he shall come again with fullness of joy to reap his entire harvest. Behold, one standeth at the door, who will complete what he hath begun, who shall ripen the seeds of grace into glory; and instead of that dew of heaven which now refreshes his soul, shall give him rivers of pleasure evermore!"

60. Hymn LX, in *Family Hymns*, 60-61.

61. *Family Hymns*, 60-61; italics added.

62. *Family Hymns*, 63-64; italicization of "seed" added.

63. Charles Wesley's theology of infant baptism as expressed in this hymn appears similar to that of William Tilly, the Church of England clergyman who influenced John Wesley's doctrine of prevenient grace. For further discussion of Tilly, see Chapter 1.

64. *Poetical Works*, 10:390; italics added. See also *Scripture Hymns*, 2:187.

65. See *HSP* [1742], 296-99.

66. *HSP* [1742], 299.

67. The action of prevenient grace should not be confused with the reality of justification. In a June 13, 1743 letter, Wesley cautioned: "I once thought several in that state who, I am now convinced, were only under the drawings of the Father." *Manuscript Journal*, 2:351.

68. *HSP* [1742], 265; *Poetical Works*, 2:324. See also the eleventh stanza of Hymn III, in *HGEL* [1742], 10, which speaks of the talent as "special saving grace."

69. *Poetical Works*, 2:325.

70. *Unpublished Poetry*, 3:156-57.

71. For a general treatment of the metaphor of light in Charles Wesley, see Gilbert Leslie Morris, "Imagery in the Hymns of Charles Wesley" (Ph.D. thesis, University of Arkansas, 1969), 135-39.

72. *HSP* [1740], 143; *Poetical Works*, 1:316.

73. *Poetical Works*, 10:142.

74. *HSP* [1739], 214; *Poetical Works*, 1:189; italics added.

75. *HSP* [1742], 169; *Poetical Works*, 2:230, italics added; Osborn changed the title to "Sinners, your hearts lift up."

76. *HSP* [1740], 141; *Poetical Works*, 1:315. See also verse one of "A Prayer Under Convictions," *HSP* [1739], 85, another instance of the "Father of light" appellation.

77. *HGEL* [1741], 11; *Poetical Works*, 3:9.

78. The title of this monograph, "Streams of Mercy," is drawn from this hymn.

79. The introduction to the on-line critical edition of this volume observes: "As the early Methodist revival spread, John and Charles Wesley found their commitment to God's universal offer of saving grace increasingly challenged by Calvinist participants in the movement...Charles' *MS Journal* reveals him becoming quite frustrated with the

'poison of Calvin' in the final months of 1740. He gave vent to this frustration in this volume, which contains some of his most pungent satirical verse." *HGEL* [1741], 1.

80. See Chapter 4 for further treatment of this anthropological theme.
81. *HSP* [1742], 218; *Poetical Works*, 2:273. See also Wesley's hymn on John 15:18-19, where Jesus was identified as the source of "glimm'ring light," in *HSP* [1739], 24-25.
82. These are treated above under the discussion of metaphors for prevenient grace.
83. *Poetical Works*, 11:218.; italics added.
84. *Poetical Works*, 11:218; italics added.
85. This phrase is from Ray Dunning, *Grace, Faith, and Holiness*, 429.
86. *Poetical Works*, 10:263; italics added.
87. *Poetical Works*, 10:236-37.
88. *Poetical Works*, 10:237.
89. *Scripture Hymns*, 2:238-39. See also Wesley's hymn on John 1:5 – found in 2:238 of the same collection – where multiple metaphors of "grain," "seed," and "ray" are employed.
90. John Wesley, *Explanatory Notes Upon the New Testament* (London: Wesleyan-Methodist Book Room, n.d.).
91. *Poetical Works*, 10:386; italics added.
92. *Poetical Works*, 10:386.
93. Conversely, the phrase in verse 1 – "we still Thy powerful drawings find" – makes it possible to interpret the poem as a *believer's* prayer, allowing a role for prevenient grace both before *and* after conversion. This broader interpretation of prevenient grace – though present in Charles Wesley's thought – is less frequent than the narrower (pre-justification) understanding. Regarding the function of the "broad" and "narrow" understandings of prevenient grace in John Wesley's theology, see Randy Maddox, *Responsible Grace* (Nashville: Abingdon Press, 1994), 84.
94. This is implied by the phrase "cords of perfect love," the means by which the Lord draws the "fallen race" to heaven. See hymn on John 12:32, in *Scripture Hymns*, 2:255.
95. *Scripture Hymns*, 2:255.
96. *Poetical Works*, 12:234.
97. This appears to be an allusion to Titus 2:11 – "For the grace of God that bringeth salvation hath appeared to all men" (KJV).
98. *Works* [BE], 19:332. On John Wesley's overtures to George Whitefield, see Herbert Boyd McGonigle, *Sufficient Saving Grace: John Wesley's Evangelical Arminianism* (Carlisle, Cumbria, and Waynesboro, Georgia: Paternoster Press, 2001), 154-60.
99. Kenneth J. Collins, *The Theology of John Wesley: Holy Love and the Shape of Grace* (Nashville, Tennessee: Abingdon Press, 2007), 80-81.
100. *Poetical Works*, 12:249; italics added.
101. *Poetical Works*, 12:249. It was only possible for one to call upon God because of the "general willingness" divinely given. See Wesley's composition on Acts 10:32 in *Unpublished Poetry*, 2:338.
102. *Poetical Works* [DE], 12:250.
103. See discussion in Robert Barclay, *An Apology for the True Christian Divinity Being an Explanation and Vindication of the Principles and Doctrines of the People Called Quakers* (1690 edition; Kessinger Publishing's Rare Mystical Reprints, at www.kessinger.net, n.d.), 109. Charles and his brother, John, read over the *Apology* with some of the London Methodists in early May 1745 in order to expose some of the errors of Quaker teaching, as indicated in John Wesley's *Journal* note in *Works* [BE], 20:65-66; also, McGonigle, *Sufficient Saving Grace*, 132, fn. 2. This censure did not indicate a

wholesale rejection of Barclay's teaching by John or Charles, as indicated by the former's abridgement of part of the *Apology*, republishing it in 1741 under the title *Serious Considerations on Absolute Predestination extracted from a late author* (Bristol, England: S. and F. Farley, 1741). For further details, see Chapter 2 of this inquiry.

104. *Poetical Works*, 12:285; italics added.

105. *Poetical Works*, 12:285.

106. *Short Hymns*, 2:272-73; *Poetical Works*, 12:333.

107. See discussion of this aspect of Wesley's anthropology in Chapter 4.

108. On Charles Wesley's anti-Catholicism, see Peter Nockles, "Charles Wesley, Catholicism and Anti-Catholicism," in *Charles Wesley: Life, Literature & Legacy* (ed. Kenneth G.C. Newport and Ted A. Campbell; Peterborough: Epworth Press, 2007), 141-64.

109. *Short Hymns*, 2:273; *Poetical Works*, 12:333.

110. *HGEL* [1742], 51.

111. *Hymn and Sacred Poems* [1740], 137.

112. *HGEL* [1742], 51; *Poetical Works*, 3:94.

113. *HSP* [1742], 169; *Poetical Works*, 2:230.

114. See stanza two of Hymn XXXVI, in *HSP* [1749], 193. This "grace enabling grace" could also appear in a post-conversion context, such as stanza eight of Hymn VI: "And grant me grace thy grace to use,/ From all the dross of nature free,/ Give me to love that soul for thee." *HSP* [1749], 270.

115. Charles Wesley, *Short Hymns on Select Passages of the Holy Scriptures* (2 vols.; Bristol: Farley, 1762), 1:194.

116. *HGEL* [1742], 49; italics added.

117. *HGEL* [1742], 47.

118. John Wesley, *Collection of Moral and Sacred Poems* (3 vols.; Bristol: Farley, 1744), 3:237. The introduction to the Duke on-line critical edition of this volume noted: "As in their other joint works, John and Charles chose not to identify who contributed specific poems. In this case, it is likely that the only poem John contributed was the translation of a German hymn by Ernst Lange. There is strong evidence to tie the other selections to Charles..."

119. *HSP* [1742], 142; italics added. On grace as alluring, see also stanza two of Hymn XIV, in Charles Wesley, *Hymns for Those that Seek and Those that have Redemption in the Blood of Jesus Christ* (London: Strahan, 1747), 18.

120. *HSP* [1742], 160; italics added.

121. Charles Wesley, *Family Hymns*, 28; italics added.

122. *Family Hymns*, 118.

123. *HGEL* [1742], 52; *Poetical Works*, 3:95.

124. *Unpublished Poetry*, 1:291-92.; italics added.

125. *Unpublished Poetry*, 3:195.

126. Dunning, *Grace, Faith, and Holiness*, 296. See Chapter 6 of this investigation for a brief comparison of prevenient grace and common grace.

127. *HGEL* [1742], 53; *Poetical Works*, 3:96.

128. The word of "general grace" and "word of power" were to be proclaimed by "labourers" working in a harvest that is "great." See "A Prayer for Labourers," *Poetical Works*, 2:342-43.

129. In "A Father's Prayer for His Son," *Family Hymns*, 118-19.

Chapter Six

Beyond the Brothers Wesley: Interpretations of Prevenient Grace

Introduction

In 18th century England, John and Charles Wesley were at the forefront of the Methodist Revival.[1] Very early in his preaching, John Wesley struck a note of "universal grace," that all God's creatures are objects of God's prevenient concern and – depending upon their divinely enabled response – heirs of salvation.[2] This was in contrast with the Calvinistic theology of his associate, George Whitefield, who held that only those predestined by God to eternal life are among the elect and therefore recipients of saving grace.

Geoffrey Wainwright traced the contours of the first Calvinistic controversy (1739-1741).[3] When John Wesley in 1739 decided to both preach and publish against predestination, including the polemical sermon *Free Grace*, a sharp division arose between Wesley and George Whitefield.[4] This sometimes heated discussion continues in one form or another to this day, part of what Wainwright called the "great debate" that characterizes "Protestant history on its Reformed side."[5]

One aspect of this historic debate is the differing ways in which Wesleyan and Calvinistic theologians have imagined grace as descriptive of God's activity. Having seen in Chapters 3, 4, and 5 the content of John and Charles Wesley's concept of prevenient grace, this chapter considers the varied responses of theologians to that doctrine.[6] Under the rubric of "the further development of a doctrine," attention is first given to three prominent 19th and 20th century Methodist theologians who appear to have slighted the role of prevenient grace as they constructed their systematic theology. Later, the chapter considers more recent Wesleyan scholars who have affirmed the validity of the Wesleys' prevenient grace concept and – in some instances – have built upon the foundation they laid. An analysis of their positive interpretations of prevenient grace is presented as answers to eight questions arising from their writings.

After the Wesleys: Further Development of a Doctrine

A. Watson, Miley, and Hills: The Muting of Prevenient Grace

While many Methodist theologians have written since the time of John Wesley, of particular prominence in the 19th and early 20th century were Richard Watson, John Miley, and Aaron Merritt Hills. Despite the emphasis in John and Charles Wesley upon prevenient grace, they de-emphasized the doctrine of grace. In Watson's two volume *Theological Institutes*, he preferred to highlight human ability:

> But as no absolute control can be externally exerted over man's actions, and he remain accountable; and on the other hand, as his actions are in fact controllable in a manner consistent with his free agency...he must be supposed to command his thoughts, his desires, his words, and his conduct, however excited, with an absolute sovereignty.[7]

Watson did speak in places of the role of "Divine gracious influence,"[8] "preventing grace,"[9] and the ministry of the Holy Spirit as a "quickening influence"[10], but these mentions were incidental and undeveloped. Grace at best appeared vestigial to his theological system.

John Miley also placed an accent upon human liberty. In the *via salutis*, prevenient grace is usually treated systematically just prior to justification. In Miley's *Systematic Theology*, however, the section on justification (chapter 5) was preceded instead by a chapter entitled "Free Agency" (chapter 3) and another labeled "Freedom of Choice" (chapter 4).[11] Despite this anthropological accent, Miley had some sense of the necessity of grace:

> Freedom is fundamental in Arminianism. The system holds accordingly the universality and provisional nature of the atonement, and the conditionality of salvation. In this matter it is thoroughly synergistic. If its doctrine of native depravity involves a moral helplessness it must set over against this the helping grace of a universal atonement. Thus the fundamental truth of freedom requires the system in the definite cast of its doctrines.[12]

Besides John Miley, Aaron Merritt Hills also underscored freedom. In his *Fundamental Christian Theology*, he presented nine "proofs of free moral agency." In the fifth proof, he addressed repentance. Is this attributable to a positive response to prevenient grace, as in John Wesley's theology? No; instead, Hills observed: "The action of a sinner's mind in repentance proves his freedom."[13] In an extended critique of the term "gracious ability," Hills appeared to allow some role for prevenient grace:

> It would be far truer to the teaching of Scripture, and consciousness and reason, to say that WE HAVE AN IMPAIRED NATURAL ABILITY PLUS GRACE,

than to say that we have lost all natural ability to obey God and have only a TEMPORARY GRACIOUS ABILITY instead. The inevitable logical inferences are too grave and startling, to accept the doctrine that lies back of this unfortunate term, inconsistent with the true doctrines of Methodism.[14]

For all three theologians, prevenient grace – where mentioned – appeared to be an afterthought. Emphasis was upon free moral agency, not upon the inability of humans to respond to God apart from grace. It remained for more recent thinkers to systematically work out the ramifications of prevenient grace for the broader Wesleyan system.

B. Contemporary Wesleyan Theology: The Prominence of Prevenient Grace

1. How have Wesleyan theologians defined prevenient grace?

Along with original sin, prevenient grace has been considered by recent scholars to be one of the twin theological *foci* of John Wesley's soteriology.[15] Sondra Higgins Matthaei called it "one of Wesley's major theological contributions."[16] Ray Dunning conceded that – while it is not a biblical term – it is a "theological category developed to capture a central biblical motif."[17]

To understand prevenient grace, a rudimentary definition of "grace" is first required. Thomas Langford defined "grace" as "God's active and continuous presence."[18] Citing John Wesley's sermons *Salvation by Faith* and *The Spirit of Bondage and Adoption*, Kenneth Collins observed that grace is both "undeserved favor" and "the power of the Holy Ghost."[19] Thomas Oden defined grace as both the "favor shown by God to the sinner" (or "divine goodwill") and the "divine disposition to work in our hearts, wills, and actions, so as to communicate effectively God's self-giving love for humanity."[20] So crucial is the activity of grace at every point in the *via salutis* that Theodore Runyon considered it to be "the key to all of Wesley's soteriological doctrines.[21] Albert Outler concurred that grace was paramount in Wesley's thinking: "The Christian life, in Wesley's view, is empowered by the energy of grace: prevenient, saving, sanctifying, sacramental. Grace is always interpreted as something more than mere forensic pardon. Rather, it is experienced as actual influence – God's love, immanent and active in human life."[22] Grace in Wesley corresponded to what Robert Rakestraw called the "three essential Wesleyan doctrines," namely, original sin, justification by faith, and holiness of heart and life.[23] To offset the dulling of conscience in depravity, God's grace *enlightened*; where pardon was necessary, grace *forgave*; and where cleansing from the flesh was needed, grace *sanctified*.

Having seen the broader meaning of "grace," it is now possible to consider more narrowly the term when preceded by the adjective "prevenient." William Burt Pope called prevenient grace "the manifestation of Divine influence which precedes the full regenerate life."[24] It is "the gracious presence of God in human life…that encounters us, calls us, and woos us from sin and self-centeredness back toward God."[25] In the same way, Orton Wiley viewed prevenient grace as "the grace which 'goes before,' preparing the soul for its entrance into the initial state of salvation."[26] Both Thomas Oden and Allan Coppedge underscored its soteriological importance, the former defining prevenient grace as "the grace that begins to enable one to choose further to cooperate with saving grace"[27] while the latter calls it the "general grace given to all people that restores in them the ability to accept God's offer of redemption."[28] Steve Harper likewise described prevenient grace as "leading grace," as "the operation of God that moves us to the place of repentance."[29] Each of these definitions captured some aspect of John Wesley's teaching on prevenient grace, and many of them admirably expressed it in language more accessible to the modern reader than is Wesley's own.

2. How are prevenient grace and the Trinity related?

If prevenient grace unresisted was understood to be instrumental in drawing the sinner away from sin and toward a saving encounter with the divine, then it was logical to ask: What role did God the Father, God the Son, and God the Holy Spirit play in the provision and workings of that grace? This question was addressed briefly in Chapter 3 of this investigation,[30] and not surprisingly, appears in the interpretive literature.

Theodore Runyon has most explicitly developed a view of prevenient grace as seen through the lens of Trinitarian theology:

> The approach suggested by a Wesleyan perspective is trinitarian rather than exclusively christological. The Spirit is wider-ranging than the explicit knowledge of God through Christ and goes where Christ is yet to be known. But the Spirit is not independent of Christ. Not only are the persons of the Trinity united in all their works *ad extra*, but the God who acts through the Spirit is the God whom Christ reveals as loving, who seeks out human beings wherever they are. Thus the authority of Christ's revelation is not undermined, because the witness of the Spirit is grounded in Christ's disclosure of God's being toward humanity always and everywhere.[31]

Leo George Cox has also discerned a Trinitarian motif when pondering the doctrine of prevenient grace. God the Father restored "to all men a measure of His Spirit." But how was this accomplished? It was "through the grace that flows from Calvary."[32] This Christological affirmation found support in John Wesley's June 25, 1744 Conference Minutes, where it was through the "obedience and death of Christ" that one received (among other blessings) "a capacity of spiritual life."[33] William Greathouse and Ray Dunning were also Trinitarian in outlook, locating the source of salvation in "God's gracious provision in the cross of Jesus," which included the work of the Holy Spirit, "God at work within our hearts *awakening*, convicting, converting, and cleansing us." As noted by Greathouse and Dunning, this underscored both the "objective" and "subjective" nature of grace as alluded to in Wesley's 1739 sermon, *Free Grace*, where grace is "free *for* all, and free *in* all."[34]

While many were Trinitarian in their formulations, Thomas Langford was unique by underscoring the Father-Son dynamic in the workings of prevenient grace. He observed: "Prevenient grace is an effect of the atonement of Jesus Christ. The grace of God in Christ creates a new possibility for human life, and to every human life God is antecedently and enablingly present."[35] More common, however, was a stress upon the dual role of Christ and the Holy Spirit. Eldon Fuhrman was typical of this twin emphasis, characterizing prevenient grace as "through Christ, by the Holy Spirit."[36] His statement provides a useful format to more closely examine the Second and Third Persons of the Trinity in relation to prevenient grace.

Prevenient grace was "through Christ." – The Christological underpinnings of prevenient grace received attention from several Wesleyan theologians. Irwin Reist called prevenient grace "a capacity for spiritual life received through Christ's death."[37] Ralph Del Colle asserted that "Wesley maintains an existential christological foundation to all anthropologically determining graced experience."[38] He presented the *ordo salutis* from the vantage point of Christ's work:

- Prevenient grace = Christ enlightening us
- justification = Christ for us
- sanctification = Christ in us[39]

The essence of Del Colle's observation was also seen in Ray Dunning, who claimed: "Wesley both explicitly and implicitly grounded prevenient grace in Christology which would appear to give the whole of his theology a Christological focus."[40]

Distinctive among Christological treatments of grace was Kenneth Collins' approach. He addressed grace not only from the vantage point of Christ's sacrificial death, but also his coming to earth: "Grace as divine empowerment is rooted in the incarnation and atonement of Jesus Christ. Grace is one of the benefits of His life, work, and sacrifice; and it is, therefore, thoroughly Christologically based."[41] This inclusion of the language of incarnation is supported by John Wesley's repeated allusions to the "light" of John 1:9 as a metaphor of prevenient grace. Collins was true to Wesley by speaking in terms both Athanasian and Anselmian.

Herbert McGonigle saw the universality of prevenient grace as intricately linked with Christ's atonement: "Because this prevenient grace originates in the merits of Christ's redemptive death, a redemption made for all men, Wesley always stressed the universal nature of this grace."[42] Skevington Wood likewise viewed the pneumatological aspects of prevenient grace from the perspective of Calvary: "He (John Wesley) realised that the specific task of the Holy Spirit is to glorify the Son and to apply the benefits of Christ's redemption…Precisely because Wesley understood from Scripture this supportive role of the Spirit, his theology remains firmly Christocentric."[43]

Prevenient grace is "by the Holy Spirit." – If God the Son was the means by which God the Father *provided* prevenient grace, then God the Holy Spirit is the means by which it is *mediated* to humanity.[44] In his systematic theology – besides briefly addressing prevenient grace as a benefit of the atonement – Ray Dunning returned to the theme under the section devoted to the work of the Holy Spirit, classifying prevenient grace as a "preparation for salvation."[45] This concurred with Albert Outler's position that "the Spirit's initiative is the dynamic of all grace."[46] All graces of the Father and the Son are communicated by the Holy Spirit, including prevenient grace.[47] Robert Vincent Rakestraw, who defined "grace" as "the Spirit in action," correctly observed:

> The grace of God, especially as divine power, is in Wesley's writings so closely linked with the workings of the Holy Spirit in a person's life that the power of God's Spirit becomes virtually indistinguishable from the power which is God's Spirit...Both the Spirit and His powerful grace effect the same activity of God in the individual, although Wesley may, in order to highlight certain truths, emphasize one more than the other.[48]

In addition to Robert Rakestraw, William Greathouse and Ray Dunning posited a close relationship between the workings of the Holy Spirit and prevenient grace. Referencing Romans 5:12, they identified prevenient grace as the "free gift" spoken of by Paul, and this gift is ministered by the Third Person of the Trinity:

> While it is true that if we are left to ourselves there is no hope of salvation, God has not left us to ourselves. The Spirit of God is at work in every sinner's heart, seeking to awaken, convict, convert, and sanctify him. This is what we mean by "prevenient" grace: God comes to every one of us by the Holy Spirit and gently strives to save us from ourselves. God's prevenient grace frees our will sufficiently to enable us to call on Christ and be delivered.[49]

This is in agreement with Ole Borgen, who considered grace under the twin optic of Christ's atonement and the work of the Holy Spirit. "Enabling grace" is only available because of Christ's work of redemption, but is bestowed by the Holy Spirit in distinctive stages, i.e. prevenient (preventing), convincing, justifying, and sanctifying grace.[50]

The prevenient work of the Holy Spirit appeared in the writings of other theologians. In a study on the Wesleyan view of the Holy Spirit, Mack Stokes asserted:

> Wesley believed that the Holy Spirit is present in everyone before conversion. No one is without the activity of the Holy Spirit on the preliminary level. The manifestation of the Spirit was called prevenient grace – the grace or the presence of the Holy Spirit that preceded the grace that comes with the acceptance of Jesus Christ as Lord.[51]

Similarly, Eldon Fuhrman affirmed that prevenient grace is descriptive of how the Holy Spirit induces "inner conflict, an accusing conscience, penitence and contrition, all of which is a preparation for the gospel."[52] Leo Cox likewise defined prevenient grace as "the power of God's Holy Spirit lifting that individual above what he had received by birth and creating in him a beginning of life which will lead on to further life if he responds to it."[53] Following John Wesley's commentary on Romans 1:19, Kenneth Collins affirmed that the "prevenient agency of the Holy Spirit" granted to humanity a "basic knowledge of God", that God is eternal and omnipotent, among other attributes.[54] In the same way, John Cobb concluded:

God's presence is, of course, grace. It is the working of the Holy Spirit in every human heart. It is prevenient. That is, there is no point in human life before it enters in. It does not exist in a human being as a separate entity. It is integral to what a human being is.[55]

A final Wesleyan theologian who delineated the relationship of the Holy Spirit and prevenient grace was Lycurgus Starkey. Speaking of the "preliminary grace of the Spirit," Starkey identified its source as the "work of Christ."[56] This grace, though available to all, may be resisted:

> Thus the pre-Christian man is convicted of sin, prompted to repentance, directed toward the knowledge and forgiveness of the one true God because he responds to the preliminary work of the Holy Spirit. The reason the conviction of sin is often ineffectual is that man resists and grieves the drawings and strivings of the Holy Spirit, until in some cases the Spirit departs reluctantly from him.[57]

Starkey called the preliminary work of the Holy Spirit the "Wesleyan bridge between nature and grace."[58] He has rightfully recognized a major emphasis in John Wesley's doctrine of prevenient grace, a doctrine that cannot be divorced from pneumatology. To speak of prevenient grace for Wesley was to speak of the work of the Holy Spirit. While "preventing grace" is a metaphor and should not be hypostasized, it is nonetheless an image useful in describing the Spirit's activity, in the same way that the image of "blood" describes the cleansing work of Christ.

3. Where in the *via salutis* should prevenient grace be classified?

The above definitions make it clear where in the *via salutis* (or "way of salvation") prevenient grace comes. It is God's grace operative *prior* to our justification. Accordingly, Steve Harper explained what he meant by "leading grace":

1. It creates in us our first sensitivity to God's will;
2. It produces a slight, transient conviction of having violated God's will;
3. It is the cause of our first wish to please God.[59]

Harper was following a traditional understanding of prevenient grace already traced by theologians such as Harald Lindström. In *Wesley and Sanctification*, Lindström treated prevenient grace immediately following the section on original sin and at the end of the chapter entitled "sanctification and the nature of man." By this ordering of his subject matter, he respected John Wesley's anthropological understanding that no individual exists purely in a state of nature, but always is a reflection of nature *plus* grace. Lindström observed: "Wesley maintains that natural man is totally corrupt, but he also maintains that God gives to all men his prevenient grace."[60] Significantly, Lindström only addressed prevenient grace in chapter one of his monograph, before turning in chapter two to Wesley's view of the atonement, justification and sanctification. In this way, it is apparent that he viewed prevenient grace as a pre-conversion concept. Kenneth Collins – like Randy Maddox – calls this the "narrow" understanding of prevenient grace.[61]

There is, however, an alternative view of the location of prevenient grace in the *via salutis*, a view that does not limit its activity to the time prior to conversion. Instead, it "views *all* grace as prevenient in that it emphasizes divine/human cooperation in terms of the *prior* activity of God as well as human response in *all* grace."[62] Randy Maddox labeled this the "broad sense" of prevenient grace and found it in John Wesley's use of the collected devotions and prayers of the Church of England.[63] Indeed, the "broad" type of language occasionally employed by the *Book of Common Prayer* sometimes appeared in Wesley's sermons. In *The Great Privilege of those that are Born of God* (1748), Wesley wrote of God: "He prevents us indeed with the blessings of his goodness."[64] This was clearly descriptive of believers, and not those who have yet to come to saving faith in Christ.

Charles Rogers repeatedly addressed the issue of where in the *via salutis* prevenient grace is located. While Rogers saw prevenient grace active before regeneration, he also understood Wesley to teach it as operative *after* conversion: "Its first soteriological role is in relation not to man's sanctification, but to his justification. However, maintaining some continuity with his earlier thought, the later Wesley holds that prevenient grace also functions as an energy or power given to man to assist him in the process of sanctification."[65] Earlier, Rogers had quoted an extract that Wesley made of a William Tilly sermon based on Phil. 2:12-13 and concluded: "Prevenient grace, for Wesley, is bestowed upon man in his new birth, and is the source of his freedom to do good works and participate in the process of sanctification. It is *not a grace which precedes regeneration*, or which somehow enables man to fulfil the conditions of regeneration: humility and faith."[66]

What is one to make of these two citations? In the first line of the first citation, Rogers appeared to be affirming the "narrow" view, i.e. that prevenient grace *precedes* the new birth. This is consistent with statements from Rogers elsewhere in the thesis where he acknowledged the pre-conversion role of prevenient grace, such as in the restoration of a measure of free-will.[67] However, in the second citation, Rogers negated what he had previously affirmed, allowing no role for prevenient grace prior to conversion, for it is "not a grace which precedes regeneration." The problem seems to reside in the use that Rogers made of the William Tilly sermon.[68] Rogers attributed the following paragraph to Wesley:

> It is only from a principle of preventing grace, laid and hidden in us at our regeneration in baptism that we are enabled to move without any other help some of the first steps toward amendment. This doctrine neither dishonours the grace of God, nor does too much honour to nature, in that is supposes nature to work only in the power and efficacy of grace itself.[69]

In fact, these were not Wesley's words, but a citation of the Tilly sermon as abridged by Wesley. Wesley appears to have been interested in Tilly's *Sixteen Sermons* primarily for their contribution to understanding how God and humans interact in the salvation encounter as an alternative to the Calvinistic predestinarian system.[70] It is questionable whether one should consider the paragraph cited as an accurate reflection in *all parts* of Wesley's theology. For example, Herbert McGonigle noted that Wesley rejected Tilly's idea that prevenient grace begins with baptismal regeneration, yet this idea was retained in Wesley's abridgement.[71] As Chapter 3 of this thesis makes clear, Wesley's own position was that prevenient grace was active even among those yet to hear the gospel. For Rogers to affirm – in an apparent reversal of his own earlier claim – that prevenient grace does not precede regeneration may have been an inappropriate superimposing of Tilly's theology upon Wesley's.

While it is true that the nature of all grace is prevenient in that God takes the initiative, is it proper to speak of "prevenient grace" in a post-justification context? Kenneth Collins argued against this practice, speaking of the "unfortunate effect of leveling key distinctions that Wesley made in his doctrine of salvation."[72] Commenting on the "broad" use of the term "prevenient grace," Collins further observed:

> It may...fail in a significant way to take note of those qualitative changes that are realized in the lives of believers as they grow from grace to grace, those alterations of tempers, that transformation of being, of which Wesley wrote repeatedly. Indeed, the distinctions of prevenient, convincing, justifying, regenerating, sanctifying, and glorifying grace are indicative of the progressive deepening of the divine/human relationship whereby love ultimately triumphs over ignorance and fear. At the very least, then, the initial activity of the Holy Spirit in calling and convicting the soul must be distinguished from that grace that makes one holy.[73]

Importantly, in his own original writings, Wesley only coupled the adjective "preventing" with the noun "grace" when describing God's awakening activity *prior* to justification. When speaking of divine enablement *after* conversion, Wesley joined other adjectives to "grace." As Collins noted, grace is active at all points of the *via salutis*, but was variously described by Wesley as "saving," "sanctifying," or with other terms. In Wesley's vocabulary, the concept of "preventing grace" was limited to describing the initial enlightening work of God's Holy Spirit in the heart of the unbeliever.[74] Of course, Wesleyan theologians are justified to speak of the *prevenience* of all grace, but to speak of "prevenient grace" as operative post-regeneration is to read into Wesley an element that is not apparent in his writings.

4. Is prevenient grace regenerative?

A second issue related to the location of prevenient grace in the *via salutis* is in what sense prevenient grace may be regenerative. In a section of *Responsible Grace* entitled "Regeneration," Randy Maddox observed:

> The affirmation of degrees of regeneration is central to Wesley's mature soteriology, and to his rejoinder to accusations that he undervalued God's prevenience in salvation. This is because Wesley came to emphasize that there was a crucial degree of regeneration prior to the New Birth: the universal nascent regenerating effect of Prevenient Grace. It is only through the benefits of this expression of God's gracious prevenience that anyone can turn to God in repentance and receive the more extensive renewal that comes from a restored pardoning relationship with God.[75]

On the other hand, Colin Williams presented a more narrowly circumscribed vision of prevenient grace. He affirmed that prevenient grace had a "very great significance in his (Wesley's) theology," yet it was limited: "This is not to say that this prevenient grace, apparent in the conscience is enough to enable man to turn to God in faith. Further gifts of grace are necessary to enable man to come to repentance and then to justification."[76] Kenneth Collins was concerned about the possible effects of Maddox's use of the language of regeneration to describe the benefits of prevenient grace. Collins cautioned: "Since all are recipients of prevenient grace and hence of rudimentary regeneration as well, the importance, indeed the cruciality of going on to regeneration, understood as initial sanctification, may lose its urgency."[77] He further noted that the evidence in Wesley's writings for a regenerative element in prevenient grace is sparse, and that Wesley in his *New Testament Notes* and *Sermons on Several Occasions* always coupled regeneration with justification, not prevenient grace.[78] Maddox replied that Wesley's *On Working Out Our Own Salvation* included the term "some degree of salvation" to describe prevenient grace, but clarified that it should not be understood as being the same thing as "saving grace."[79] He viewed his use of "regeneration" in the same limited way, as a reference to the universal restoration of conscience and the ability to respond to the offer of grace.[80] Since the publication of *Responsible Grace*, Maddox appears to have qualified his terminology to the point that he is in agreement with the consensus of Wesleyan theologians.

Kenneth Collins' concern did not include addressing the missiological ramifications of an expanded doctrine of prevenient grace, yet Randy Maddox's initial position – if left unqualified – clearly would have missiological consequences. While John Wesley purposely used soft words like "glimmering rays" to describe prevenient grace, Maddox's view in *Responsible Grace* at first reading appears far more robust.[81] If prevenient grace is universal *and* regenerative – even in a rudimentary sense – then the rationale for preaching the gospel is weakened. Colin Williams steered clear of this consequence by considering prevenient grace (via conscience) a "preliminary" way that God is revealed, whereas the gospel is a "direct" way and the vehicle of "convincing grace."[82] Similarly, Robert Hillman viewed prevenient grace in Wesley's sermon, *On Working Out Our Own Salvation*, as part of the "initial stages" of one's move toward Christ. However, justification and regeneration were the result of further grace, a "gift of the Spirit, *working through the Gospel.*"[83] Lycurgus Starkey acknowledged the "possibility of an extrascriptural redemption," calling it "implicit in several of the Wesleyan statements."[84] However, he continued: "Socrates, the greatest to have enjoyed the preliminary inspiration of the Spirit of grace, is still unacquainted with the true scriptural religion. The work of the hidden Christ must be fulfilled in the gospel's revelation of the Saviour."[85] Prevenient grace was for Starkey a "witness in the outer court of the gentiles."[86] Nonetheless, it was "not of sufficient brightness to work justification and sanctification without the gospel confrontation of a redeeming Saviour."[87] Too great an emphasis upon prevenient grace could lead to a neglect of what it points to, namely, God's saving grace, and this pardon is typically appropriated in response to the proclamation of the gospel.[88]

5. Conscience and restored faculties: Is prevenient grace "irresistible"?

Though prevenient grace is not regenerative, is it irresistible? Kenneth Collins raised this issue, noting that speaking of prevenient grace as irresistible "may come as a surprise to those Methodists who have been schooled on the notion that irresistible grace is a topic more suited to Calvinists."[89] If a Wesleyan accepts total depravity, but denies unconditional election, then Collins argued that "graciously restored faculties, the first aspect of prevenient grace, cannot be refused."[90] Elsewhere Collins asserted: "Since Wesley's doctrine of original sin underscores the notion of total depravity, then it logically follows that 'irresistible grace' has to operate at least at some point in the Wesleyan order of salvation."[91]

In what sense was Ken Collins' observation correct? Randy Maddox – while calling the word "irresistible" potentially misleading – agreed that grace in general and prevenient grace in particular are "enduring realities in human life."[92] If by "irresistible" Collins meant "universal," then he clearly had the weight of John Wesley's own teaching on his side.[93] Wesley believed that conscience 1) resides in all human beings, and 2) is animated by prevenient grace.[94] Harald Lindström affirmed the first point when speaking of depravity: "It is clear that Wesley cannot reconcile the idea of a knowledge of God arising from the human resources of natural man with his doctrine of original sin. The insight accorded by conscience acquires therefore the character of supernatural grace."[95] Richard Heitzenrater confirmed the second point, i.e. the universal character of prevenient grace:

> This enlightenment (knowledge of the good) that comes through prevenient grace Wesley associates with conscience, which he felt was commonly understood to be present in all humankind. He disclaims an exact parallel between conscience and prevenient grace in order to avoid any misconception that prevenient grace was part of created human nature instead of a divine gift offered to sinful humanity. But he claims the analogy in order to press its universal application to humankind.[96]

Likewise, Theodore Runyon maintained that conscience – characterizing those being awakened by prevenient grace – "plays the healthy role of bringing us to awareness of our distance from God, the seriousness of our sin, and our need for *repentance*."[97] Conscience is not reserved for a select few, but is the "unknown companion of each of us."[98] However, for Wesley, conscience must be informed by the more perfect knowledge only available through the revelation of God in Christ.[99]

In the end, despite his provocative use of the term "irresistible," Collins appeared to be affirming nothing more than what Lindström and Heitzenrater maintained, since he conceded that prevenient grace "may be resisted, and indeed often is."[100] Though prevenient grace is frequently stifled, all beginning at birth are its recipients.

6. Is prevenient grace a convincing alternative to determinism and moralism?

Prevenient grace is frequently described as a *via media* between two extremes, namely, determinism and moralism. Robert Cushman detailed the logic of these two positions:

> If salvation is by faith, and faith is altogether God's gift (grace); then clearly if a man is saved, it is because he was chosen, viz, God willed to give him the gift. If a man is not saved (justified), it is because he was not given the gift of grace unto faith; therefore he was not chosen. Thus if salvation is not by works, it must be by decrees. If it is not by decrees, then it must be by works.[101]

Colin Williams saw in prevenient grace an escape from this either/or dilemma. Prevenient grace breaks "the pattern of logical necessity involved in the traditional doctrine of predestination."[102] At the same time, it "may well have real ecumenical significance in speaking to the Catholic fear that the Classical Protestant emphasis on justification by faith alone involves a devaluation of the significance of works in man's saving relation to God, and leads to a relaxation of ethical endeavour."[103] From the Wesleyan vantage point, the measure of free-will restored by prevenient grace makes the doctrine of predestination "superfluous."[104] On the other hand, Pelagianism is avoided since no one can claim that salvation is his or her own doing. It is only because of prevenient grace that an individual is enabled to turn to God.[105]

The strength of the Wesleyan position on prevenient grace is its relationship to the doctrine of original sin or depravity. John Prince was a proponent of this viewpoint: "He (John Wesley) believed in the depravity of human nature but at the same time joined it to an ameliorating doctrine of grace whereby every man born into the wolrd is enabled to sense his pitiable condition, to sigh for deliverance, and to make a start toward it."[106] Calling John Wesley's doctrine of original sin "near-Augustinian," Herbert McGonigle described prevenient grace in Wesley as a "supernatural gift of God, and it gives to every human being that power of choice which is the prerequisite for all moral responsibility."[107] This "gift" is crucial precisely because – in the words of Richard Heitzenrater – "fallen humanity has lost both the ability to discern the good and the capability to choose it."[108] Randy Maddox likewise summarized the soteriological essence of the Wesleyan *via media*:

> There is no clearer expression of the dialectic between God's gift and human responsibility in Wesley's thought than his well-known conjunction of a strong doctrine of original sin with an equally strong doctrine of God's universal prevenient grace. This conjunction allows Wesley to deny all natural human merit and power while at the same time calling sinners to respond to God's offer of grace and take responsibility for their lives in Christ.[109]

Noting that some see little difference between a doctrine of natural ability and a doctrine of prevenient grace, Umphrey Lee nevertheless maintained that prevenient grace differs in two vital ways: 1) It puts a proper emphasis upon human proneness to evil, and 2) It safeguards divine initiative.[110]

Thomas Langford[111] has helpfully grouped Wesleyan theologians into three schools of thought on the issue of divine/human interaction in the salvation encounter:

1. Positive human initiative – Langford cited Umphrey Lee as the chief proponent of this point of view. In his *John Wesley and Modern Religion*, Lee employed the language of liberty. When describing the effects of the fall on the *imago Dei*, he observed: "Man lost not only the moral image of God, but in part at least, he lost the natural image. His will became infirm, since his affections were not guided by an unerring reason. Likewise, his liberty ceased to be freedom 'wholly guided by his understanding'"[112] In the Calvinistic system, according to Lee, humans are compelled to obey, whereas Wesley believed that prevenient grace was an empowerment allowing for choice.[113] Though not mentioned by Langford, William Burt Pope more clearly expressed this optimism about post-fall human ability. On the relationship between grace and human freedom, he observed: "There is a divine operation which works the desire and acts in such a way as not to interfere with the *natural freedom of the will*. The man determines himself, through Divine grace, to salvation: never so free as when swayed by grace."[114] Earlier, Pope had affirmed that "the will is not bound." Prevenient grace "is not needed to restore to the faculty of will its power of originating action: that has never been lost. But it is needed to suggest to the intellect the truth on which religion rests, and to sway the affections of hope and fear by enlisting the heart on the side of that truth."[115]

What can be concluded regarding Umphrey Lee's and William Pope's position? Lee and Pope failed to adequately weigh the dark picture Wesley painted of the human condition apart from grace in sermons like *Original Sin*.[116] It is true that they allowed for the operation of grace, but it was not always clear how this interfaced with their view of free will.

2. Graciously enabled response – This is the majority opinion expressed in the literature, a viewpoint shared by William Cannon, Randy Maddox, Harald Lindström, Theodore Runyon, Colin Williams, John Cobb, and others. Leon Hynson summarized this position:

> Wesley proclaimed the prevenient grace of God in and through Jesus Christ. Conscience, will, repentance, the act of justification, faith – all spring from the grace of God as their source. They are always, everywhere preceded by and surrounded by God's grace, giving, enabling, empowering. Man is a free creature, but only because he is a sinful creature under the grace of God which enables him to respond within the sphere of grace.[117]

John Cobb called John Wesley "second to none in his insistence on human sinfulness and the total inability of fallen human beings to save themselves. Indeed, he went to great lengths in his conviction that apart from divine grace human beings are capable of no good whatsoever."[118] In the same way, Thomas Langford characterized John Wesley's idea of "faith" as "a graciously enabled response to grace."[119] Irwin Reist affirmed that for Wesley, "there is no neutrality of natural ability to respond to God's grace, but this response is created by God himself in grace."[120] Einar Nilsen noted that "God acts; man reacts. God always has the initiative."[121] God, through prevenient grace, restored to fallen humanity the capacity either to respond to God's calling, or else resist it.[122] Where *all* was of grace, there was no room for human merit, and Wesley's "third way" thus escapes the charge of Pelagianism. Herein lies the importance of George Croft Cell's observation: "The Wesleyan reconstruction of the Christian ethic of life is an original and unique synthesis of the Protestant ethic of grace with the Catholic ethic of holiness."[123]

Not all have favorably viewed this *via media*. While John Wesley argued vigorously for a traditional understanding of original sin, was he guilty of theological sleight-of-hand by softening the doctrine with the concept of prevenient grace? Robert Hillman criticized Wesley at exactly this point, claiming that he has created "an abstract doctrine of original sin." How was this so? "For there is no one who is a real 'natural man': man is utterly corrupt, but thanks to prevenient grace, natural man does not exist."[124] John Peters answered this charge:

> It has been stated that Wesley's doctrine of prevenient grace made his concept of the "natural man" a "logical abstraction." This statement, while perceptive, tends to suggest inferences that are invalid. It cannot be inferred, that is, that Wesley looked upon man with the optimistic eye of nineteenth and twentieth century humanism. While Wesley taught that prevenient grace might free man from his "total inability," he still pictured him as the corrupted and impaired creature of the semi-Augustinian tradition. Wesley did have a doctrine of total depravity. He also had a doctrine of grace.[125]

Yoshio Noro concurred, noting that in Wesley "there is no idea of nature as absolutely separated from grace."[126]

Robert Monk discerned a weakness in this "response-able grace" school of thought. If response to the gospel is predicated not upon divine election to salvation but rather response to prevenient grace, then why does it appear that some possess more prevenient grace than others? Put differently, why does conscience appear to be weaker in some? Does God show favoritism, endowing some with greater amounts of prevenient grace? If so, then is this not just a variation of the same charge leveled against the predestinarian system, where some are graced with salvation, while others are not? Having raised the objection, Monk answered it himself:

> Although some may be more richly endowed through prevenient grace, none are without it – "in all and for all." All are elected to receive prevenient grace and the opportunity for saving grace even if in varying degrees; by the same token, all are made responsible no matter to what degree. Wesley's construction may leave one with unexplained discrepancies which appear to indicate "degrees" of election; yet at least it avoids the predestinarian discrepancy whereby grace is offered to some while it is withheld from others. In addition, it does provide an explanation for each man's being a responsible moral agent.[127]

3. "Despair" – Both Robert Cushman and Robert Chiles were unsatisfied with either the Lee-Pope accommodation to free-will or the graciously enabled response position. Cushman maintained that "Wesley's provision for prevenient grace only pushes the problem back a step."[128] There could be no "cooperative assistance" with God. The best that could be done is to *not* resist grace. This non-resistance allowed for the effectual operation of further grace. In other terms, non-resistance was an "abdication of self through despair."[129] Likewise, Robert Chiles objected to active language used in relation to prevenient grace. It was *not* the means by which a sinner is able to "will God." Rather, it produced in the individual a "radical self-knowledge, a conviction of sin and helplessness, which drives him to despair so that God can have full course in his life."[130]

The net effect of the Cushman-Chiles corrective was positive. Their emphasis upon words like "abdication" and "despair" was in keeping with the tenor of John Wesley's language.[131] Only reluctantly did Robert Monk qualify Wesley's system as synergistic, and even then it was "still within a Reformation context."[132] Albert Outler called Wesley's doctrine a "synergism of grace"[133] while Randy Maddox spoke of the "gift of grace upon which salvation depends" as functioning to "empower us to respond without compelling us to obey."[134] As can be seen in this careful choice of words, the emphasis of the "despair" school of thought provided theological counterbalance, preventing Wesleyan theologians from veering too far toward a free-will emphasis.[135]

7. Are prevenient grace and common grace equivalent?

Charles Hodge in his *Systematic Theology* gave an extended treatment of common grace.[136] He defined the concept as the "influence of the Spirit common to all men."[137] Hodge continued:

> The great truth, however, that concerns us is that the Spirit of God is present with every human mind, restraining from evil and exciting to good; and that to his presence and influence we are indebted for all the order, decorum, and virtue, as well as the regard for religion and its ordinances, which exist in the world.[138]

Though common grace is a restraint on evil, Hodge differentiated it from the influence of the Holy Spirit that leads to "genuine conversion" or "regeneration."[139]

Dale Yocum has noted that the Wesleyan concept of prevenient grace and the Calvinistic doctrine of common grace appear to overlap. He described the latter as "similar to prevenient grace, in that it is directed toward all men, and in that it brings wholesome influences to all, such as the restraint of conscience."[140] Likewise, Robert Johnston described the primary purpose of common grace as restraining evil, but also as a motivation to do what is good, an impulse stemming from the ministry of the Holy Spirit.[141] The convergence of the two concepts, particularly in relation to the restraint of evil, was affirmed by Ray Dunning, who argued that prevenient grace could be extended by Wesleyans to cover what Calvinistic theologians refer to as "common grace."[142]

Having acknowledged this area of convergence, it is important to underscore the important divergences between the two concepts. This becomes clear when considering the five characteristics of prevenient grace outlined by Leo Cox:

1. Prevenient grace is common or universal grace;
2. It is ministered through the Holy Spirit;
3. It leads to salvation;
4. It provides for personal responsibility;

5. It preserves the *sola gratia* and the *sola fide*.[143]

Common grace is universal, and is ministered through the Holy Spirit. However, the last three characteristics cannot be ascribed to common grace. Dale Yocum noted that in the Calvinistic system, common grace "is not sufficient to bring sinners to repentance. The effectual calling is necessary for that, and is accompanied by irresistible grace unto salvation for the elect only."[144] For the Calvinist, prevenient grace functions primarily for the conviction of sins, but even here, its operation is limited to convicting the sins of the elect.[145]

8. How did prevenient grace inform Wesley's view of other religions?

Theodore Runyon acknowledged the relevance of prevenient grace to any discussion of religious pluralism.[146] However, it is Randy Maddox who systematically presented John Wesley's views on the question of whether "truth" and "salvation" may be found in other religions.[147] Acknowledging the "lack of consensus" in the current discussion of Christianity's relation to other religions, Maddox nevertheless maintained that Wesley "offers a distinctive contribution to this discussion."[148]

It is the rubric of John Wesley's understanding of prevenient grace that informed Maddox's essay. He delineated two categories, namely, "initial universal revelation" and "definitive Christian revelation." The latter "took place in Christ and is found in Scripture,"[149] while the former is knowledge about God that is "universally available."[150] This "inward voice" is the means by which God may have instructed the unevangelized on the tenets of true religion, or holiness. Maddox clarified:

> (Wesley) raised the possibility that Prevenient Grace might involve more than simply strengthening our human faculties and testifying to us through creation. It might also provide actual overtures to our "spiritual senses"! With provisions such as this, some people would surely pursue virtuous lives, and the late Wesley appeared willing to acknowledge some attainment. However, he was quick to add that such cases would be less pure and less common than in the Christian dispensation. Moreover, he was convinced that these persons would not have the assurance that is available to Christians through the Spirit.[151]

Maddox underscored Wesley's repeated refusal to condemn those who only have available "initial universal revelation," i.e. prevenient grace. Instead, according to Wesley, individuals would be judged according to the light they receive.[152] The value of evangelization and proclamation of the "definitive Christian revelation" lies in the power it provides for a life of obedience.[153]

Conclusion

Through the answers to these eight questions, one may see that in no case studied has there been a radical departure from the foundation laid by John Wesley.[154] Wesleyan theologians have rendered a service by describing prevenient grace in terms more accessible to the contemporary reader.

Furthermore, they have systematized Wesley by applying prevenient grace to a variety of broader questions, including those with missiological significance. His interpreters in the centuries following him have arguably more clearly than Wesley himself understood the importance of the doctrine of prevenient grace in tracing a constructive *via media* between the determinism of Augustine and Calvin and the moralism of Roman Catholicism and some prominent thinkers of the 17th and 18th century Church of England. In the future, interpretations of the contribution of Charles Wesley to the prevenient grace concept will further enrich discourse on this topic so significant in Wesleyan theology.

Notes

1. Two works that chronicled the Methodist Revival against the broader backdrop of 18th century English society are Henry D. Rack, *Reasonable Enthusiast: John Wesley and the Rise of Methodism* (3rd ed.; London: Epworth Press, 2002), and Richard P. Heitzenrater, *Wesley and the People Called Methodists* (Nashville: Abingdon Press, 1995).

2. Only with time would Wesley begin to attach the adjective "preventing" to the noun "grace," but the concept is already present in his 1739 sermon *Free Grace*.

3. Geoffrey Wainwright, "Charles Wesley and Calvinism," in Kenneth G.C. Newport and Ted A. Campbell, eds., *Charles Wesley: Life, Literature, and Legacy* (Werrington, Peterborough: Epworth Press, 2007), 184-203. The second controversy erupted following the poorly worded Minutes of the 1770 Methodist conference. See Allan Coppedge, *Shaping the Wesleyan Message: John Wesley in Theological Debate* (Nappanee, Illinois: Francis Asbury Press/Evangel Publishing House, 2003), 157-218.

4. Details of the episode are found in John Pollock, *Whitefield: the Evangelist* (Eastbourne, England: Kingway Publications, 1972), 181-86.

5. Wainwright, 184.

6. Since the doctrine of prevenient grace in Charles Wesley has not been researched outside of the present investigation, secondary literature studied in this chapter references only John.

7. Richard Watson, *Theological Institutes, or a View of the Evidences, Doctrines, Morals and Institutions of Christianity* (2 volumes; New York: T. Mason and G. Lane, 1836), 2:31-32.

8. Watson, 2:248.

9. Watson, 2:258.

10. Watson, 2:57.

11. See chapters 3-4 in John Miley, *Systematic Theology* (2 volumes; New York: Hunton & Eaton, 1892), 2:271-307.

12. Miley, *Systematic Theology*, 2:275; italics added.

13. A.M. Hills, *Fundamental Christian Theology: A Systematic Theology* (2 volumes; Pasadena, California: C.J. Kinne and Pasadena College, 1931), 1:366.

14. Hills, *Fundamental Christian Theology*, 1:373; capitalization is Hill's. For full discussion, see 1:368-75.

15. Herbert Boyd McGonigle, *Sufficient Saving Grace: John Wesley's Evangelical Arminianism* (Carlisle, Cumbria, and Waynesboro, Georgia: Paternoster Press, 2001), 329.

16. Sondra Higgins Matthaei, *Making Disciples: Faith Formation in the Wesleyan Tradition* (Nashville: Abingdon Press, 2000), 46.

17. H. Ray Dunning, *Grace, Faith, and Holiness* (Kansas City, Missouri: Beacon Hill Press, 1989), 338.

18. Thomas A. Langford, *Theology in the Wesleyan Tradition*, Vol. 1 in the *Practical Divinity* Series (rev. ed.; Nashville: Abingdon Press, 1998), 20.

19. Kenneth J. Collins, *The Scripture Way of Salvation: The Heart of John Wesley's Theology* (Nashville: Abingdon Press, 1997), 19-20.

20. Thomas C. Oden, *The Transforming Power of Grace* (Nashville: Abingdon Press, 1993), 206.

21. Theodore Runyon, *The New Creation: John Wesley's Theology Today* (Nashville: Abingdon Press, 1998), 26.

22. Albert Outler, *John Wesley* (New York: Oxford University Press, 1964), 33. Thomas Noble cautioned against making grace an "impersonal intermediary entity" or an "impersonal force" as opposed to a legitimate metaphor describing the direct and personal action of God. (From e-mail correspondence with the author, May 1, 2008). Outler's use of the word "energy" would appear to be an example of the language Noble is critiquing; however, he was not alone in speaking this way. Charles Rogers also adopted the metaphor, defining prevenient grace as "energy enabling action." In Charles Allen Rogers, "The Concept of Prevenient Grace in the Theology of John Wesley" (Ph.D. thesis, Duke University, 1967), 257. In defense of Outler and Rogers, it may be questioned in what sense "energy" differs from the term "power," a term that John Wesley – as Kenneth Collins showed (see above) – employed in connection with the gracious activity of the Holy Spirit.

23. Robert V. Rakestraw, "John Wesley as a Theologian of Grace," *Journal of the Evangelical Theological Society* Vol. 27 (June 1984), 195.

24. William Burt Pope, *A Compendium of Christian Theology* (2 vols.; London: Wesleyan Conference Office, 1877), 2:359.

25. Michael Lodahl, *The Story of God: Wesleyan Theology and Biblical Narrative* (Kansas City, Missouri: Beacon Hill Press, 1994), 45.

26. H. Orton Wiley and Paul Culbertson, *Introduction to Christian Theology* (Kansas City, Missouri: Beacon Hill Press, 1946), 261.

27. Thomas C. Oden, *John Wesley's Scriptural Christianity: A Plain Exposition of His Teaching on Christian Doctrine* (Grand Rapids: Zondervan Publishing Company, 1994), 243.

28. Allan Coppedge, *Shaping the Wesleyan Message: John Wesley in Theological Debate* (Nappanee, Indiana: Francis Asbury Press/Evangel Pub. House, 2003), 111.

29. Steve Harper, *The Way to Heaven: The Gospel According to John Wesley* (Grand Rapids, Michigan: Zondervan, 2003), 35.

30. See p. 109.

31. Runyon, 34-35.

32. Leo Cox, "Prevenient Grace: A Wesleyan View," *Journal of the Evangelical Theological Society* 12 (Summer 1969): 145.

33. *Works* [BE], 8:278-279. This entry is also consistent with what John Deschner called Wesley's "concern to give a Christological grounding to his doctrine of prevenient grace and conscience." In John Deschner, *Wesley's Christology: An Interpretation* (1960; repr., Dallas: Southern Methodist University Press, 1985), 110.

34. William Greathouse and H. Ray Dunning, *An Introduction to Wesleyan Theology* (Kansas City, Missouri: Beacon Hill Press, 1989), 73; italics added.

35. Langford, *Wesleyan Tradition*, 28.

36. Eldon Fuhrman, "The Concept of Grace in the Theology of John Wesley" (Ph.D. thesis, University of Iowa, June, 1963), 123.

37. Irwin W. Reist "John Wesley's View of Man: A Study in Free Grace vs. Free Will," *Wesleyan Theological Journal* Vol. 7, Number 1 (Spring 1972), 29.

38. Ralph Del Colle, "John Wesley's Doctrine of Grace in Light of the Christian Tradition," *International Journal of Systematic Theology*, Vol. 4, No. 2 (July 2002), 187.

39. Del Colle, 179-180.

40. H. Ray Dunning, "Systematic Theology in a Wesleyan Mode," *Wesleyan Theological Journal*, Vol. 17, No. 1 (Spring 1982), 21.

41. Kenneth J. Collins, *Wesley on Salvation: A Study in the Standard Sermons* (Grand Rapids: Francis Asbury Press/Zondervan Publishing Company, 1989), 24.

42. McGonigle, *Sufficient Saving Grace*, 327. Besides universality in *space*, prevenient grace is universal in *time*, as it is – in the words of Weldon Smith – the "proleptic result of Christ's atoning work." See J. Weldon Smith III, "Some Notes on Wesley's Doctrine of Prevenient Grace," *Religion in Life* Vol. 34, No. 1 (Winter 1964-1965), 75. This helps explain, for example, how the ancient philosophers, like Socrates, could have been the recipients of the enlightenment provided by prevenient grace.

43. A. Skevington Wood, "John Wesley, Theologian of the Spirit," *Evangelical review of theology* 4 (1980), 177.

44. This pneumatological motif was apparent in some writers abridged by John Wesley in his *Christian Library*. For further details, see Chapter 1 of this monograph.

45. Dunning, *Grace, Faith, and Holiness*, 338-39, 431-36.

46. Outler, *John Wesley*, 33.

47. Albert Outler, in *Works* [BE], 1:99.

48. Robert Vincent Rakestraw, "The Concept of Grace in the Ethics of John Wesley" (Ph.D. thesis, Duke University, 1985), 138, 142. Theodore Runyon likewise affirms that Wesley was "concerned that a capacity within the human not be substituted for the necessary intervention of the divine Spirit in the renewal process." *New Creation*, 22.

49. Greathouse and Dunning, 60.

50. Ole E. Borgen, *John Wesley on the Sacraments: A Theological Study* (Nashville: Abingdon Press, 1972; repr., Eugene, Oregon: Wipf and Stock Publishers, 2000), 122-23.

51. Mack B. Stokes, *The Holy Spirit in the Wesleyan Heritage* (Nashville: Abingdon/ Graded Press, 1985), 47. Stokes has mischaracterized Wesley's position. Wesley taught that – while the Holy Spirit (via prevenient grace) influences all – the Holy Spirit only resides in believers. See the 1746 sermon, *The Spirit of Bondage and Adoption*, in *Works* [BE], 1:260; also, see Wesley's *New Testament Notes* on Romans 8:9, where a "Christian" is one who has the Spirit of Christ "dwelling and governing in him."

52. Fuhrman, 223. Mary Elizabeth Mullino-Moore viewed the law as a necessary supplement to prevenient grace in eliciting sensibility to sin, since the latter in most persons is usually stifled. In "Poverty, Human Depravity, and Prevenient Grace," *The Quarterly Review* Vol. 16 (Winter 1996), 354.

53. Cox, "Prevenient Grace," 147. Cox's remarks anticipated Randy Maddox's qualified use twenty years later of the language of regeneration to describe the working of prevenient grace.

54. Kenneth J. Collins, *The Theology of John Wesley: Holy Love and the Shape of Grace* (Nashville: Abingdon Press, 2007), 77.

55. John B. Cobb, Jr., "Human Responsibility and the Primacy of Grace," in Bryan P. Stone & Thomas Jay Oord, eds., *Thy Nature and Thy Name is Love: Wesleyan and Process Theologies in Dialogue* (Nashville: Kingswood Books/Abingdon Press, 2001), 99. Cobb's language approximates that of Mack Stokes. See endnote 49 above.

56. Lycurgus Starkey, *The Work of the Holy Spirit: A Study in Wesleyan Theology* (New York and Nashville: Abingdon Press, 1962), 41.

57. Starkey, 42-43.

58. Starkey, 45.

59. Harper, *Way to Heaven*, 35.

60. Harald Lindström, *Wesley and Sanctification* (1950; repr. Nappanee, Indiana: Francis Asbury Press/Evangel Publishing House, 1996), 45.

61. Collins, *Scripture Way*, 40. See also Albert Outler's comment on John Wesley's sermon, *On Conscience*, in *The Works of John Wesley*, Bi-Centennial edition (Frank Baker, ed. 35 vols. projected. Nashville: Abingdon Press, 1984), 2:479; hereafter, *Works* [BE].

62. Collins, *Scripture Way*, 40. Outler observed: "Wesley's pneumatology begins with an awareness of the religious and ethical import of a valid integration of Christology, soteriology, and pneumatology; the vital linkage between theo-logy, Christo-logy, and pneumato-logy held together by a consistent emphasis on the prevenience of all grace, an habituated awareness of the Holy Spirit as the Giver of all Grace." In Thomas C. Oden and Leicester R. Longden, eds., *The Wesleyan Theological Heritage: Essays of Albert C. Outler* (Grand Rapids: Zondervan Publishing House, 1991), 165.

63. Randy Maddox, *Responsible Grace: John Wesley's Practical Theology* (Nashville: Kingswood Books/Abingdon Press, 1994), 84. An example is the Collect for Easter-Day: "Almighty God...we humbly beseech thee, that as by thy special grace preventing us thou dost put into our minds good desires..." In *The Book of Common Prayer* (Glasgow: Collins' Clear-Type Press, n.d.), 134

64. *Works* [BE], 1:442.

65. Rogers, 205. This appears to be the position of Cary Balzer, who wrote: "Prevenient grace...is not a distinct stage that gives way to a new stage of growth in grace, but rather prevenience is an aspect of grace that operates throughout the life of the believer." In Cary Balzer, "John Wesley's Developing Soteriology and the Influence of the Caroline Divines" (Ph.D. thesis, University of Manchester, England, 2005), 30-31.

66. Rogers, 129; italics added.

67. "For Wesley, the prevenient grace of God restores to unregenerate man a measure of freedom requisite for choice and action in moral matters." Rogers, 195.

68. For a detailed analysis of sermons from Tilly's *Sixteen Sermons* that touched upon prevenient grace and that appear to have affected John Wesley's prevenient grace doctrine, see Chapter 1 of this inquiry.

69. Cited by Rogers, 128-129, as taken from the Colman collection, vol. 19 (Rogers, 295, bibliographical entry # 11).

70. McGonigle, *Sufficient Saving Grace*, 321.

71. McGonigle, *Sufficient Saving Grace*, 321.

72. Collins, *Scripture Way*, 40.

73. Collins, *Scripture Way*, 40.

74. Eldon Fuhrman noted: "Although Wesley did occasionally distinguish between various stages of grace, his usual method was to include everything prior to regeneration in the one category of prevenient grace." Fuhrman, 125.

75. Maddox, *Responsible Grace*, 159. See also Maddox, "Continuing the Conversation," *Methodist History* 30, no. 4 (July 1992), 235-241.

76. Colin W. Williams, *John Wesley's Theology Today* (New York and Nashville: Abingdon Press, 1960), 41-42.

77. Kenneth J. Collins, "Recent Trends in Wesley Studies and Wesleyan/Holiness Scholarship," *Wesleyan Theological Journal* 35:1 (Spring 2000), 73.

78. Collins, "Recent Trends," 73, fn. 14.

79. From an e-mail exchange between Randy Maddox and Greg Crofford, February 27-28, 2007. For the relevant portion from *On Working Out Our Own Salvation*, see *Works* [BE], 3:203-04. Weldon Smith, on the other hand, appears to have espoused an even more expansive understanding of prevenient grace as presented in *Our Own Salvation*: "I am persuaded that when Wesley says in the same sermon 'preventing

grace...implies some degree of salvation,' he is not speaking of the gift of conscience or other manifestations of imputed grace, but of the gift of faith, active grace." Smith, "Prevenient Grace," 78.

80. E-mail exchange, Maddox/Crofford, February 27-28, 2007.

81. Leo Cox twenty years prior made similar comments in an article for the *Wesleyan Theological Journal*, calling prevenient grace "a beginning of life which will lead on to further life if he responds to it." Cox, "Prevenient Grace," 147. Maddox affirmed that this accurately reflects his own position. From e-mail correspondence, March 3, 2007.

82. Williams, *Wesley's Theology*, 42.

83. Robert John Hillman, "Grace in the Preaching of Calvin and Wesley: A Comparative Study" (Ph.D. thesis, Fuller Theological Seminary, 1978), 157-58; italics are Hillman's. He further noted: "In his (Wesley's) preaching, the focus is on the preaching of the Gospel as *the* means by which grace comes to man to lead him to salvation." Hillman, "Calvin and Wesley," pp. 170-71. Hillman's view – while admirable for defending the role of preaching – would appear too narrow even from Wesley's point of view, where the "means of grace" included practices like the taking of Eucharist and the reading of Scripture. See Wesley's sermon, "The Means of Grace," *Works* [BE], 1: 376-97. The work of the Gideons confirms that prevenient and regenerating grace can operate via the reading of Scripture unaccompanied by proclamation. While these cases are exceptional, Hillman's conception failed to take them into account.

84. Starkey, *Holy Spirit*, 43.

85. Starkey, 43. Wesley was non-committal regarding the fate of those who hear no gospel preaching. In the 1784 sermon, *On Charity*, he commented on Mark 16:16: "Accordingly that sentence, 'He that believeth not shall be damned,' is spoken of them to whom the gospel is preached. Others it does not concern; and we are not required to determine anything touching their final state." In *Works* [BE], 3:295-96.

86. Starkey, 62.

87. Starkey, 62. John Wesley's father, Samuel Wesley, in a 1703 letter to the *Athenian Gazette*, wrote: "There is a natural religion written on every man's heart and these that are denied a greater light shall be judged according to that." Cited by Balzer, 45.

88. Hillman, 163.

89. Collins, *Scripture Way*, 43; also, *Holy Love and the Shape of Grace*, 80-82.

90. Collins, *Scripture Way*, 44.

91. *Holy Love and the Shape of Grace*, 80.

92. *Responsible Grace*, 88; see also 300, fn. 168. In a *Journal* entry for August 24, 1743, Wesley wrote regarding saving grace: "With regard to the Second, Irresistible Grace, I believe, That the grace which brings faith, and thereby salvation into the soul, is irresistible at that moment: That most believers may remember some time when God did irresistibly convince them of sin: That most believers do, at some other times, find God irresistibly acting upon their souls: Yet I believe that the grace of God, both before and after those moments, may be, and hath been, resisted..." In Nehemiah Curnock, ed., *The Journal of the Rev. John Wesley* (8 vols.; London: Epworth Press, 1938), 3:85. See also McGonigle, *Sufficient Saving Grace*, 154-55.

93. Albert Outler said that for Wesley, conscience was a "universal moral sense." He credited this understanding to Wesley's reading of the classics, including Lucretius, Sophocles, and Homer. See *Works* [BE], 1:73. Charles Rogers noted: "By virtue of Christ's work, the prevenient grace of God is bestowed upon man *universally*, as well before as after the historical event of the life and death of Jesus Christ." In Rogers, 243-44; italics added. Brian Shelton credited prevenient grace as a "way to reconcile inherited depravity and a world full of good deeds." In W. Brian Shelton, forthcoming as *Prevenient Grace* (Wilmore, Kentucky: Asbury Press, 2008), n.p.

94. Richard P. Heitzenrater, "God with Us: Grace and the Spiritual Senses in John Wesley's Theology," in Robert K. Johnston et. al., eds., *Grace Upon Grace: Essays in Honor of Thomas A. Langford* (Nashville: Abingdon Press, 1999), 94.

95. Lindström, 49.

96. Richard P. Heitzenrater, "Spiritual Senses," 94.

97. Theodore Runyon, *The New Creation: John Wesley's Theology Today* (Nashville: Abingdon Press, 1998), 32.

98. Runyon, 32. If conscience makes us aware of what is good, then prevenient grace, according to Heitzenrater, is God's way of providing "universally to fallen humanity the possibility of knowing the good and thereby the potential of restoring the capability of doing the good." Heitzenrater, "Spiritual Senses," 93.

99. Runyon, 33.

100. Collins, *Scripture Way*, 44.

101. Robert Cushman, "Salvation for All: Wesley and Calvinism," in William K. Anderson, ed., *Methodism: A Summary of basic information concerning The Methodist Church* (Cincinnati: The Methodist Publishing House, 1947), 105.

102. Williams, 46.

103. Williams, 46.

104. Del Colle, "Doctrine of Grace," 178.

105. Coppedge, 112.

106. John W. Prince, *Wesley on Religious Education* (New York and Cincinnati: The Methodist Book Concern, 1926), 40.

107. Herbert Boyd McGonigle, "Arminius and Wesley on Original Sin," *European Explorations in Christian Holiness*, Issue 2 (Summer 2001), 104-105. Leon Hynson concurred, explaining: "Ethics is grounded in the grace of God. Because of prevenient grace, every man is capable of moral action, and is morally responsible. Morality is an intimate expression and consequence of grace." In Leon O. Hynson, "Creation and Grace in Wesley's Ethics," *Drew Gateway*, Vol. 46, Nos. 1-3 (1975-1976), 50.

108. Heitzenrater, "Grace and the Spiritual Senses," 92.

109. Randy L. Maddox, "Responsible Grace: The Systematic Nature of Wesleyan Theology," *Wesleyan Theological Journal*, Vol. 19, No. 2 (Fall, 1984), 16.

110. Umphrey Lee, *John Wesley and Modern Religion* (Nashville, Tennessee: Cokesbury Press, 1936), 125.

111. Thomas Langford, *Wesleyan Tradition*, 28.

112. Lee, *Modern Religion*, 122.

113. Lee, 127.

114. Pope, *Compendium*, 2:367; italics added. Pope can seem inconsistent. One page earlier, he noted: "The fact that man is since the Fall, still a free agent is not more essentially a necessity of his moral nature than it is the effect of grace."

115. Pope, 2:364. Charles Rogers appeared to have a position like Pope's in-mind when he remarked: "It has been too quickly and uncritically assumed that Wesley's statements concerning free will are adequately understood as meaning that unregenerate man, through prevenient grace, is able as an act of free will to respond to grace when offered, and cooperate actively with grace in offering repentance or accepting faith." Rogers, 17.

116. See *Works* [BE], 2:172-85.

117. Hynson, "Free Grace vs. Free Will," 33.

118. John B. Cobb, Jr., *Grace & Responsibility: A Wesleyan Theology for Today* (Nashville: Abingdon Press, 1995), 37.

119. Langford, *Wesleyan Tradition*, 25.

120. Irwin W. Reist, "John Wesley's View of Man: A Study in Free Grace Versus Free Will," *Wesleyan Theological Journal* Vol. 7, No. 1 (Spring 1972), 26.

121. Einar A. Nilsen, "Prevenient Grace," *The London Quarterly & Holborn Review*, Vol. 184 (1959), 191.

122. H. Ray Dunning, *Reflecting the Divine Image: Christian Ethics in Wesleyan Perspective* (Downer's Grove: InterVarsity Press, 1998), 57.

123. George Croft Cell, *The Rediscovery of John Wesley* (New York: Henry Holt and Company, 1934), 347. See similar quote on pp. 359-60. Cell's larger thesis was presented earlier in his work: "Wesley was at heart, and what is more, openly, avowedly a Calvinist" (p. 244). To this sweeping claim, Herbert McGonigle replied: "To label Cell's conclusion misleading would be a gross understatement...Cell virtually ignored Wesley's fifty-year protest against the 'Five Points' of classic Calvinism." In *Sufficient Saving Grace*, 330. McGonigle's critique, while valid, does not undermine the validity of Cell's separate observation about the Protestant-Catholic synthesis. Cell anticipates by nearly 20 years a more developed interpretation of divine-human interaction in salvation that will become mainstream, beginning with Harald Lindström's 1950 *Wesley and Sanctification*, but more clearly with Colin Williams' 1964 *John Wesley's Theology Today*.

124. Hillman, "Calvin and Wesley," 171.

125. John L. Peters, *Christian Perfection and American Methodism* (Nashville, Tennessee: Pierce & Washabaugh, 1956; repr., Grand Rapids: Francis Asbury Press/Zondervan Publishing Company, 1985), 42-43. Peters does not clarify what he means by "semi-Augustinian."

126. Yoshio Noro, trans. John W. Krummel, "The Character of John Wesley's Faith," *The Wesleyan Quarterly Review*, Vol. 4 (1967), 20.

127. Robert C. Monk, *John Wesley: His Puritan Heritage—A Study of the Christian Life* (New York and Nashville: Abingdon Press, 1966), 102.

128. Cushman, 111.

129. Cushman, 115.

130. Robert E. Chiles, *Theological Transition in American Methodism* (New York and Nashville: Abingdon Press, 1965), 151.

131. An example of this despair is found in the 1746 sermon, *The Spirit of Bondage and Adoption*, where Wesley described at-length the struggle of one who has been awakened to his or her sinful condition and wishes not to sin, but has yet to receive the grace of justification: "And the more he frets against it (i.e. inward/outward sin), the more it prevails; he may bite, but cannot break his chain. Thus he toils without end, repenting and sinning, and repenting and sinning again, till at length the poor sinful, helpless wretch is even at his wit's end, and can barely groan, 'O wretched man that I am, who shall deliver me from the body of this death?'" *Works* [BE], 1:258.

132. Monk, 101. He continued: "Man cooperates in his salvation only in the sense of accepting or rejecting saving grace, and even this ability – or responsibility – is given by God's free gift of prevenient grace."

133. Albert C. Outler, *Evangelism and Theology in the Wesleyan Spirit* (1996; repr., Nashville: Discipleship Resources, 2000), 108.

134. Maddox, "Responsible Grace: Systematic Perspective," 13.

135. Michael Leffel, on the other hand, called the "despair" perspective "not consistent with Wesley's understanding of the cooperative quality of Grace." See G. Michael Leffel, "Prevenient Grace and the Re-Enchantment of Nature: Toward a Wesleyan Theology of Psychotherapy and Spiritual Formation," *Journal of Psychology and Christianity* Vol. 23, No. 2 (2004), 130-39. However, non-resistance to God's grace is a helpful image, safeguarding both God's initiative in salvation and human moral responsibility.

136. Charles Hodge, *Systematic Theology* (3 vols.; New York: Charles Scribner's Sons, 1871), 2:654-75.

137. Hodge, 2:670.

138. Hodge, 2:674.

139. Hodge, 2:671, 74.

140. Dale M. Yocum, *Creeds in Contrast* (Salem, Ohio: Schmul Pub. Company, 1986), 109.

141. Robert K. Johnston, "Rethinking Common Grace: Toward a Theology of Co-relation," in Robert K. Johnston et al., eds., *Grace Upon Grace: Essays in Honor of Thomas A. Langford* (Nashville: Abingdon Press, 1999), 153-68.

142. Dunning, *Grace, Faith, and Holiness*, 296. In *Predestination Calmly Considered*, Wesley conceded that common grace was a legitimate category for understanding how reprobates were restrained from hurting the elect. See *Works*, 10:228. Thomas Oden, however, went beyond Wesley by explaining conscience not in reference to prevenient grace but common grace. See Thomas C. Oden, *The Transforming Power of Grace* (Nashville: Abingdon Press, 1993), 71-73.

143. Leo Cox, "Prevenient Grace: A Wesleyan View," 143-49. Cox's summary was incomplete, since he neglected to root prevenient grace in the atonement of Christ.

144. Yocum, 109.

145. Neil R. Livingston, "A Calvinistic Concept of Prevenient Grace (M.Th. thesis, Dallas Theological Seminary, 1961), 57-66, 68.

146. Runyon, *New Creation*, 34.

147. Randy L. Maddox, "Wesley and the Question of Truth or Salvation through Other Religions," *Wesleyan Theological Journal* 27:1-2 (Spring-Fall 1992), 7-29. The broader missiological application of prevenient grace is beyond the scope of this work. See the "Appendix" for a partial listing of relevant sources and research suggestions in this area.

148. Maddox, "Question of Truth," 8.

149. Maddox, "Question of Truth," 16.

150. Maddox, "Question of Truth," 14.

151. Maddox, "Question of Truth," 15.

152. Maddox, "Question of Truth," 17-18. For a treatment of this theme as found in Wesley's sermons *On Charity* (1784) and *On Faith* (1788), see Chapter 3.

153. Maddox, "Question of Truth," 18. See especially Wesley's *New Testament Notes* on Acts 17:28, where Wesley recommended the hymn of Cleanthes to Jupiter as "one of the purest and finest pieces of natural religion in whole world of pagan antiquity." For other references in Wesley to what Albert Outler called "the salvability of the heathen," see *Works* [BE], 3:296, fn. 16.

154. For other instances (not addressed in this investigation) where significant departures from Wesley's theology occurred, consult Robert E. Chiles, *Theological Transition in American Methodism* (New York: Henry Holt and Company, 1934).

Appendix

Summary of Findings and Suggestions for Further Research

At the beginning of this investigation, it was noted the extent to which the doctrine of prevenient grace has become normative in the formulation of Wesleyan theology. In the dialogue with both moralistic and deterministic systems of thought, prevenient grace is a key to forging a dynamic *via media* that in the salvation encounter safeguards both divine initiative and human responsibility. Because John Wesley put a premium on Scripture as authoritative for theology,[1] he was intent on holding in creative tension the truths of divine sovereignty, justice, and love. To that end, prevenient grace became for Wesley what Ray Dunning calls "a theological category developed to capture a central biblical motif."[2]

This biblical motif was not apparent to John Wesley alone. Though rarely using the term itself, prominent Church of England, Puritan, and Quaker theologians from the 17th and early 18th century – many of whose writings are abridged in Wesley's *Christian Library* – employed anthropological, cosmological, and pneumatological terminology that was similar, helping forge the context in which the Wesley brothers' more developed prevenient grace doctrine developed. Fortified by the language of the *39 Articles* and the *Book of Common Prayer*, John Wesley taught prevenient grace from key Johannine passages such as John 1:9, 6:44, and 12:32. He recognized in the parable of the talents (Matt. 25) and the story of Cornelius (Acts 10) allusions to the workings of prevenient grace. Nevertheless, it was the place of his brother, Charles, to reinforce the doctrine through the poetic use of biblical metaphor (seed, talent, and light) and versifications upon other passages in the Gospels and Acts of the Apostles where he discerned the action of prevenient grace. In so doing, Charles made a contribution that was significant for its breadth and poetic simplicity.

The richness of prevenient grace entails not only its charting a mid-course between moralism and determinism, but also its usefulness as a missiological concept. Important work has already been done in this area, including theses by Mark Powell Royster[3] and Tae Hyoung Kwon.[4] In the ongoing discussion of religious pluralism, Clark Pinnock, Al Truesdale, and Mark Mann appropriated prevenient grace as a helpful rubric.[5] A further study in prevenient grace would examine not only these writers, but especially those who have written on the work of the Holy Spirit in relation to world religions.[6] The purpose would be to identify the diverse ways in which the prevenient grace concept has been used, and in what ways similar concepts have been employed by non-Wesleyan theologians. Such a study would be ecumenical in nature, allowing Wesleyan theologians to better communicate with their peers in other traditions by pursuing common goals, while learning ways to supplement the sometimes parochial jargon of prevenient grace.

An undeveloped theme that appears in the writings of John and Charles Wesley is the relationship between the Sacraments and prevenient grace. A follow-up study to the present inquiry would begin with the passing references in the Wesley brothers, then trace this motif through 19th and 20th century Methodism and up to the present day. On the Lord's Supper, Ole Borgen has already provided some helpful insights on John Wesley, but other subsequent theologians also merit research.[7] Regarding the baptism of infants, Rob Staples asserted: "Prevenient grace is not conveyed by infant baptism but is declarative of it."[8] Discovering the roots and development of this idea would be a worthwhile investigation in historical theology. Also worthwhile would be an exploration of Charles Wesley's doctrine of baptism, since at times he appears to espouse the baptismal regeneration of infants.

Some of non-Wesleyan persuasion have rightly criticized the Methodist tradition for its lack of exegetical spadework on the doctrine of prevenient grace.[9] The biblical basis of prevenient grace merits further elaboration. It is hoped that in addition to the soon to appear study by Brian Shelton[10], specialists in Old and New Testament studies will take up the challenge to more carefully exegete Scriptures germane to this important concept in Wesleyan theology.

While this inquiry has both revisited some of the theologians identified by Charles Rogers and gone beyond him by investigating the *Christian Library*, Jeremy Taylor, and Robert Barclay, research has necessarily been limited in scope. Future investigations would do well to explore those writing on prevenient grace between Augustine and Thomas Aquinas, tracing the development of the doctrine through the Middle Ages.

Prevenient grace – an element of the Wesley brothers' own theological heritage – is part of the legacy handed down to all reasoning Wesleyans. Rooted in Scripture and attested to by tradition, the prevenience of God's grace has been confirmed by generations of believers. May the same vital experience of grace be transmitted to those who follow in our footsteps.

Notes

1. See Scott J. Jones, *John Wesley's Conception and Use of Scripture* (Nashville: Kingswood Books/Abingdon Press, 1995).

2. H. Ray Dunning, *Grace, Faith, and Holiness* (Kansas City, Missouri: Beacon Hill Press, 1988), 338.

3. Royster, Mark Powell. "John Wesley's Doctrine of Prevenient Grace in Missiological Perspective." D.Miss. diss., Asbury Theological Seminary, 1989. Royster also examined the contribution to the doctrine made by John Fletcher and select early American Methodist theologians.

4. Tae Houng Kwon, "John Wesley's Doctrine of Prevenient Grace: It Impact on Contemporary Missiological Dialogue" (Ph.D. thesis, Temple University, 1996).

5. See Clark H. Pinnock, *A Wideness in God's Mercy: The Finality of Jesus Christ in a World of Religions* (Grand Rapids, Michigan: Zondervan Publishing House, 1992) ;Al Truesdale, *With Cords of Love: A Wesleyan Response to Religious Pluralism* (Kansas City, Missouri: Beacon Hill Press, 2006); Mark Mann, "Religious Pluralism," in Thomas J. Oord, ed., *Philosophy of Religion: Introductory Essays* (Kansas City, Missouri: Beacon Hill Press, 2003), 259-74.

6. An example is Amos Yong, *Beyond the Impasse: Toward a Pneumatological Theology of Religions* (Grand Rapids: Baker Academic, 2003).

7. Ole E. Borgen, *John Wesley on the Sacraments: A Theological Study* (1972; reprint, Eugene, Oregon: Wipf and Stock Publishers, 2000).

8. Rob Staples, *Outward Sign and Inward Grace: The Place of Sacraments in Wesleyan Spirituality* (Kansas City, Missouri: Beacon Hill Press, 1991), 179.

9. See Thomas R. Schreiner, "Does Scripture Teach Prevenient Grace in the Wesleyan Sense?," in *Still Sovereign? Contemporary Perspectives on Election, Foreknowledge, and Grace* (ed. Thomas R. Schreiner and Bruce A. Ware; Grand Rapids: Baker Books, 1995, 2000), 229-46; and William W. Combs, "Does the Bible Teach Prevenient Grace?", in *The Sovereignty of God and the Spread of the Gospel* (Allen Park, Michigan: Detroit Baptist Theological Seminary, 2002), 37-49.

10. W. Brian Shelton, forthcoming as *Prevenient Grace* (Wilmore, Kentucky: Francis Asbury Press, 2008).

Bibliography

Primary sources

Albin, Thomas R., and Beckerlegge, Oliver A. *Charles Wesley's Earliest Evangelical Sermons: Six Shorthand Manuscript Sermons now for the first time Transcribed from the Original.* Clayhall, Ilford: Wesley Historical Society, 1987.

Ambrose, Isaac. *The Complete Works of Isaac Ambrose.* London: Printed for R. Chiswel, B. Tooke, and T. Sawbridge, 1689.

Annesley, Samuel, ed. *The Morning Exercises at Cripplegate, or, Several Cases of Conscience Practically Resolved, by Sundry Ministers.* London: T. Milbourn and Joshua Johnson, 1671.

Barclay, Robert. *An Apology for the True Christian Divinity Being an Explanation and Vindication of the Principles and Doctrines of the People Called Quakers.* 1690 edition. Kessinger Publishing's Rare Mystical Reprints (www.kessinger.net), n.d.

Beckerlegge, Oliver A., and Kimbrough, S.T., Jr., eds. *The Unpublished Poetry of Charles Wesley.* 3 vols. Nashville: Kingswood Books/Abingdon Press, 1988.

Benson, Joseph, ed. *The Works of the Rev. John Fletcher, Late Vicar of Madeley* 9 vols. London: Wesleyan Conference Office, 1877.

The Book of Common Prayer. Glasgow: Collins' Clear-Type Press, n.d.

Carroll, Thomas K., ed. *Jeremy Taylor: Selected Works.* In *The Classics of Western Spirituality: A Library of the Great Spiritual* Masters. Edited by Bernard McGinn. New York and Mahwah, New Jersey: The Paulist Press, 1990.

Certain Sermons or Homilies appointed to be read in churches in the time of Queen Elizabeth of famous memory. Oxford: University Press, 1844.

Curnock, Nehemiah, ed. *The Journal of John Wesley, A.M.* 8 vols. London: Epworth Press, 1913; repr. 1938.

Eden, Charles Page, ed. *The Whole Works of the Right Rev. Jeremy Taylor, D.D., Lord Bishop of Down, Connor, and Dromore.* 10 vols. London: Longman, Brown, Green, et. al., 1847-52.

Grosart, Alexander B., ed. *Works of Richard Sibbes: Exposition and Treatises from Portions of Several of the Epistles of St. Paul.* Carlisle, Pennsylvania: Banner of Truth Trust, 1977.

Heber, Reginald, ed. *The Whole Works of the Right Rev. Jeremy Taylor.* 15 vols. London: Printed for C. and J. Rivington and others, 1828.

Jackson, Thomas. *The Journal of Charles Wesley*. 1849; Repr., Staffordshire: Tentmaker Publications, 2002.

Kimbrough, S.T., Jr., and Newport, Kenneth G.C., eds. *The Manuscript Journal of the Reverend Charles Wesley, M.A.* 2 vols. Nashville: Kingswood Books/Abingdon Press, 2008.

Law, William. *A Serious Call to a Devout and Holy Life, Adapted to the State and Condition of All Orders of Christians.* London: William Innys, 1729.

Locke, John. *An Essay Concerning Human Understanding.* Edited by Peter H. Niddich. Oxford: Clarendon Press, 1975.

Lucas, Richard. *An Enquiry After Happiness in Several Parts.* 6th ed. London: Printed for R. Gosling, 1734.

McNeill, John T., ed. *Calvin: Institutes of the Christian Religion.* Vols. 20 and 21 of the *Library of Christian Classics.* Translated by Ford Lewis Battles. London and Louisville: Westminster/John Knox Press, 1960.

Minutes of the Methodist Conferences from the First, held in London, by the Late Rev. John Wesley, A.M., in the year 1744. London: Thomas Cordeaux/Conference Office, 1812.

Newport, Kenneth G.C. *The Sermons of Charles Wesley: A Critical Edition with Introduction and Notes.* Oxford: Oxford University Press, 2001.

Osborn, G., ed. *The Poetical Works of John and Charles Wesley: Reprinted from the Originals, with the Last Corrections of the Authors; Together with the Poems of Charles Wesley not before Published.* 13 vols. London: Wesleyan-Methodist Conference Office, 1868-1872.

Outler, Albert C., ed.. *John Wesley.* New York: Oxford University Press, 1964.

Preston, John. *The Breast-Plate of Faith and Love.* London: R.Y. for Nicholas Bourne, 1634.

Reynolds, Edward. *The Whole Works of Edward Reynolds.* 6 vols. London: Printed for Holdsworth, 1826.

South, Robert. *Twelve Sermons Upon Several Subjects and Occasions.* London: Thomas Warren, 1698.

Taylor, John. *The Scripture Doctrine of Original Sin Proposed to a Free and Candid Examination.* 4th ed. London: J. Wilson, 1767.

Telford, John, ed. *The Letters of the Rev. John Wesley, A.M.* 8 vols. 1931; Repr., London: The Epworth Press, 1960.

_____. *The Life of the Rev. Charles Wesley, M.A.* London: Methodist Book Room, 1900.

Tillotson, John. *Sermons.* London: Printed for R. Chiswell, at the Rose and Crown in St. Paul's Church-yard, 1701.

Tilly, William. *Sixteen Sermons Upon Several Occasions, All (except One) Preached Before the University of Oxford at St. Mary's Church.* 2nd ed. London: Printed for John Osborn, 1737.

Tyson, John R., ed. *Charles Wesley: A Reader.* New York: Oxford University Press, 1989.

Wallace, Charles Jr., ed. *Susanna Wesley: The Complete Writings.* New York and Oxford: Oxford University Press, 1997.

Wesley, Charles. *The Journal of the Rev. Charles Wesley, M.A., Sometime Student of Christ Church, Oxford – The Early Journal, 1736-1739*. New Edition; Taylors, South Carolina: Methodist Reprint Society, 1977.
_____. *The Journal of Charles Wesley*. 2 vols. Stoke-on-Trent, Staffordshire, United Kingdom: Tentmaker Publications, 2002.
Wesley, John. *The Works of John Wesley*. Bi-Centennial edition. 35 vols. projected. Edited by Frank Baker. Nashville: Abingdon Press, 1984 to present.
_____. *The Works of John Wesley*. 3rd ed. 14 vols. 1872; reprint, Kansas City, Missouri: Beacon Hill Press, 1978.
_____. *Explanatory Notes Upon the New Testament*. London: Wesleyan-Methodist Book Room, n.d.
_____. *Serious Considerations on Absolute Predestination extracted from a late author*. Bristol: S. and F. Farley, 1741.
Wesley, John, ed. *A Christian Library*. 50 vols. Bristol: Felix Farley and Son, 1751-1755.
_____. *A Christian Library*. 30 vols. London: T. Cordeaux for T. Blanshard, 1819-1827.
Whitefield, George. "A Letter from the Reverend Mr. George Whitefield to the Reverend Mr. John Wesley in Answer to his Sermon entitled 'Free Grace.'" London: Printed by G. Rogers, for S. Kneeland and T. Green, Cornhill, 1740.
Williams, Griffith. *Discourses upon the existence and attributes of God, abridged from the writings of the late learned and venerable Stephen Charnock, B.D.* London: W. Smith, 1797.
Williams, Henry Griffin. *Select Discourses by John Smith, M.A., Formerly Fellow of Queen's College, Cambridge*. Cambridge: University Press, 1859.

Secondary sources

1. Monographs or Books in a Series

Allison, C. Fitzsimons. *The Rise of Moralism: The Proclamation of the Gospel from Hooker to Baxter*. Vancouver: Regent College Publishing, 1966.
Baker, Frank. *Charles Wesley's Verse: An Introduction*. 2nd Ed. London: The Epworth Press, 1988.
_____. *Charles Wesley As Revealed by His Letters*. London: The Epworth Press, 1948.
_____. *Representative Verse of Charles Wesley*. London: The Epworth Press, 1962.
Berger, Teresa. *Theology in Hymns? A Study of the Relationship of Doxology and Theology According to* A Collection of Hymns for the People Called Methodists (1780). Translated by Timothy E. Kimbrough. Nashville: Kingswood Books/Abingdon Press, 1995.
Bett, Henry. *The Hymns of Methodism in Their Literary Relations*. London: The Epworth Press, 1913.
Bicknell, E.J. *A Theological Introduction to the Thirty-Nine Articles*. 2nd edition. New York: Longmans, Green, and Co., 1925.

Borgen, Ole E. *John Wesley on the Sacraments: A Theological Study.* 1972; reprint, Eugene, Oregon: Wipf and Stock Publishers, 2000.

Brailsford, Mabel Richmond. *A Tale of Two Brothers: John and Charles Wesley.* London: Rupert Hart-Davis, 1954.

Brantley, Richard E. *Locke, Wesley, and the Method of English Romanticism.* Gainesville: University of Florida Press, 1984.

Brown-Lawson, Albert. *John Wesley and the Anglican Evangelicals of the Eighteenth Century.* Edinburgh, Cambridge, and Durham: The Pentland Press, 1994.

Burkill, T.A. *The Evolution of Christian Thought.* Ithaca and London: Cornell University Press, 1971.

Burnet, Gilbert. *An Exposition of the 39 Articles of the Church of England.* Oxford: Clarendon Press, 1814.

Butler, David. *Methodists and Papists: John Wesley and the Catholic Church in the 18th Century.* London: Dartman, Longman, and Todd, 1995.

Cairns, Earle Edwin. *Christianity Through the Centuries: A History of the Christian Church.* 3rd ed. Grand Rapids: Zondervan Publishing Co., 1996

Cannon, William Ragsdale. *The Theology of John Wesley.* New York and Nashville: Abingdon/Cokesbury Press, 1946.

Cell, George Croft. *The Rediscovery of John Wesley.* New York: Henry Holt and Company, 1934.

Chiles, Robert E. *Theological Transition in American Methodism.* New York and Nashville: Abingdon Press, 1965.

Cobb, John B., Jr. *Grace & Responsibility: A Wesleyan Theology for Today.* Nashville: Abingdon Press, 1995.

Collins, Kenneth J. *John Wesley: A Theological Journey.* Nashville: Abingdon Press, 2003.

_____. *The Scripture Way of Salvation: The Heart of John Wesley's Theology.* Nashville: Abingdon Press, 1997.

_____. *The Theology of John Wesley: Holy Love and the Shape of Grace.* Nashville: Abingdon Press, 2007.

_____. *Wesley on Salvation: A Study in the Standard Sermons.* Grand Rapids: Francis Asbury Press/Zondervan Publishing Company, 1989.

Coppedge, Allan. *Shaping the Wesleyan Message: John Wesley in Theological Debate.* 1987; Repr., Nappanee, Indiana: Francis Asbury Press/Evangel Publishing House, n.d.

Creamer, David. *Methodist Hymnology, Comprehending Notices of the Poetical Works of John and Charles Wesley.* New York: Joseph Longking, 1848.

Dallimore, Arnold. *A Heart Set Free: The life of Charles Wesley, Evangelist, Hymn-writer, Preacher.* Welwyn, Hertfordshire: Evangelical Press, 1988.

De Pauley, W.C. *The Candle of the Lord: Study in the Cambridge Platonists.* London: SPCK, 1937, 42.

Deschner, John. *Wesley's Christology: An Interpretation.* 1960; repr., Dallas: Southern Methodist University Press, 1985.

Dunning, H. Ray. *Grace, Faith, and Holiness.* Kansas City, Missouri: Beacon Hill Press, 1989.

_____. *Reflecting the Divine Image: Christian Ethics in Wesleyan Perspective.* Downer's Grove, Illinois: InterVarsity Press, 1998.

Eeg-Olofsson, Leif. *The Conception of the Inner Light in Robert Barclay's Theology: A Study in Quakerism.* Lund: CWK Gleerup, 1954.

Fairweather, A.M., trans. and ed. *Nature and Grace: Selections from the Summa Theologica of Thomas Aquinas.* In the *Library of Christian Classics* (Ichthus Edition), no volume numbers. Philadelphia: The Westminster Press, 1954.

Findlay, George H. *Christ's Standard Bearer: A Study in the Hymns of Charles Wesley as they are contained in the last edition (1876) of* A Collection of Hymns for the Use of the People Called Methodists, *by the Rev. John Wesley, A.M.* London: The Epworth Press, 1956.

Flew, R. Newton. *The Hymns of Charles Wesley: A Study of Their Structure.* London: The Epworth Press, 1953.

Gill, Frederick C. *Charles Wesley: the first Methodist.* London: Lutterworth Press, 1964.

Greathouse, William M., and Dunning, H. Ray. *An Introduction to Wesleyan Theology* Kansas City, Missouri: Beacon Hill Press, 1989.

Green, V.H.H. *The Young Mr. Wesley.* London: Edward Arnold Publishers, 1961.

Harper, Steve. *The Way to Heaven: The Gospel According to John Wesley.* Grand Rapids: Zondervan, 2003.

Heitzenrater, Richard P. *Wesley and the People Called Methodists.* Nashville: Abingdon Press, 1995.

Hills, Aaron Merritt. *Fundamental Christian Theology: A Systematic Theology.* 2 volumes. Pasadena, California: C.J. Kinne and Pasadena College, 1931.

Hodge, Charles. *Systematic Theology.* 3 vols. New York: Charles Scribner's Sons, 1871.

Houghton, Edward. *The Handmaid of Piety and other papers on Charles Wesley's Hymns.* Petergate, York: Wesley Fellowship/Quack Books, 1992.

Jackson, Thomas. *The Life of the Rev. Charles Wesley, sometime Student of Christ-Church Oxford.* 2 vols. London: Wesleyan Methodist Conference Office, 1841.

Jones, Scott J. *John Wesley's Conception and Use of Scripture.* Nashville: Kingswood Books/Abingdon Press, 1995.

Kendall, R.T. *Calvin and English Calvinism to 1649.* Rev. ed. New York: Oxford Univ. Press, 1981.

Kimbrough, S.T., Jr., ed. *Charles Wesley: Poet and Theologian.* Nashville: Kingswood Books/Abingdon Press, 1992.

Klaiber, Walter, and Marquardt, Manfred. *Living Grace: An Outline of United Methodist Theology.* Translated and adapted by J. Steven O'Malley and Ulrike R.M.Guthrie. Nashville: Abingdon Press, 2001.

Langford, Thomas A. *Theology in the Wesleyan Tradition.* Vol. 1 in the *Practical Divinity* Series. Rev. ed. Nashville: Abingdon Press, 1998.

Lawson, John. *The Wesley Hymns as a Guide to Scriptural Teaching.* Grand Rapids: Zondervan/Francis Asbury Press, 1987.

Lee, Umphrey. *John Wesley and Modern Religion.* Nashville: Cokesbury Press, 1936.

Lindström, Harald. *Wesley and Sanctification.* London: Epworth Press, 1950; repr., Napannee, Illinois: Francis Asbury/Evangel Publishing House, 1996.
Lloyd, Gareth. *Charles Wesley and the Struggle for Methodist Identity.* Oxford: Oxford University Press, 2007.
Lodahl, Michael. *The Story of God: Wesleyan Theology and Biblical Narrative.* Kansas City, Missouri: Beacon Hill Press, 1994.
Long, D. Stephen. *John Wesley's Moral Theology: The Quest for God and Goodness.* Nashville: Kingswood Books/Abingdon Press, 2005.
MacCulloch, Diarmaid. *Thomas Cranmer: A Life.* New Haven and London: Yale University Press, 1996.
Maddox, Randy L. *Responsible Grace: John Wesley's Practical Theology.* Nashville: Kingswood Books/Abingdon Press, 1994.
Manning, Bernard Lord. *The Hymns of Wesley and Watts: Five Informal Papers.* London: The Epworth Press, 1942.
Marquardt, Manfred. *John Wesley's Social Ethics: Praxis and Principle.* Translated by John E. Steely and W. Stephen Gunter. Eugene, Oregon: Wipf and Stock Publishers, 2000.
Matthaei, Sondra Higgins. *Making Disciples: Faith Formation in the Wesleyan Tradition.* Nashville: Abingdon Press, 2000.
McAdoo, H.R. *The Spirit of Anglicanism: A Survey of Anglican Theological Method in the Seventeenth Century.* New York: Charles Scribner's Sons, 1965.
_____. *The Structure of Caroline Moral Theology.* London, New York, and Toronto: Longmans, Green, and Co., 1949.
_____. *The Eucharistic Theology of Jeremy Taylor Today.* Norfolk: The Canterbury Press Norwich, 1988.
McGonigle, Herbert Boyd. *Sufficient Saving Grace: John Wesley's Evangelical Arminianism.* Carlisle. Cumbria, and Waynesboro, Georgia: Paternoster Press, 2001.
_____. *John Wesley's Doctrine of Prevenient Grace.* Derbys: Wesley Fellowship/Mooreley's Print and Publishing, 1995.
McReynolds, Kathy. *Susanna Wesley.* Minneapolis: Bethany House Publishers. 1988.
Miley, John. *Systematic Theology.* 2 vols. New York: Hunt & Eaton, 1892. Reprint, Peabody, Massachusetts: Hendrickson Publishers, 1989.
Monk, Robert C. *John Wesley, His Puritan Heritage: A Study of the Christian Life.* Nashville and New York: Abingdon Press, 1966.
Newport, Kenneth G.C., and Campbell, Ted A., eds. *Charles Wesley: Life, Literature, and Legacy.* Werrington, Peterborough: Epworth Press, 2007.
Newton, John A. *Susanna Wesley and the Puritan Tradition in Methodism.* 2nd Edition. London: Epworth Press, 2002.
Oden, Thomas C. *John Wesley's Scriptural Christianity: A Plain Exposition of His Teaching on Christian Doctrine.* Grand Rapids: Zondervan Publishing Company, 1994.
_____. *The Transforming Power of Grace.* Nashville: Abingdon Press, 1993.
O'Donovan, Oliver. *On the Thirty-Nine Articles: A Conversation with Tudor Christianity.* Exeter: Paternoster Press, 1986.

Outler, Albert C., ed. *John Wesley*. New York: Oxford University Press, 1964.

―――――. *The Wesleyan Theological Heritage: Essays of Albert C. Outler*. Edited by Thomas C. Oden, and Leicester R. Longden. Grand Rapids: Zondervan Publishing House, 1991.

Packer, James I. *Evangelism and the Sovereignty of God*. London: InterVarsity Fellowship, 1961.

Peters, John L. *Christian Perfection and American Methodism*. Nashville: Pierce & Washabaugh, 1956; repr., Grand Rapids: Francis Asbury Press/Zondervan Publishing Company, 1985.

Pollock, John. *Whitefield the Evangelist*. Eastbourne: Kingsway Publications, 2000.

Pope, William Burt. *A Compendium of Christian Theology*. 2 vols. London: Wesleyan Conference Office, 1877.

Prince, John W. *Wesley on Religious* Education. New York and Cincinnati: The Methodist Book Concern, 1926.

Purkiser, W.T., ed. *Exploring our Christian Faith*. Kansas City, Missouri: Beacon Hill Press, 1960, 1978.

Rack, Henry D. *Reasonable Enthusiast: John Wesley and the Rise of Methodism*. 3d ed. London: Epworth Press, 2002.

Rattenbury, J. Ernest. *The Eucharistic Hymns of John and Charles Wesley*. London: Epworth Press, 1948. Repr., 2nd American Edition, Akron, Ohio: OSL Publications, 1996.

―――――. *The Evangelical Doctrines of Charles Wesley's Hymns*. London: The Epworth Press, 1941.

Routley, Erik. *The Musical Wesleys*. New York: Oxford University Press, 1968.

Runyon, Theodore. *The New Creation: John Wesley's Theology Today*. Nashville: Abingdon Press, 1998.

Shelton, W. Brian. Forthcoming as *Prevenient Grace*. Wilmore, Kentucky: Francis Asbury Press, 2008.

Staples, Rob L. *Outward Sign and Inward Grace: The Place of the Sacraments in Wesleyan Spirituality*. Kansas City, Missouri: Beacon Hill Press, 1991.

Starkey, Lycurgus. *The Work of the Holy Spirit: A Study in Wesleyan Theology*. New York and Nashville: Abingdon Press, 1962.

Stokes, Mack B. *The Holy Spirit in the Wesleyan Heritage*. Nashville: Abingdon/Graded Press, 1985.

Stranks, C.J. *The Life and Writings of Jeremy Taylor*. London: S.P.C.K., 1952.

―――――. *Anglican Devotion: Studies in the Spiritual Life of the Church of England between the Reformation and the Oxford Movement*. London: SCM Press Ltd., 1961.

Tabraham, Barrie W. *Brother Charles*. Vol. 6 in the *Exploring Methodism* series. Peterborough: Epworth Press, 2003.

Telford, John. *The Life of the Rev. Charles Wesley, M.A*. London: Wesleyan-Methodist Book Room, 1900.

Tomkins, Stephen. *John Wesley: A Biography*. Grand Rapids: Wm. B. Eerdmans, 2003.

Trueblood, D. Elton. *Robert Barclay: A portrait of the life and times of a great Quaker intellectual leader.* New York, Evanston, and London: Harper and Row, 1968.
Truesdale, Al. *With Cords of Love: A Wesleyan Response to Religious Pluralism.* Kansas City, Missouri: Beacon Hill Press, 2006.
Tyson, John R., ed. *Charles Wesley: A Reader.* Oxford: Oxford University Press, 1989.
Watson, Richard. *Theological Institutes, or a View of the Evidences, Doctrines, Morals and Institutions of Christianity.* 2 volumes. New York: T. Mason and G. Lane, 1836.
Wiley, H. Orton, and Culbertson, Paul T. *Introduction to Christian Theology.* Kansas City, Missouri: Beacon Hill Press, 1946.
Williams, Colin. *John Wesley's Theology Today.* New York and Nashville: Abingdon Press, 1964.
Wiseman, F. Luke. *Charles Wesley: Evangelist and Poet.* London: The Epworth Press, 1932.
Woodberry, J. Dudley, ed. *Muslims and Christians on the Emmaus Road.* Monrovia, California: Marc Publications, 1989.
Woods, F.H., and Johnston, J.O., trans. *Three Anti-Pelagian Treatises of S. Augustine.* London: David Nutt, 1887.
Yocum, Dale M. *Creeds in Contrast.* Salem, Ohio: Schmul Pub. Company, 1986.
Yong, Amos. *Beyond the Impasse: Toward a Pneumatological Theology of Religions.* Grand Rapids, Michigan, and Carlisle, Cumbria: Baker Academic Books and Paternoster Press, 2003.
Young, Carlton R. *Music of the Heart: John & Charles Wesley on Music and Musicians.* Carol Stream, Illinois: Hope Publishing Company, 1995.
Yrigoyen, Charles, Jr. *Praising the God of Grace: The Theology of Charles Wesley's Hymns.* Nashville: Abingdon Press, 2005.

2. Chapters or Essays in an Edited Book

Albin, Thomas R. "Charles Wesley's Other Prose Writings." Pages 85-94 in *Charles Wesley: Poet and Theologian.* Edited by S.T. Kimbrough, Jr. Nashville: Abingdon/Kingswood Books, 1992.
Campbell, Ted A. "Charles Wesley, *Theologos.*" Pages 264-277 in *Charles Wesley: Life, Literature & Legacy.* Edited by Kenneth G.C. Newport and Ted A. Campbell. Werrington, Peterborough: Epworth Press, 2007.
Cobb, John B., Jr. "Human Responsibility and the Primacy of Grace." Pages 95-110 in *Thy Nature & Thy Name is Love.* Edited by Bryan P. Stone and Thomas Jay Oord. Nashville: Kingswood Books/Abingdon Press, 2001.
Combs, William W. "Does the Bible Teach Prevenient Grace? Pages 37-49 in *The Sovereignty of God and the Spread of the Gospel* (Allen Park, Michigan: Detroit Baptist Theological Seminary, 2002).
Cushman, Robert. "Salvation for All: Wesley and Calvinism." Pages 103-15 in *Methodism: A Summary of basic information concerning The Methodist Church.*

Edited by William K. Anderson. Cincinnati: The Methodist Publishing House, 1947.

Dale, James. "The Singer's Response to the Word: Charles Wesley's Hymns of Invitation." Pages 237-256 in *The Contribution of Methodism to Atlantic Canada*. Edited by Charles H.H. Scobie and John Webster Grant. Montreal: McGill-Queen's University Press, 1992.

Heitzenrater, Richard P. "Charles Wesley and the Methodist Tradition." Pages 176-185 in *Charles Wesley: Poet and Theologian*. Edited by S.T. Kimbrough, Jr. Nashville: Abingdon/Kingswood Books, 1992.

_____. "God with Us: Grace and the Spiritual Senses in John Wesley's Theology." Pages 87-109 in *Grace Upon Grace: Essays in Honor of Thomas A. Langford*. Edited by Robert K. Johnston et al. Nashville: Abingdon Press, 1999.

Knight, John Allan. "Aspects of Wesley's Theology After 1770." Pages 33-42 in *Methodist History*. Lake Junaluska, North Carolina: Commission on Archives and History, The United Methodist Church, 1968.

Johnston, Robert K. "Rethinking Common Grace: Toward a Theology of Co-relation."

Pages 153-168 in Robert K. Johnston et al., eds., *Grace Upon Grace: Essays in Honor of Thomas A. Langford*. Nashville: Abingdon Press, 1999.

Langford, Thomas A. "Charles Wesley as Theologian." Pages 97-106 in *Charles Wesley: Poet and Theologian*. Edited by S.T. Kimbrough, Jr. Nashville: Abingdon/Kingswood Books, 1992.

Mann, Mark Grear. "Religious Pluralism." Pages 259-74 in *Philosophy of Religion: Introductory Essays*. Edited by Thomas J. Oord. Kansas City, Missouri: Beacon Hill Press, 2003.

Outler, Albert C. "The Place of Wesley in the Christian Tradition." Pages 11-38 in *The Place of Wesley in the Christian Tradition*. Edited by Kenneth E. Rowe. 1976; reprint, Metuchen, New Jersey: Scarecrow Press, 1980.

Schreiner, Thomas R. "Does Scripture Teach Prevenient Grace in the Wesleyan Sense?" Pages 229-246 in *Still Sovereign: Contemporary Perspectives on Election, Foreknowledge, and Grace*. Edited by Thomas R. Schreiner and Bruce A. Ware. Grand Rapids: Baker Books, 1995, 2000.

Smith, Timothy L. "The Theology of the Wesleys' Hymns." Pages 1011-1042 in *A Contemporary Wesleyan Theology: Biblical, Systematic, and Practical*. Edited by Charles W. Carter. Grand Rapids: Zondervan/Francis Asbury Press, 1983.

Wainwright, Geoffrey. "Charles Wesley and Calvinism." Pages 184-203 in *Charles Wesley: Life, Literature & Legacy*. Edited by Kenneth G.C. Newport and Ted A. Campbell. Werrington, Peterborough: Epworth Press, 2007.

White, Susan J. "Charles Wesley and Contemporary Theology." Pages 515-531 in *Charles Wesley: Life, Literature & Legacy*. Edited by Kenneth G.C. Newport and Ted A. Campbell. Werrington, Peterborough: Epworth Press, 2007.

3. Dissertations, Theses, and Unpublished Papers

Balzer, Cary. "John Wesley's Developing Soteriology and the Influence of the Caroline Divines." Ph.D. thesis, University of Manchester, England, 2005.

Benefiel, Ron. "John Wesley's Doctrine of Original Sin." Unpublished paper, Nazarene Theological College, Manchester, England, May 29, 2002.

Crofford, James Gregory. "Justification in John Calvin and John Wesley: A Comparative Study." M.A. diss.., Nazarene Theological College/University of Manchester, 2005.

Dale, James. "The Theological and Literary Qualities of the Poetry of Charles Wesley in Relation to the Standards of His Age." Ph.D. thesis, Univ. of Cambridge, 1960.

Downes, J. Cryril. "Eschatological Doctrines in the Writings of John and Charles Wesley." Ph.D. thesis, University of Edinburgh, 1960.

Ekrut, James Charles, Jr. "Universal Redemption, Assurance of Salvation, and Christian Perfection in the Hymns of Charles Wesley, with Poetic Analyses and Tune Examples." M. Mus. thesis, Southwestern Baptist Theological Seminary, 1978.

Fuhrman, Eldon . "The Concept of Grace in the Theology of John Wesley." Ph.D. thesis, University of Iowa, June, 1963.

Gallaway, Craig B. "The Presence of Christ with the Worshipping Community: A Study in the Hymns of John and Charles Wesley." Ph.D. thesis, Emory University, 1988.

Gerlach, Harlan R. "The Arminian Doctrine of Prevenient Grace." M.Th. thesis, Dallas Theological Seminary, 1956.

Griggs, Geoffrey. "An Assessment of Charles Wesley's Contribution to the Evangelical Awakening 1739-1751." M. Phil. thesis, University of Manchester, 2005.

Heitzenrater, Richard Paul. "John Wesley and the Oxford Methodists, 1725-35." Ph.D. thesis., Duke University, 1972.

Hillman, Robert John. "Grace in the Preaching of Calvin and Wesley: A Comparative Study." Ph.D. thesis, Fuller Theological Seminary, 1978.

Kwon, Tae Hyoung. "John Wesley's Doctrine of Prevenient Grace: Its Impact on Contemporary Missiological Dialogue." Ph.D. thesis, Temple University, 1996.

Livingston, Neil R. "A Calvinistic Concept of Prevenient Grace." M.Th. thesis, Dallas Theological Seminary, 1961.

Lloyd, Gareth. "Charles Wesley: A New Evaluation of his Life and Ministry." Ph.D. thesis, University of Liverpool, 2002.

Lohrstorfer, Chris. "Know Your Disease, Know Your Cure: A Critical Analysis of John Wesley's Sources for his Doctrine of Original Sin." Ph.D. thesis, University of Manchester, 2006.

Marquardt, Manfred. *John Wesley's Social Ethics: Praxis and Principle*. Translated by John E. Steely and W. Stephen Gunter. Eugene, Oregon: Wipf and Stock Publishers, 2000.

McGonigle, Herbert Boyd. "Christianity or Deism? John Wesley's Response to John Taylor's Denial of the Doctrine of Original Sin." Unpublished paper, Nazarene Theological College, Manchester, England, June, 2005.

Morris, Gilbert Leslie. "Imagery in the Hymns of Charles Wesley." Ph.D. thesis, University of Arkansas, 1969.
Quantrille, Wilma Jean. "The Triune God in the Hymns of Charles Wesley." Ph.D. thesis, Drew University, 1989.
Rainey, David. "John Wesley's Doctrine of Salvation in Relation to His Doctrine of God." Ph.D. thesis, King's College/University of London, 2006.
Rakestraw, Robert Vincent. "The Concept of Grace in the Ethics of John Wesley." Ph.D. thesis, Duke University, 1985.
Renshaw, John Rutherford. "The Atonement in the Theology of John and Charles Wesley." Th.D. thesis, Boston University School of Theology, 1965.
Rogers, Charles Allen. "The Concept of Prevenient Grace in the Theology of John Wesley." Ph.D. thesis, Duke University, 1967.
Royster, Mark Powell. "John Wesley's Doctrine of Prevenient Grace in Missiological Perspective." D.Miss. diss., Asbury Theological Seminary, 1989.
Selleck, Jerald Brian. "The Book of Common Prayer." Ph.D. thesis, Drew University, 1983.
Shepherd, Neville Thomas. "Charles Wesley and the Doctrine of the Atonement." Ph.D. thesis, University of Bristol, 1999.
Taek Kim, Young. "A Comparative Study of the Doctrine of Grace Between Calvin and Wesley." M.Th. thesis, Southwestern Baptist Theological Seminary, 1999.

4. Internet Documents

Charles Wesley's published verse (Duke Divinity School criticial edition). Cited April 4, 2007. Online: http://www.divinity.duke.edu/wesleyan/texts/cw_published_verse.html.
Concise Oxford English Dictionary. "Nature." No pages. Cited October 11, 2007. Online: http://www.askoxford.com/concise_oed/nature?view=uk.
"The Homilies." No pages. Cited August 1, 2005. Online: http://www.anglicanlibrary.org/homilies.
Huckabee, Davis W. "Studies on Strong Doctrine, Chapter One: Prevenient Grace." No pages. Cited June 2, 2002. Online: http://www.pbsministries.org/baptists.htm.
Paton, Jeff. "Prevenient Grace." n.p. [cited June 16, 2003]. Online: http://biblicaltheology.webhostme.com/prevenient_grace.htm.

5. Dictionary, Encyclopedia, and Journal Articles

Atherton, Ian. "Reynolds, Edward." Pages 529-30 of vol. 46 in the *Oxford Dictionary of National Biography, from the Earliest Times to the year 2000*. Edited by H.C.G. Matthew and Brian Harrison. 60 vols. Oxford, England: Oxford University Press, 2004.
Baker, Frank. "Wesley's Puritan Ancestry." *London Quarterly and Holborn Review* 187 (1962): 180-186.
_____. "Charles Wesley's Productivity as a Religious Poet." *Proceedings of the Wesley Historical Society* Vol. XLVII (February 1989): 1-12.

Bailey, John Eglington. "Ambrose, Isaac." Pages 350-51 in vol. 1 of the *Dictionary of National Biography*. Edited by Leslie Stephen and Sidney Lee. 22 vols. London: Smith, Elder, & Co., 1908.

Barnard, Toby. "Browne, Peter." Pages 187-88 in vol. 8 of the *Oxford Dictionary of National Biography, from the Earliest Times to the year 2000*. Edited by H.C.G. Matthew and Brian Harrison. 60 vols. Oxford, England: Oxford University Press, 2004.

Beck, Brian. "Rattenbury Revisited: The Theology of Charles Wesley's Hymns." *Epworth Review* 26:2 (April 1999): 71-81.

Bennett, David. "How Arminian was John Wesley?" *The Evangelical Quarterly* 72:3 (July 2000): 237-248.

Bible, Ken. "The Wesleys' Hymns on Full Redemption and Pentecost: A Brief Comparison." *Wesleyan Theological Journal* 17:2 (Fall 1982): 79-87.

Blaikie, William Gordon. "Charnock, Stephen." Pages 134-5 in vol. 4 of the *Dictionary of National Biography*. Edited by Leslie Stephen and Sidney Lee. 22 vols. London: Smith, Elder, & Co., 1908.

Burrows, Clive. "Prevenient Grace: A Wesleyan Perspective." *European Explorations in Christian Holiness* 1 (September 1999): 60-68.

Collins, Kenneth J. "Recent Trends in Wesley Studies and Wesleyan/Holiness Scholarship," *Wesleyan Theological Journal* 35:1 (Spring 2000): 67-86.

Cope, Jackson I. "Seventeenth Century Quaker Style" *PMLA* 71:4 (September 1956): 725-54.

Cox, Leo. "Prevenient Grace: A Wesleyan View." *Journal of the Evangelical Theological Society* 12 (Summer 1969): 143-49.

Dever, Mark E. "Sibbes, Richard." Pages 486-88 in vol. 50 of the *Oxford Dictionary of National Biography, from the Earliest Times to the year 2000*. Edited by H.C.G. Matthew and Brian Harrison. 60 vols. Oxford: Oxford University Press, 2004.

Del Colle, Ralph. "John Wesley's Doctrine of Grace in Light of the Christian Tradition," *International Journal of Systematic Theology*, 4:2 (July 2002): 172-189.

"Didymus." " Mr. Wesley's Christian Library." *The Wesleyan Methodist* XXVII. Vol. 50, from the beginning, or vol. 6 in the 3rd series, No. 27 (1827), 315.

Dunning, H. Ray. "Systematic Theology in a Wesleyan Mode." *Wesleyan Theological Journal*, 17:1 (Spring 1982): 15-22.

Ellingsworth, Paul. " 'I' and 'we' in Charles Wesley's Hymns." *The London Quarterly and Holborn Review*, 188 (April 1963): 153-164.

Fox, Harold G. "John Wesley and Natural Philosophy." *The University of Dayton Review* 7:1 (1970): 31-39.

Frost, J. William. "The Dry Bones of Quaker Theology." *Church History* 39:4 (December 1970): 503-523.

Gordon, Alexander. "Preston, John, D.D." Pages 308-12 in vol. 16 of the *Dictionary of National Biography*. Edited by Leslie Stephen and Sidney Lee. 22 vols. London: Smith, Elder, & Co., 1908.

_____. "Sibbes, Sibbs, or Sibs, Richard, D.D." Pages 182-83 in vol. 18 of the *Dictionary of National Biography*. Edited by Leslie Stephen and Sidney Lee. 22 vols. London: Smith, Elder, & Co., 1908.

_____. "South, Robert, D.D." Pages 683-85 in vol. 18 of the *Dictionary of National Biography*. Edited by Leslie Stephen and Sidney Lee. 22 vols. London: Smith, Elder, & Co., 1908.

_____. "Taylor, Jeremy, D.D." Pages 422-29 in vol. 19 of the *Dictionary of National Biography*. Edited by Leslie Stephen and Sidney Lee. 22 vols. London: Smith, Elder, & Co., 1908.

_____. "Tillotson, John." Page 874 in vol. 19 of the *Dictionary of National Biography*. Edited by Leslie Stephen and Sidney Lee. 22 vols. London: Smith, Elder, & Co., 1908.

Gordon, James G. "Impassive He Suffers; Immortal He Dies; Rhetoric and Polemic in Charles Wesley's Portrayal of the Atonement." *Scottish Bulletin of Evangelical Theology* 18:1 (Spring 2000), 56-70.

Greaves, Richard L. "Charnock, Stephen." Pages 203-05 in vol. 11 of the *Oxford Dictionary of National Biography, from the Earliest Times to the year 2000*. Edited by H.C.G. Matthew and Brian Harrison. 60 vols. Oxford: Oxford University Press, 2004.

Grider, J. Kenneth. "Prevenient Grace." Pages 415-16 in *The Beacon Dictionary of Theology*. Edited by Richard S. Taylor et al. Kansas City, Missouri: Beacon Hill Press, 1984.

Griggs, Burke. "South, Robert." Page 679 in Vol. 51 of the *Oxford Dictionary of National Biography, from the Earliest Times to the year 2000*. Edited by H.C.G. Matthew and Brian Harrison. 60 vols. Oxford: Oxford University Press, 2004.

Grosart, Alexander Balloch . "Annesley, Samuel." Page 480 in vol. 1 of the *Dictionary of National Biography*. Edited by Leslie Stephen and Sidney Lee. 22 vols. London: Smith, Elder, & Co., 1908.

_____. "Bolton, Robert." Pages 792-94 in Vol. 2 of the *Dictionary of National Biography*. Edited by Leslie Stephen and Sidney Lee. 22 vols. London: Smith, Elder, & Co., 1908.

Heitzenrater, Richard. "The Current State of Wesley Studies." *Methodist History* 22:4 (July 1984): 221-233.

Hendricks, M. Elton. "John Wesley and Natural Philosophy." *Wesleyan Theological Journal* 18:2 (Fall 1983): 7-17.

Hoskins, Steven T. "Eucharist and Eschatology in the Writings of the Wesleys." *Wesleyan Theological Journal* 19:1-2 (Spring-Fall 1994): 64-80.

Hutton, Sarah. "Smith, John." Pages 200-01 in vol. 51 of the *Oxford Dictionary of National Biography, from the Earliest Times to the year 2000*. Edited by H.C.G. Matthew and Brian Harrison. 60 vols. Oxford: Oxford University Press, 2004.

Hynson, Leon O. "Creation and Grace in Wesley's Ethics." *Drew Gateway* 46:1-3 (1975-1976): 41-55.

Key, Newton E. "Annesley, Samuel." Pages 238-39 in vol. 2 of the *Oxford Dictionary of National Biography, from the Earliest Times to the year 2000*. Edited by H.C.G.Matthew and Brian Harrison. 60 vols. Oxford: Oxford University Press, 2004.

Kirby, Ethyn Williams. "The Quakers' Efforts to Secure Civil and Religious Liberty, 1660-96." *The Journal of Modern History* 7:4 (December 1935): 401-21.

Leffel, G. Michael. "Prevenient Grace and the Re-Enchantment of Nature: Toward a Wesleyan Theology of Psychotherapy and Spiritual Formation." *Journal of Psychology and Christianity* 23:2 (2004): 130-39.

Maddox, Randy. "The Collection of Books Owned by the Charles Wesley Family." *Wesleyan Theological Journal*, 38:2 (Fall 2003): 175-216.

_____. "Responsible Grace: The Systematic Nature of Wesleyan Theology," *Wesleyan Theological Journal*, 19:2 (Fall, 1984): 7-22.

_____. "Wesley and the Question of Truth or Salvation Through Other Religions." *Wesleyan Theological Journal*, 27:1-2 (Spring-Fall 1992): 7-29.

McGonigle, Herbert Boyd. "Arminius and Wesley on Original Sin," *European Explorations in Christian Holiness* Issue 2 (Summer, 2001): 96-108.

Mitchell, T. Crichton. "Response to Dr. Timothy Smith on the Wesley Hymns." *Wesleyan Theological Journal* 16:2 (Fall 1981): 48-57.

Moore, Jonathan D. "Preston, John." Pages 260-64 in vol. 45 of the *Oxford Dictionary of National Biography, from the Earliest Times to the year 2000*. Edited by H.C.G. Matthew and Brian Harrison. 60 vols. Oxford, England: Oxford University Press, 2004.

Mullino-Moore, Mary Elizabeth. "Poverty, Human Depravity, and Prevenient Grace." *The Quarterly Review* 16 (Winter 1996): 343-60.

Newport, Kenneth G.C. "Charles Wesley, 'Warts and All'": The Evidence of the Prose Works." *Proceedings of the Wesley Historical Society*. 56:4 (February 2008): 165-85.

Nilsen, Einar A. "Prevenient Grace." *The London Quarterly & Holborn Review*. 184 (1959): 188-94.

Noll, Mark A. "Romanticism and the Hymns of Charles Wesley." *The Evangelical Quarterly* XLVI:4 (Oct-Dec 1974): 195-223.

Noro, Yoshio. "The Character of John Wesley's Faith." Translated by John W. Krummel. *The Wesleyan Quarterly Review* 4 (1967): 10-26.

_____. "Wesley's Theological Epistemology." Translated by John W. Krummel. *The Iliff Review* 28 (Winter 1971): 59-76.

Olleson, Philip. "The Wesleys at Home: Charles Wesley and His Children." *Methodist History* 36 (April 1998): 139-152.

Overton, John Henry. "Lucas, Richard, D.D." Pages 239-40 of the *Dictionary of National Biography*. Edited by Leslie Stephen and Sidney Lee. 22 vols. London: Smith, Elder, & Co., 1908.

Peterson, Raymond A. "Jeremy Taylor in Conscience and Law." *Anglican Theological Review* 48 (July '66): 243-63.

Pooley, Roger. "Ambrose, Isaac." Page 921 in vol. 1 of the *Oxford Dictionary of National Biography, from the Earliest Times to the year 2000*. Edited by H.C.G. Matthew and Brian Harrison. 60 vols. Oxford: Oxford University Press, 2004.

Rakestraw, Robert V. "John Wesley as a Theologian of Grace." *Journal of the Evangelical Theological Society* 27 (June 1984):193-203.

Reist, Irwin W. "John Wesley's View of Man: A Study in Free Grace Versus Free Will," *Wesleyan Theological Journal* 7:1 (Spring 1972): 25-35.

Rivers, Isobel. "Tillotson, John." Pages 791-801 in vol. 54 of the *Oxford Dictionary of National Biography, from the Earliest Times to the year 2000*. Edited by H.C.G. Matthew and Brian Harrison. 60 vols. Oxford, England: Oxford University Press, 2004.

Rogers, Charles A. "John Wesley and William Tilly." *Proceedings of the Wesley Historical Society* 35 (June 1966): 137-41.

Sedgwick, Timothy F. "Revisioning Anglican Moral Theology." *Anglican Theological Review* 63:1 (January 1981): 1-20.

Slights, Camille. "Ingenious Piety: Anglican Casuistry of the Seventeenth Century." *Harvard Theological Review* 63 (1970): 409-32.

Smith, J. Weldon III. "Some Notes on Wesley's Doctrine of Prevenient Grace." *Religion in Life* 34:1 (Winter 1964-1965): 68-80.

_____, Timothy Dudley. "Charles Wesley: A Hymnwriter for Today." *The Hymn* 39:4 (October 1988): 7-25.

_____, Timothy L. "The Holy Spirit in the Hymns of the Wesleys." *Wesleyan Theological Journal* 16:2 (Fall 1981): 20-47.

Somerville, C. John. "Anglican, Puritan, and Sectarian in Empirical Perspective." *Social Science History* 13:2 (Summer 1989):109-35.

Spurr, John. "Taylor, Jeremy." Pages 921-28 in vol. 53 of the *Oxford Dictionary of National Biography, from the Earliest Times to the year 2000*. Edited by H.C.G. Matthew and Brian Harrison. 60 vols. Oxford: Oxford University Press, 2004.

Stephen, Leslie. "Barclay, Robert." Pages 1087-1090 in volume 1 of the *Dictionary of National Biography*. Edited by Leslie Stephen and Sidney Lee. 22 vols. London: Smith, Elder, & Co., 1908.

Tiessen, Terrance. "Divine Justice and Universal Grace: A Calvinistic Proposal." *Evangelical Review of Theology* 21 (January 1999): 63-83.

Tracy, Wesley D. "Economic Policies and Judicial Oppression as Formative Influences on the Theology of John Wesley." *Wesleyan Theological Journal* 27(Spring-Fall, 1992): 30-56.

Tyson, John R. "Charles Wesley, Evangelist: The Unpublished New Castle Journal." *Methodist History* 25:1 (October 1986): 41-60.

_____. "Charles Wesley's Sentimental Language." *The Evangelical Quarterly* Vol. 57:3 (July 1985): 269-275.

_____. "Charles Wesley's Theology of Redemption: A Study in Structure and Method." *Wesleyan Theological Journal* 20:2 (Fall 1985): 7-28.

_____. "Christian Liberty as Full Redemption." *Wesleyan Theological Journal* 38:2 (Fall 2003): 143-174.

_____. "God's Everlasting Love: Charles Wesley and the Predestinarian Controversy." *Journal of the Evangelical Theological Society* 3:2 (Fall 1985): 47-62.

Vallance, Edward. "Lucas, Richard. Pages 688-89 Pages 486-88 in vol. 34 of the *Oxford Dictionary of National Biography, from the Earliest Times to the year 2000*. Edited by H.C.G. Matthew and Brian Harrison. 60 vols. Oxford: Oxford University Press, 2004.

Watson, J.R. "Pitying Tenderness and Tenderest Pity: The Hymns of Charles Wesley and the Writings of St Luke: The A.S. Peake Memorial Lecture, 2005." *Epworth Review* 32:3 (July 2005): 33-38.

Williams-Kirby, Ethyn. "The Quakers' Efforts to Secure Civil and Religious Liberty, 1660-96." *The Journal of Modern History* 7:4 (December 1935): 401-421.

Wood, A. Skevington. "John Wesley, Theologian of the Spirit." *Evangelical Review of Theology* 4 (1980):177.

Wright, Stephen. "Bolton, Robert." Pages 491-93 in vol. 6 of the *Oxford Dictionary of National Biography, from the Earliest Times to the year 2000*. Edited by H. C. G. Matthew and Brian Harrison. 60 vols. Oxford: Oxford University Press, 2004

Index

Aldersgate, 19, 21, 43, 68, 77
Ambrose, 46, 207, 218, 220
Ambrose, Isaac, 26, 27, 28
Annesley, 14, 47, 48, 102, 207, 219
Annesley, Samuel, 19, 22, 31, 32, 35, 90
Anselm, 183
Anti-Christ, 60
Aquinas, Thomas, 13, 204, 211
Aristotle, 24
Articles, Thirty-Nine, 19, 20, 42, 203, 210
Athanasius, 183
atonement, 12, 78, 84, 87, 93, 98, 99, 114, 128, 143, 166, 173, 183, 184, 185, 202, *See* prevenient grace and Christ's atonement
   extent of, 82, 142, 143, 144, 145, 149, 156, 157, 164, 180
   limited, 109, 164
   provisional, 180
Augustine, 10, 13, 20, 67, 84, 195, 204, 214, *See* prevenient grace in Augustine

Baker, Frank, 12, 14, 15, 43, 47, 94, 105, 110, 111, 130, 131, 132, 133, 134, 174, 198, 205, 209, 214, 215, 217
Balzer, Cary, 38, 41, 49, 50, 51, 72, 96, 198, 199, 216
baptism, 30, 37, 38, 99, 126, 153, 176, 186, 204
Barclay, 15, 62, 63, 64, 65, 66, 98, 100, 175, 177, 207, 211, 214, 221
Barclay, Robert, 12, 13, 42, 53, 54, 55, 56, 57, 58, 59, 60, 61, 62, 78, 79, 82, 166, 172, 204
Barnes, Robert, 14, 19
Beckerlegge, Oliver, 107, 110, 111, 122, 131, 132, 134, 135, 137, 176, 207
Berger, Teresa, 107, 108, 112, 117, 132, 209
Bett, Henry, 111, 209
Beveridge, William, 14, 19
Böhler, Peter, 21, 115, 116, 135
Bolton, Robert, 26, 28, 30, 31, 47, 219, 222
Book of Common Prayer, 19, 20, 42, 43, 132, 186, 198, 203, 207, 217
Brailsford, Mabel, 106, 114, 130, 135, 210
Brown-Lawson, Albert, 94, 142, 173, 210
Burnet, Gilbert, 14, 19, 42, 210

Calvin, John, 10, 47, 67, 72, 75, 79, 82, 101, 177, 195, 199, 201, 208, 211, 216, 217

Campbell, Ted, 12, 15, 109, 132, 133, 178, 195, 212, 214, 215
Catholic ethic, 11, 192
Cell, George Croft, 11, 14, 192, 201, 210
Charnock, Stephen, 25, 26, 45, 209, 218, 219
Chiles, Robert, 71, 192, 193, 201, 202, 210
Christian Library, 13, 22, 23, 24, 25, 26, 27, 29, 30, 31, 32, 33, 34, 35, 42, 44, 90, 103, 197, 203, 204, 209, 218
Christian perfection, 76, 107, 108, 131
Circumcision of the Heart, 48
Collins, Kenneth, 9, 11, 13, 43, 50, 75, 86, 94, 96, 97, 98, 99, 101, 102, 103, 112, 131, 164, 174, 177, 181, 183, 184, 185, 187, 188, 189, 196, 197, 198, 199, 200, 207, 210, 218
conscience, 23, 24, 30, 36, 38, 39, 40, 42, 45, 47, 50, 60, 90, 103, 196, 199, 200, 202, *See* light of conscience; prevenient grace and conscience
    and light of Christ, 60
    and the Holy Spirit, 40, 184
    as human faculty, 24, 83, 84, 85, 88, 89, 90, 189
    as restraint, 193
    as supernatural gift, 90, 91
    defined by Annesley, 32
    defined by Jeremy Taylor, 39
    defined by Robert Barclay, 60
    impaired, 23, 24, 28, 89, 124, 181, 192
    remnant of the fall, 23, 91
conversion, 10, 20, 31, 36, 58, 80, 121, 162, 168, 170, 175, 177, 178, 184, 185, 186, 187, 193, *See* prevenient grace and conversion
    prepared by Holy Spirit, 27, 28, 30, 35
Coppedge, Allan, 11, 12, 14, 46, 66, 94, 98, 100, 101, 173, 182, 195, 196, 200, 210
Cornelius, 79, 88, 102, 164, 165, 203
Cox, Leo, 182, 184, 193, 196, 197, 199, 202, 218
Cranmer, Thomas, 20, 21, 43, 212
Cushman, Robert, 190, 192, 193, 200, 201, 214

death
    consequence of sin, 38, 69, 73
    eternal, 73, 75
    of Christ, 37, 57, 79, 142, 143, 144, 145, 153, 182, 183
    redemption from, 116, 119
    spiritual, 73, 76, 122
Del Colle, Ralph, 183, 197, 200, 218
depravity, 10, 11, 56, 68, 72, 73, 74, 75, 77, 84, 93, 124, 180, 181, 189, 190, 199, *See* sin, original; prevenient grace and depravity/original sin
    total, 9, 75, 76, 94, 189, 192
determinism, 11, 21, 84, 94, 154, 190, 195, 203
devil, 24, 55, 67, 75, 95, 123, 125, 145
docetism, 56
Downing, George, 72
drawing, 27, 28, 35, 85, 102, 145, 147, 149, 159, 161, 172, 182
Dunning, Ray, 97, 99, 100, 102, 139, 171, 173, 177, 178, 181, 182, 183, 184, 193, 196, 197, 201, 202, 203, 204, 210, 211, 218

elect, 67, 78, 79, 89, 102, 142, 144, 157, 179, 194, 202

election, 10, 11, 14, 100, 101, 189, 192
enablement, divine, 10, 46, 80, 139, 153, 156, 157, 170, 187
Epictetus, 75
evil, 25, 32, 37, 39, 40, 41, 46, 56, 58, 59, 64, 71, 73, 74, 78, 83, 86, 88, 90, 99, 101, 123, 141, 158, 171, 190, 193

faith, 10, 11, 20, 21, 27, 30, 33, 54, 59, 72, 73, 76, 81, 86, 91, 191
   and grace, 164, 190, 191
   justifying, 92, 113, *See* justification by faith
   light of, 162
   nature of, 21, 29, 31, 91, 117
   of "heathens", 92
   related to reason, 26, 29
   saving, 31, 72, 82, 116, 186
   temporary, 30
   working by love, 85, 116, 117, 130
fall, the, 12, 23, 24, 33, 37, 38, 40, 56, 58, 64, 68, 69, 70, 71, 72, 74, 76, 93, 95, 124, 125, 126, 137, 143, 154, 191
Farley, Felix, 13, 22, 44, 66, 103, 173, 174, 175, 178, 209
fatalism, 36
fate, 33, 34, 59, 67, 88, 166, 199
Findlay, George, 118, 124, 136, 211
forgiveness, 41, 73, 139, 140, 160, 166, 185
Fox, George, 53, 64, 218
free will, 10, 37, 48, 71, 72, 82, 93, 97, 191, 200
freedom, 37, 68, 69, 71, 82, 93, 180, 186, 191, 198
Fuhrman, Eldon, 183, 184, 196, 197, 198, 216

Gill, Frederick, 116, 130, 211
Gordon, James, 25, 29, 44, 45, 46, 47, 49, 145, 175, 218, 219
grace
   and liberty, 41, 71
   as forgiveness, 139
   as mercy, 80, 143
   assisting, 71
   baptismal, 37, 38
   concomitant, 39
   convincing, 184, 188
   covenant of, 73
   economy of, 128, 130
   free, 35, 71, 72, 78, 79, 169
   glorifying, 187
   growth in, 40, 83
   increase of, 41
   irresistible, 163, 164, 189, 194
   justifying, 79, 81, 149
   means of, 81
   persevering, 39
   renewal through, 74, 84
   sacramental, 181
   sanctifying, 81, 128, 130, 149, 150, 184

saving, 30, 62, 79, 89, 140, 143, 153, 154, 161, 164, 179, 182, 188, 189, 192
secret, 159, 161, 165
source of spiritual knowledge, 35
source of strength, 41
sovereign, 86, 121, 143
Spirit of, 41, 145, 146, 188
sufficient, 141, 143
supernatural, 83, 189
throne of, 128
universal, 72, 172, *See prevenient grace*
violence of, 40
Greathouse, William, 100, 102, 182, 184, 196, 197, 211
Gregory, Theophilus, 105, 130
Grider, Kenneth, 10, 14, 219

Harper, Steve, 15, 62, 182, 185, 196, 197, 211, 214
Heathen, 165
Heitzenrater, Richard, 10, 14, 35, 44, 46, 48, 50, 68, 94, 174, 189, 190, 195, 200, 211, 215, 216, 219
Hillman, Robert, 188, 192, 199, 201, 216
Hills, Aaron Merritt, 180, 195, 211
Hodge, Charles, 193, 201, 202, 211
holiness, 11, 33, 36, 38, 67, 69, 72, 73, 74, 116, 117, 148, 152, 192, 194, *See* righteousness
as love, 76, 77
as sinlessness, 154
moral image, 70, 74, 124, 127
Holy Spirit. *See* prevenient grace: pneumatological, prevenient grace and the Holy Spirit
Homilies, 12, 19, 20, 21, 22, 43, 116, 207, 217
Hooker, Richard, 14, 19, 43, 94, 209
human nature, 45

illumination, 23, 30, 31, 35, 54
image of God, 34, 68, 69, 72, 73, 74, 118, 124, 125, See *imago Dei*
impaired, 126, 127
moral, 69, 70, 71, 74, 76, 124, 127, 128, 191
natural, 69, 70, 74, 76, 128, 191
political, 69, 70, 71, 76, 128
relics of, 32, 56, 71, 90
restored, 126, 127, 128, 152
image of the devil, 75
imago Dei, 12, 25, 56, 70, 74, 76, 91, 97, 124, 125, 126, 127, 128, 129, 137, 139, 153, 191
incarnation, 124, 183
initiative, divine, 10, 20, 67, 79, 82, 87, 123, 149, 150, 157, 159, 160, 162, 163, 165, 167, 168, 172, 175, 184, 187, 190, 191, 201, 203

Johnston, Robert, 13, 14, 193, 200, 202, 214, 215
justice, 59, 203
justification by faith, 21, 72, 77, 86, 116, 117, 125, 130, 175, 181, 190, *See* faith, justifying

Kimbrough, S.T. Jr., 15, 106, 107, 108, 109, 110, 111, 131, 132, 133, 174, 176, 207, 208, 209, 211, 214, 215
Knight, John, 71, 96, 215
Kwon, Tae Hyoung, 203, 205, 216

Langford, Thomas, 14, 108, 181, 182, 191, 196, 200, 202, 211, 215
Law, William, 98, 115, 117, 135
Lawson, John, 111, 134, 211
Lee, Umphrey, 5, 44, 62, 75, 94, 97, 134, 190, 191, 192, 200, 211, 218, 219, 220, 221
liberty, 36, 37, 38
Liberty, 63, 220, 221, 222
light
   and grace, 25, 41
   and the Holy Spirit, 28, 30, 36, 59, 91, 146
   basis of judgment, 194
   divine, 26, 33, 56, 80, 82
   of Christ, 57, 58, 59, 60, 61, 62, 78, 85, 88, 119, 121
   of conscience, 23, 31, 89, 90
   of creation, 25
   of reason, 24, 28, 32
   resistance to, 161, 169
   saving, 59, 61
   sufficient, 83
   universal, 59, 61, 62, 83, 88, 89, 91, 155, 160, 161, 166
   weakness of, 24, 92, 155, 161, 165, *See* prevenient grace: weakness of
Lindström, Harald, 11, 14, 72, 96, 185, 189, 191, 198, 200, 201, 212
Liturgy, 19, 20
Lloyd, Gareth, 17, 105, 130, 133, 212, 216
Lord's Supper, 81, 93, 99, 174, 204
love, 26, 33, 41, 69, 80, 84, 85, 95, 102, 116, 117, 120, 125, 130, 136, 146, 148, 150, 151, 152, 153, 159, 161, 163, 164, 169, 170, 171, 175, 176, 177, 178, 187
   and holiness, 76
   as an affection, 69, 71
   as God's decree, 172
   component of natural image, 71
   divine, 10, 34, 57, 59, 69, 78, 80, 125, 127, 142, 143, 144, 145, 148, 151, 154, 156, 162, 171, 181, 203
   everlasting, 109, 143, 172
   for the world, 40
   of Christ, 114, 159, 167, 170
   of neighbor, 88
   of the Father, 78, 143, 145, 160
   perfect, 77, 127, 129, 140, 148, 150, 162
   restores divine image, 125
   universal, 109, 142, 145, 156
Lucas, Richard, 33, 34, 48, 208, 220, 221
Luther, Martin, 75, 116, 139

Maddox, Randy, 9, 10, 11, 13, 14, 20, 68, 71, 94, 96, 131, 177, 185, 186, 187, 188, 189, 190, 191, 193, 194, 197, 198, 199, 200, 201, 202, 212, 220
Mann, Mark, 204, 205, 215

Matthaei, Sondra Higgins, 181, 195, 212
McGonigle, Herbert, 12, 15, 17, 35, 46, 48, 49, 63, 72, 82, 88, 93, 96, 97, 98, 100, 102, 103, 177, 183, 187, 190, 195, 197, 198, 199, 200, 201, 212, 216, 220
Melanchthon, 55
mercy, 9, 28, 34, 41, 59, 88, 119, 123, 143, 144, 153, 157, 163, 164, 169, *See* grace as mercy
Mercy, 176, 205
merit, 9, 67, 78, 79, 85, 86, 90, 98, 109, 115, 152, 157, 165, 168, 190, 192, 204
Miley, John, 44, 180, 195, 212
monergism, 168
Monk, Robert, 12, 14, 43, 44, 47, 192, 193, 201, 212
Morris, Gilbert, 118, 136, 176, 217
Murray, Grace, 105

natural theology, 12, 74
nature
   asleep, 122, 167
   corrupt/fallen, 24, 36, 70, 71, 72, 73, 74, 75, 83, 84, 89, 114, 118, 119, 120, 121, 123, 124, 125, 130, 156, 158, 168, 171
   created order, 23, 70, 74, 118
   divine, 24, 33, 35, 79, 125, 152, 153, 164
   human, 10, 24, 25, 26, 34, 37, 38, 39, 40, 56, 57, 58, 69, 82, 83, 84, 86, 87, 93, 118, 120, 123, 124, 130, 150, 185, 186, 189, 190, 192
   law of, 39, 40, 42, 84, 113
   light of, 25, 32, 34, 90
   spiritual, 57
new birth, 70, 74, 75, 115, 187, *See* regeneration
new covenant, 40
Newport, Kenneth, 12, 15, 105, 106, 110, 130, 131, 132, 133, 136, 137, 174, 176, 178, 195, 208, 212, 214, 215, 220
Nilsen, Einar, 191, 201, 220
Noro, Yoshio, 192, 201, 220

Oden, Thomas, 181, 182, 196, 198, 202, 212, 213
Outler, Albert, 11, 14, 43, 47, 76, 81, 83, 85, 87, 91, 98, 99, 100, 101, 102, 103, 134, 181, 184, 193, 196, 197, 198, 199, 201, 202, 208, 213, 215

Pearson, John, 14, 19
Pelagianism, 11, 37, 56, 78, 84, 154, 190, 192
Pelagius, 10, 78
Penn, William, 53, 62, 64
perfection, 31, 37, 44, 69, 76, 77, 95, 132, 136
Peters, John, 75, 97, 192, 201, 213
Pinnock, Clark, 204, 205
Plato, 34
Platonists, Cambridge, 26, 49, 210
Pope, William Burt, 181, 191, 192, 196, 200, 213
prayer, 81, 93, 116, 125, 127, 130, 147, 174, 177
preaching, 25, 27, 28, 30, 31, 35, 48, 59, 65, 85, 86, 87, 88, 101, 109, 110, 115, 151, 158, 166, 172, 179, 188, 199
predestination, 9, 33, 41, 59, 61, 67, 78, 79, 82, 89, 100, 101, 142, 143, 168, 179, 190
Preston, John, 26, 27, 46, 208, 218, 220

prevenient grace
  alternative to Pelagianism (moralism) and determinism, 11, 89, 190
  and baptism, 38, 153
  and Christian education, 10
  and Christ's atonement, 37, 78, 79, 82, 84, 93, 94, 142, 143, 148, 162, 182, 183
  and common grace, 193
  and conscience, 12, 32, 34, 35, 90, 93, 188, 189, 192
  and conversion, 79
  and conviction of sin, 194
  and depravity/original sin, 72, 75, 94, 157, 189, 190, 192
  and other religions, 194
  and preaching, 85, 87, 155, 172, 188
  and revelation, 11, 32
  and saving faith, 154
  and saving grace, 170
  and the Holy Spirit, 38, 77, 91, 93, 141, 183, 184, *See* prevenient grace: pneumatological
  and the *imago Dei*, 130
  and the incarnation, 183
  and the law, 84, 93
  and the Lord's Supper, 81, 144
  and the means of grace, 81, 93
  and the Trinity, 10, 93, 182
  anthropological, 12, 23, 32
  as "preventing" grace, 10, 140, 141
  as heat, 41
  as light, 30, 56, 78, 142, 149, 154
  as quickening, 77
  as seed, 56, 79, 142, 151, 152
  as talent, 142, 153
  as theological catergory, 203
  broad definition, 11, 20, 186
  cosmological, 12, 25
  drawing, 78, 144, 159, 162, 172
  enablement, 75, 87, 93, 153, 154, 157, 169, 182, 191
  enlightening, 78, 183, 189
  fate of unevangelized, 88
  in Augustine, 20, 192
  in English Protestant theology, 19
  in the *Book of Common Prayer*, 20
  in the *Homilies*, 12, 20, 21
  irresistible, 164, 189
  Latin root, 10
  location in *via salutis*, 11, 85, 106, 157, 180, 184, 185
  narrow definition, 11, 185
  necessary for salvation, 41, 183
  pneumatological, 12, 26, 38, 145
  regenerative, 187
  resisted, 38, 83, 93, 154, 161, 166, 169, 189, 192
  restores a measure of free will, 42, 93, 168, 182, 190
  restraint from sin, 170, 171

universal, 12, 78, 79, 81, 83, 89, 142, 144, 153, 155, 157, 162, 189, 190
   weakness of, 26, 89, 91, 158, 165, *See* light: weakness of
   working definition, 10
Prince, John, 10, 11, 14, 190, 200, 213
Protestant ethic, 11, 192
providence, divine, 22, 34, 40, 48, 80, 81
Puritanism, 28, 43
Pythagoras, 34

Quakers, Quakerism, 12, 13, 15, 42, 53, 54, 56, 57, 62, 63, 65, 67, 78, 83, 177, 203, 214, 218
Quantrille, Wilma Jean, 108, 132, 217
quickening, 26, 30, 35, 77, 119, 180

Rakestraw, Robert Vincent, 181, 184, 196, 197, 217, 220
Rattenbury, Ernest, 106, 107, 109, 111, 112, 131, 132, 133, 174, 213, 218
reason
   and light of Christ, 60
   as erring, 191
   as faculty, 60
   as instrument of faith, 26
   corrupted, 24
   natural, 39, 54, See light: of reason, faith: related to reason and light of Christ
   Quaker view, 55
redemption, 75, 123, 182, 183, 184
   extrascriptural, 188
   universal, 12, 54, 57, 109, 142, 183
regeneration, 28, 31, 36, 37, 70, 74, 153, 186, 187, 188, 193, *See* new birth
   baptismal, 37, 186, 187, 204
regneration, 28
Reist, Irwin, 183, 191, 196, 200, 221
remonstrants, 57
repentance, 29, 61, 97, 102, 109, 168, 180, 182, 185, 187, 188, 189, 191, 194, 200
Repentance, 97
reprobation, 78, 82, 164
revelation
   basis of Christian morals, 39
   by preaching, 92
   by Scripture, 35, 92
   by the Holy Spirit, 35, 55
   divine, 12, 25, 32, 35
   immediate, 54, 55
   in Creation, 25
   initial and universal, 194
   inward illumination, 54
   of Christ, 25, 55, 182, 189
   of divine law, 25
   special, 39
   supplementary to conscience, 39
Reynolds, Edward, 23, 24, 25, 45, 208, 217
righteousness, 56, 57, 64, 69, 70, 71, 73, 74, 77, 88, 95, 114, 138, 150, 165, 166
   imputed, 29

Rogers, Charles, 9, 11, 13, 14, 15, 19, 20, 21, 32, 33, 42, 43, 48, 78, 91, 93, 94, 96, 98, 103, 186, 187, 196, 198, 199, 200, 204, 209, 217, 221
Rogers, Thomas, 14, 19
Roman Catholicism, 67, 195
Royster, Mark Powell, 101, 203, 205, 217
Runyon, Theodore, 11, 14, 95, 102, 181, 182, 189, 191, 194, 196, 197, 200, 202, 213

salvation, 29, 41, 43, 46, 57, 58, 59, 66, 72, 78, 85, 89, 93, 99, 100, 102, 109, 112, 114, 116, 125, 128, 132, 134, 142, 144, 145, 152, 154, 164, 167, 168, 169, 172, 174, 177, 179, 182, 183, 185, 187, 191, 192, 193, 194, 199, 201
   a prayer for, 125
   available to all, 59, 143, 154, 157
   by faith, 72, 116, 190
   by grace, 9, 94, 140
   conditional, 180
   degree of, 89, 188
   elected to, 82
   encounter, 37, 67, 107, 159, 163, 186, 191, 203
   free, 119
   hope of, 184
   of the "heathen", 88
   refused, 61
   uncertainty, 67
   without preaching, 59
   working out our own, 37, 88, 115, 117, 190
   working with God, 82
sanctification, 11, 14, 31, 65, 70, 75, 76, 83, 89, 97, 102, 117, 131, 137, 139, 140, 151, 183, 185, 186, 188
Satan, 82, 84, 85, 136, 141, 158
seed, 31, 56, 57, 58, 60, 61, 64, 65, 76, 79, 98, 100, 142, 150, 151, 152, 153, 154, 172, 175, 176, 177, 203
Shepherd, Neville, 111, 112, 133, 134, 217
Sibbes, Richard, 26, 29, 30, 47, 207, 218, 219
sin, 14, 21, 24, 28, 35, 40, 45, 57, 70, 74, 77, 80, 89, 96, 97, 99, 100, 102, 113, 116, 119, 121, 122, 123, 127, 130, 136, 137, 141, 144, 148, 154, 157, 158, 159, 166, 168, 170, 174, 181, 182, 189, 197, 199, 201
   and self-will, 113
   brings ruin, 33
   conviction of, 78, 164, 185, 193
   God author of, 59
   high-handed, 36
   leads to hardness, 31
   original, 9, 10, 24, 37, 38, 56, 58, 68, 69, 71, 72, 73, 74, 75, 76, 77, 79, 90, 118, 120, 122, 123, 127, 128, 139, 144, 152, 157, 167, 168, 181, 185, 189, 190, 192, *See* depravity
   practice of, 24, 114
   redemption from, 55
   unsatisfying, 40
   weariness of, 30
sleep (spiritual), 28, 80, 121, 122, 124, 167
Smith, John, 26, 44, 45, 46, 62, 145, 175, 197, 198, 199, 209, 215, 218, 219, 220, 221

Socinianism, 23, 29
Socrates, 34, 59, 60, 75, 188, 197
South, Robert, 23, 24, 25, 44, 45, 87, 103, 133, 208, 209, 219
sovereignty of God, 10
spark, 24, 31, 35, 79, 120, 123, 147, 161, 175
Staples, Rob, 17, 99, 204, 205, 213
Starkey, Lycurgus, 185, 188, 197, 199, 213
Stookey, Lawrence Hull, 108, 109, 132
synergism, 82, 159, 193

Tabraham, Barrie, 12, 15, 115, 116, 130, 135, 213
talents,, 61, 83, 85, 101, 153, 154, 166, 203
Taylor, Jeremy, 13, 38, 39, 40, 41, 42, 49, 50, 72, 75, 94, 96, 97, 204, 207, 208, 212, 213, 216, 219, 220, 221
Telford, John, 96, 97, 98, 100, 101, 112, 208, 213
Tillotson, John, 26, 28, 29, 35, 44, 46, 208, 219, 221
Tilly, William, 13, 14, 19, 35, 36, 37, 38, 41, 48, 49, 176, 186, 187, 198, 208, 221
Trueblood, Elton, 12, 15, 59, 62, 63, 64, 65, 66, 214
Truesdale, Al, 204, 205, 214
Tucker, Josiah, 79, 98
Tyson, John, 12, 15, 107, 112, 131, 132, 133, 134, 208, 214, 221

understanding, 26, 43, 69, 71, 80, 95, 102, 103, 114, 173, 177, 198, 199, 201, 202, See reason
  and light of Christ, 61
  and natural image of God, 69, 70
  as faculty of knowledge, 25
  as guide to liberty, 191
  before the fall, 68, 70
  darkened, 28, 73, 123
  depraved, 69
  enlightened by Holy Spirit, 30, 55, 70, 82
  related to faith, 27
  strengthened by God, 86

via salutis, 20, 80, 85, 102, 106, 126, 128, 150, 154, 170, 180, 181, 185, 186, 187
Voltaire, 54

Wainwright, Geoffrey, 109, 132, 179, 195, 215
Whitefield, George, 21, 29, 61, 78, 86, 98, 115, 142, 143, 164, 177, 179, 195, 209, 213
Whitehead, Thomas, 82
Wiley, Orton, 10, 14, 181, 196, 214
Williams, Colin, 11, 13, 14, 45, 63, 89, 101, 102, 188, 190, 191, 198, 199, 200, 201, 209, 214, 220, 222
Würtemberg, Confession of, 20

Yocum, Dale, 193, 194, 202, 214

Zinzendorf, Count Nicolaus von, 115